THE CORPORATE SPONSORSHIP TOOLKIT

THE CORPORATE SPONSORSHIP TOOLKIT

SECOND EDITION

KIM SKILDUM-REID

FREYA
PRESS

FREYA
PRESS

First published 2025

National Library of Australia Cataloguing-in-Publication data:

Skildum-Reid, Kim
The Corporate Sponsorship Toolkit, Second Edition

ISBN: 978-1-921097-05-8
ISBN (ePub): 978-1-921097-07-2

1. Corporate sponsorship
2. Marketing
3. Advertising

Published in Australia by
Freya Press
FreyaPress.com
Editor: Claire McGregor, ClaireMcgregor.com.au
Designer: Luke Causby, Blue Cork, BlueCork.com
Typesetter: Post Pre-Press Group, PostPrePress.com.au
Illustrator: Henry Ceballos, Henry.lat

Contents

Foreword –
Jeremy Edwards

The world of sponsorship is changing – fast.

The initial phase of this transformative era saw sponsorship move away from the passions and whims of Chairs and CEOs and the emphasis on logos, eyeballs, and brand affiliations, towards deeper, more strategic partnerships focused on business objectives, targeting, engagement, conversion, values, and social impact.

This change occurred as the space itself became more complex: with more platforms, changing consumer behaviour, and an evolution of the balance of power amongst the industry's various stakeholders.

It may sound counterintuitive, but the world of sponsorship is simultaneously fragmenting and converging. The proliferation of channels and platforms is driving ever more specialist niches, and yet the once distinct cultural and entertainment silos that separated art, music, sport are breaking down and blurring into one another.

The accelerating pace of technology change and access to communication channels isn't only providing rights owners and sponsors with more platforms and spaces, but giving talent (the stars and the players) and consumers (audiences and fans) with the reach and the stage to assume more direct control and power.

This communication and platform democratisation is freeing up creation, self-expression, and passion sharing, and yet the loss of professional and expert control is also leading to an overload of mixed-quality content and a lack of message clarity.

On top of this, the rise of artificial intelligence, bots, and marketing neuroscience is challenging our established ideas about authentic passion, genuine creativity, original ideas, and even human control.

All this means that navigating through the world of sponsorship is more challenging than ever, and books like this – which offer a big, broad vision for sponsorship alongside credible, nuanced detail drawn from years of experience – are ever more vital. The latest version of *The Corporate Sponsorship Toolkit* offers updated angles and approaches on the changing landscape.

Whether you are a student or in the early stages of industry training, a mid-career professional or even an experienced sponsorship leader, this *Toolkit* is THE essential partner to a successful brand- or company-side sponsorship career.

It is a practical, useable, and nuanced guide to all aspects and all sides of the industry. For those on the sponsorship start-line, I recommend reading it cover-to-cover. For those already established in the industry, keep a copy to hand — for experienced advice, valuable tips, and even just reassurance.

From established principles and contemporary trends, through objectives and outcomes, through to thinking and doing, the *Toolkit* covers the breadth and depth of the evolving sponsorship landscape from the company perspective.

As well as laying out frameworks and strategies, processes and tips, this substantially updated new edition is packed full of contemporary ideas, inspiration, and best-practice examples from around the world. It explores evolving sponsorship mindsets and processes, provides useable tools and templates, as well as practical exercises. In fact, I recommend that you not only read the book, but actively participate in it.

Like its author, this no-nonsense book is authentic, to the point, refreshingly free from bullshit and jargon, inspirational, passionate, and above all, genuinely practical.

Jeremy Edwards
Founder of Activative: Inspiring Sports Marketing

Foreword –
Angeline Ngunjiri

The African sponsorship landscape is undergoing a dynamic transformation, transitioning from outdated practices to a new era of strategic partnerships. Gone are the days of logo placement and event association; today's brands are being challenged to recognise the power of authentic connections with consumers, leveraging shared passions and values to create meaningful engagement. This shift has given rise to the three Rs of modern sponsorship: Relevance, Reach, and Returns. The experiences we create need to resonate with our brand's identity, reaching a broad spectrum of consumers, while delivering tangible results that justify the investment.

The current landscape also reveals a stark reality of the lack of strategic clarity in defining the optimal marketing mix. Even when well-chosen, some sponsorships are leveraged to their full potential, while others remain underutilised or completely ignored. This disparity is alarming, especially considering that *effective leverage*, not the sponsorship itself, is the true driver of impactful results. As an African brand marketer, we have a unique opportunity to tap into the rich cultural tapestry and diverse passions of the continent and craft strategic sponsorships that resonate with our audiences and elevate our brand experiences to foster loyalty, and achieve measurable business outcomes.

This book is an essential guide to navigating the complexities and opportunities of the African – and global – sponsorship market. It provides a comprehensive framework for developing a strategic approach to sponsorship, equipping you with the necessary skills and tools to:

1. **Make informed decisions**: Analyse data, understand your audience, and identify the right partners.
2. **Build impactful partnerships**: Create meaningful connections with consumers through shared values and passions.
3. **Maximise returns**: Develop activation strategies that deliver tangible results and measure their impact.

It goes beyond mere tactics and strategies — it challenges you to demand more from your sponsorships and strive for excellence in every aspect of partnership leverage. It encourages you to move away from haphazard decision-making and embrace a data-driven, results-oriented approach. By embracing the principles outlined in this book, you can transform your sponsorship program into a strategic engine for growth.

It is time to move beyond random acts and create meaningful connections that resonate with your audience, drive measurable results, and ultimately contribute to the overall development and maturity of the sponsorship industry, particularly in developing markets, like Africa.

Angeline Ngunjiri
Senior Manager, Brand Assets and Sponsorship
Safaricom

How to use this book

Welcome to *The Corporate Sponsorship Toolkit, 2nd Edition*! This massively updated, new edition is your cutting-edge guide to making sponsorship work for your brand and company.

In this book, as with the first edition, I've endeavoured to establish a vision for what best-practice sponsorship is all about, and how it can work for you. This is balanced with specific, practical strategies and tools, so you have a roadmap for implementing best practice.

As with my other books, *The Corporate Sponsorship Toolkit, 2nd Edition* was created to be a desk reference — something you'll turn to and annotate on a regular basis. But before it turns into that desk reference for you, you've got to get through it once, so you know what's in here.

With that in mind, I suggest you initially use the book like this:

➤ Ensure key stakeholders within your organisation know what you're doing. There is every chance you'll want to make some big changes around sponsorship, and you need to ensure you have support for that change. You may even recommend that they read the book themselves.

➤ Read through the book once, taking notes as you go.

➤ Pay close attention to case studies and lists of sponsorship ideas. Make notes or highlight any of them that you could replicate or rework for your sponsorships. They'll go a long way to augmenting your sponsorship idea bank. (Much more on that in Part 3: Leverage.)

➤ Go back through the book, doing the exercises along the way. In most cases, working collaboratively will get you the best result. In addition, it can serve as soft education on best-practice sponsorship for your peers.

➤ Encourage everyone involved to let themselves get really creative in the brainstorm exercises. If you don't provide the latitude to have a few big, blockbuster, occasionally crazy ideas, you aren't being creative enough!

The Corporate Sponsorship Toolkit, 2nd Edition was created to be a desk reference.

If you're in a rush and need immediate insight on a specific area of sponsorship (eg, measurement), go ahead and skip to that part. My strong recommendation, however, is that you read Chapter 1 first, as that will ground you in the right mindset for all of the advice and strategies in this book.

Examples and case studies

This book is full of examples and case studies, illustrating a range of skills and angles you can use with your own sponsorships, and an overarching approach that's as flexible as it is creative.

The case studies are mostly displayed in groups, demonstrating a specific angle. I'll admit this is somewhat imperfect, as many of the case studies showcase multiple angles. They're scattered throughout the book, but particularly prevalent in Part 3: Leverage.

These case studies come from around the world. Some are recent, while others are vintage, but don't let the vintage nature of some of them deter you. They're still great ideas, executed well, and many of them come from sponsors that were well ahead of their time.

There are lots of great case studies around COVID lockdowns, but these ideas can be repurposed for remote fans at any time. There are also great case studies about equity, inclusion, sustainability, and coming out of the explosion of women's sport.

I'm the first to admit that the case studies are a bit heavy on sport. This is due to a few factors, including that more money is spent in sport than any other category of sponsorship. It's also extremely cluttered and competitive, with many sponsors turning to innovative, best-practice thinking to get a strong result. Finally, there is simply more coverage of sports sponsorship than other types, so there are more case studies out there.

If you're reading this and you don't sponsor a lot of sport, don't despair. There are still a lot of case studies and examples of non-sport sponsorship, and most of the sports ideas are built on a framework — a basic premise — that can be repurposed for almost any type of sponsorship.

Many of these case studies come from industry must-read Activative. I can't recommend this platform enough as a motherlode of sports sponsorship ideas. For more information and to subscribe, visit Activative.co.uk.

Finally, in past books I've included links to videos or landing pages for each case study. More often than not, those links went dead before the book was updated, so I've decided not to include links this time. I do strongly urge you to search for more information and videos for case studies that grab you, because there's plenty more info available on these fantastic ideas.

Downloading the tools

This book comes with a series of tools and templates to help you implement best-practice sponsorship in your organisation. Downloadable tools are marked in the book text by this symbol: ⏻

You'll need a computer with an internet connection. You'll also need your copy of this book handy (hardcopy or ebook). When you're all set, follow these steps:

1. Go to CorporateSponsorshipToolkit.com.
2. Answer five simple questions about the book. All questions can be easily answered if you're looking at the book, particularly if you use the Contents pages as a quick reference.
3. After answering all five questions correctly, you'll be asked to enter your email address. A one-time download link will be emailed to you straightaway. Note, your email will not be added to a database or used for any other purpose.
4. When you receive the email, click the link to download the zip file containing the templates. All templates are in MS Word format (docx).

If you have any difficulties, contact details are on the download site.

Warning

These tools and templates are copyrighted and provided as an added value to owners of this book. If you return or sell the book, you no longer have a licence to use them, and they, and any derivative works, must be deleted or destroyed immediately. If you continue to use them, you will be breaching copyright, and I may exercise legal options. Plus, they will be very difficult to use without the context provided in the book. The same rules apply to people borrowing the book from the library or someone else. If you don't own the book, you don't have a licence to the tools and templates.

I've gone to a lot of effort to provide you with a book that will make sponsorship as effective and straightforward as it can possibly be. Please, do the right thing.

Acknowledgements

This is my eighth book, and wow, I can tell you that it doesn't get any easier. There are lots of people to thank for helping me bring this book to fruition.

First off, I'd like to thank my editor, Claire McGregor, for her wonderful job on this book, and particularly for letting me sound like me. Thank you, Luke Causby, for your beautiful cover. Thanks also to Post Pre-press Group for making the inside of the book so handsome.

Thank you very much to Jeremy Edwards and Angeline Ngunjiri for your fantastic forewords.

Lionel Hogg, your ability to put complex legal concepts into words fit for a marketer is unparalleled. Thanks so much once again for your advice, contribution, and a killer contract template.

I'd also like to thank all of my writing colleagues from Shut Up & Write, who supported me through the seemingly endless task of finishing this book. You made banging out the words so much easier.

Special thanks to my family and friends who kept my head from exploding when it all felt like too much. Particular thanks to my amazing husband, Rob, for being my biggest cheerleader, even when I was stuck. Special thanks to Baris for all his support. I also need to thank my bandmates, Jeff, Christopher, and Guillermo. There's nothing like roaring through a few punkers to get the writing frustrations out!

Finally, I want to thank the sponsorship industry and all of the professionals I've worked with and got to know over the years. You've inspired and taught me so much. I love this industry, and I'm so happy I've found a home here.

Part **1**

PREPARATION

Chapter 1

The best-practice mindset

Sponsorship provides you with the privilege of connecting with people through something they care about.

This book is about how to do sponsorship as well as you can possibly do it. It's about the strategy, the process, and the tools that will get you to best practice. It's about the skills you and your team need to open up a gulf between the effectiveness of your sponsorship program and that of your competitors. By the time you're done, you'll have checklists, templates, countless ideas, a to-do list as long as your arm, and a reinvigorated sense of excitement about this most amazing marketing discipline.

However, before we roll up our sleeves and get into it, we have to get the mindset right.

When I wrote the first edition of this book, it was right on the cutting edge. And while the bones of best-practice sponsorship are similar, the strategies, challenges, media, and technology have advanced substantially. There are more ways to make sponsorship deliver, but it's also more complex. There are more channels for leverage and accountability, but it requires even more buy-in.

Since the first edition, many sponsors have made big changes to best-practice sponsorship and are now reaping the benefits. Many others have either struggled to make change in a company stuck in the past, made a half-arsed attempt, for equally half-arsed results, or want to make the leap to best practice, but just don't know where to start. Getting all sponsors to best practice is what this book is all about.

Doing sponsorship well does take work, and it requires a certain mindset and organisational culture, but none of that is unachievable. And, frankly, doing sponsorship well is a lot of fun, both for the frontline people and the other stakeholders who are using it to achieve their objectives. Once the best-practice mindset is instilled and adopted as part of your corporate culture, just try to stop your team from doing it well!

In this section, we will be concentrating on the big picture:

- Why sponsorship is the most powerful marketing tool in the toolbox.
- The ultimate goal of sponsorship.
- How sponsorship fits with your brand and business objectives.
- How great sponsorship really works (and how it doesn't).

> The trends driving sponsorship.
> The mantras that will keep the focus in the right place.

Why sponsorship?

Sponsorship is the most powerful marketing media there is. This is because sponsorship has a combination of four things that no other marketing media has:

1. Meaning
2. Authenticity
3. Flexibility
4. Integratability

Meaning

Sponsorship provides you with the privilege of connecting with people through something they care about — something they have already decided is important enough to invest their time, money, and heart. This meaning is not only a benefit of best-practice sponsorship, it is also a threshold need for it to work.

Forget huge visibility numbers or "mass-market appeal", as neither of those big, sexy numbers tells you whether anyone gives a rat's arse about it. What matters now is how much your target markets care about what you're sponsoring; how relevant it is to their lives. If it's not relevant, don't sponsor it. If it is relevant — if it has meaning — there is almost no limit to what you can do with it. This brings me to why this is an important benefit of sponsorship.

Nothing else gets you closer to your target markets' passions than sponsorship. Nothing else puts you in a position to align your brand to those passionate fans or, even better, amplify their passion. Nothing else gives you such a powerful platform for adding value to your relationships with those fans, becoming a welcome and valued part of the experience. Meaning is sponsorship's superpower.

Contrast that with advertising. People care about what you're *interrupting* with the ad, not the ad itself. Even great ads get tired after just a few viewings. With few exceptions — ad nerds — people don't love the medium of advertising. It doesn't make people's lives better.

Authenticity

Sponsorship gives sponsors a way to *demonstrate* brand values and attributes — to *demonstrate* corporate culture and purpose — in an authentic and meaningful way.

Sure, a brand can go on and on about how helpful they are, but the only people experiencing that helpfulness are their customers. But that same brand can authentically demonstrate that helpfulness to customers and potential customers alike by sponsoring things they care about in a way that is legitimately helpful.

A company can talk about supporting LGBTQ+ rights, and plaster their company with

> Meaning is sponsorship's superpower.

rainbows during Pride. But that's not nearly as powerful as authentically demonstrating a commitment to the movement by sponsoring properties that are doing meaningful work in this space, and collaborating on projects that support this community.

Sponsorship provides the ideal platform for sponsors to demonstrate who they are, what they're about, and what they stand for. With recent research indicating that upwards of 60% of people (and growing) agree with the statement, "I tend to buy brands that reflect my personal values",* effectively demonstrating those values is an increasingly important component of brand marketing.

Flexibility

Without question, sponsorship is the most flexible of all marketing media. All other marketing media are like paintings — they can be masterpieces, but they are in some way constrained by their formats. Sponsorship, on the other hand, is like sculpture — it can be made out of anything, into anything you want, as long as it is structurally sound.

Sponsorship has a degree of flexibility that is unparalleled. If you've got a sponsorship with the requisite amount of relevance — it *means* something to people — you can create leverage activities that will make it deliver on virtually any marketing or business objective you could have.

Stop thinking about just the obvious benefits of sponsorship to your brand, and start thinking broadly. You can absolutely make a charitable sponsorship drive sales. You can create staff-retention programs around a cultural investment. You can use a flower show to launch a new product. Need to make a local or regional sponsorship work on a national level? Or a short event work for longer? Take a step back and look at the larger relevance of the theme and leverage that. (Lots more on that later!)

Integratability

Apparently, "integratability" isn't even a word, but until someone comes up with a word that means the same thing, I'm sticking with it. Like meaning, integration is both a reason and a requirement for being a great sponsor.

The value in sponsorship isn't in the sponsorship itself, but in what you do with it. We'll go into leverage in great detail later in the book, but suffice to say that much of the value sponsorship will bring to your brand is in making everything else you do more effective and efficient. It's a marketing powerhouse — a catalyst — that will make all of your other marketing channels work harder.

Let's say you've got a sponsorship that is relevant and meaningful to at least one of your core target markets. Doesn't it make sense to use it across your other marketing activities? Could you use it:

- To generate content for social media? For storytelling?
- To make your advertising more interesting or relevant?

Ipsos Global Trends 2021

> 60% of people (and growing) "tend to buy brands that reflect my personal values".

CHAPTER 1/THE BEST-PRACTICE MINDSET

- To hero your staff, customers, the communities in which you operate, or fans?
- To anchor promotions – sales, media, online, staff, in- or on-pack, retail, or B2B?
- To build a database of qualified prospects?
- To grow your social following and engagement?
- As a hook for PR?
- On your website?
- In EDMs?
- In your key customer management strategy?
- To underpin your corporate culture or purpose?
- To anchor incentive programs?

Terminology

Here are a few key terms that are used extensively throughout the book. Some of these have replaced outmoded terms, just in the past few years.

Fans

"Fans" refers to anyone who cares about what you're sponsoring and/or the larger themes around it (eg, sustainability, adventure, gourmet food, etc.). The shift to this term reflects the passion and meaning around what you're sponsoring, in contrast to dry terms, like "audience".

Leverage

Leverage is what you do with the sponsorship, turning the opportunity you've invested in into a result against your objectives. This can range from social content to promotions to on-site activities, and much more. Some organisations prefer the term "activation", although there are some issues with that, which I'll address later in the book.

Rightsholders and properties

The rightsholder is your partner. It's literally the organisation that owns the rights you're buying; the organisation you're contracting with. The property is what you're sponsoring. Some examples:

- The art gallery is the rightsholder; the exhibition you're sponsoring is the property.
- The local government is the rightsholder; the festival you're sponsoring is the property.
- The governing body is the rightsholder; the development league you're sponsoring is the property.

It's worth noting that some rightsholders can also be properties. For instance, you could sponsor a blockbuster science exhibition, or you can sponsor the science museum as a whole.

> Sponsorship is a catalyst that makes your existing activities work harder.

> In your marketing collateral?

> To attract quality new hires?

> To reward loyal customers?

> To inspire or launch a new product?

The list could go on and on and encompass all of your marketing to internal, external, and intermediary markets. Only sponsorship can integrate across everything else you do. It can even integrate across other sponsorships!

One mission, three objectives

Sponsorship is amazing and multifaceted. It is reflective of changes in society and technology and marketing media, so it changes all the time. You can be in the industry for decades, like I have, and still be learning new things every day.

At its core, though, sponsorship is exceedingly simple. There is one mission and three objectives that drive every single decision a good sponsor makes.

One mission

Every single sponsor — every single brand marketer — has the exact same mission. As I write this, I can feel your scepticism, but it's true.

Your mission is to be the natural choice for your target markets. You want your brand to be the one they believe is right for them; the one they naturally gravitate towards. Because when you achieve that, it's very difficult for the competition to get a foothold.

The issue for many brands is that they're functionally very commoditised. There's just not that much difference from one product to another in the category. For this reason, marketers often try to imbue brands with emotional points of difference, driving that natural choice, and sponsorship is an exceptionally powerful way to do that.

Your mission is to be the natural choice for your target markets.

What's in a brand?

When I refer to your "brand", I'm referring to whatever area within your company is doing the sponsoring. It could be your entire company, like Unilever, a master brand like Unilever's Lipton, or a brand line, like Lipton Iced Tea or Lipton Cup-a-Soup.

You don't sell a physical product? That doesn't mean you don't have a brand. Every service you market is a brand. Your brand can even be a message, which is the case for many government sponsors, such as the Transport Accident Commission's "Drink Drive, Bloody Idiot", or "Virginia is for Lovers".

Three objectives

When I ask sponsors what they are trying to achieve with sponsorship, the answers are often geared towards the mechanisms of sponsorship, and not the results. These sponsors seem to forget that sponsorship is just another marketing tool — albeit a powerful one — and lose sight of the bigger picture.

Your objectives should not be about the sponsorship, or specific to the sponsorship, but a subset of your overall marketing objectives, and every single one of those objectives falls into one of three categories:

1. Changing or reinforcing perceptions around your brand.
2. Changing or reinforcing behaviours around your brand.
3. Aligning with your target markets.

One of the easiest and most effective things you can do to increase your results is to consistently ask the three questions below. Make them part of your selection process, your leverage brainstorms, your measurement plan, your mantra:

1. What perceptions are we trying to change or reinforce with this?
2. What behaviours are we trying to change or reinforce with this?
3. In what ways are we trying to demonstrate alignment with the target markets?

Sponsorship vs partnership

Every year or so, somebody in the industry raises the old sponsorship vs partnership thing. What do we call what we do? What is the future? Most pundits come down squarely on the side of "partnership", but I disagree.

Clearly, the industry's approach to sponsorship has shifted to one that is partnership oriented. The problem with shifting to the *word* "partnership" is that a) it means something different to every department within a company; and b) it has a specific legal definition that goes way beyond the relationship outlined in a sponsorship contract.

I don't believe "partnership" is ever going to be redefined in the general business vernacular, and that is what we're talking about. Our industry needs a term that is specific to what we do, and is recognised as the same thing from the CEO to marketing to finance to sales to HR and beyond.

Until, or unless, a better term comes along, "sponsorship" is immediately recognisable by people across the gamut of organisations. And as certainly as the terms "media" and "public relations" mean something different now than they did 10 years ago, the meaning of "sponsorship" has grown - and will continue to grow and change - as our industry changes.

Do just that and your sponsorship program will change. Why? Because it will snap you and your team out of the old habit of focusing on the sponsorship and into the habit of focusing on your target markets, and the desired result.

To get you started, I've listed a few of the goals you could find under these three overarching objectives.

Changing or reinforcing perceptions

- Increasing or reinforcing the understanding of positive brand attributes
- Increasing the relevance of the brand
- Increasing trust in the brand
- Increasing the desirability of the brand, compared to the competition
- Increasing staff morale and/or pride
- Becoming a preferred employer

Changing or reinforcing behaviours

- Inciting your target markets to try the brand for the first time
- Increasing enquiries and consideration of the brand
- Increasing the number of ways and times your target markets use the brand
- Increasing brand preference
- Increasing brand loyalty
- Increasing brand advocacy
- Increasing staff retention
- Increasing sales
- Upselling or incremental sales to existing customers

Increasing alignment

- Increasing belief that your brand reflects their values or priorities
- Increasing your target markets' belief that they are understood and valued by the brand
- Increasing staff uptake and belief in the organisational purpose or values

Sponsorship and brand marketing

Brand marketers may be tempted to skip this section, but I encourage you not to. Best-practice sponsorship is derived directly from brand planning, yet for many sponsors, that link is either tenuous, misplaced, or missing completely. Honestly, it amazes me how many great brand marketers get sponsorship so wrong.

Customer cycle

Brands have their cycles, as do customers. The following graphic shows the customer cycle. The entry point is brand awareness, and at every stage around the cycle, the customer becomes more valuable to the brand.

Figure 1: Customer cycle

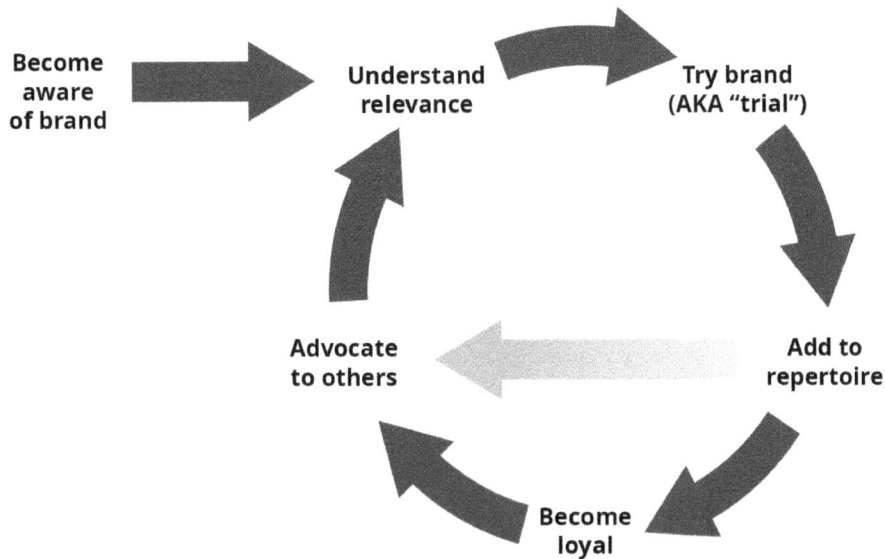

Aware of brand

If someone is aware your brand exists but has no idea what the brand does, they are of negligible value to you. Not convinced? Surf some of the sports channels that show the more obscure or overseas sports. You'll probably see plenty of signage featuring logos of companies and brands you've never heard of. Tah-dah! Now you're aware. But are you of any value to those companies? Not yet.

Understand relevance

At this point on the cycle, your potential customer understands the brand, but has never used it, or even considered it. You can probably name plenty of brands that would fall into that category for you. For me, I'm thinking Ferrari, Jimmy Choo, Viagra. I understand all of those brands perfectly, but they are not in my consideration set, so my value to those companies is extremely limited.

Try the brand

The minute one of your potential customers makes a move towards your brand under their own power, they are "trying" your brand and have become much more valuable to you. This includes buying your brand for the first time, as well as taking a test drive, checking out product features on your website, asking for a quote, taking a brochure, or giving a friend's new smartphone a spin.

One of the easiest, lowest-drag ways for someone to try a brand is to engage on social media. Smart brands will use this trial to nurture the relationship with this new connection, providing regular, relevant content around things they care about. More often than not, however, brands get this wrong – hammering people with ads and offers until they regret connecting at all.

One note on "forced trial": I don't consider "forced trial" to be the same as getting your target to make a move towards your brand by their own choice. A common example would be allowing spectators to drink only your brand of beer at a festival, because you have exclusive pouring rights. Selling beer to a captive audience may be a good sales decision, but how many of them keep drinking that brand at the pub afterwards? If it's not a brand they already know and like, the answer is "very few".

Add to repertoire

Let's say for a moment that you're successful at getting a potential customer to buy your brand for the first time. Even if they really like it, it's unlikely that they will become immediately 100% loyal. Instead, they will add your brand to their repertoire – the selection of brands within a given category they know, like, and trust.

Don't think because you're sharing loyalty with a few other brands that getting into somebody's repertoire isn't big, because it is. These are the brands they will choose from, when they have a choice. This is in stark contrast to the dozens – maybe hundreds – of brands in that category they don't know, like, or trust enough to consider. Wouldn't you rather your brand was in the repertoire?

Once your brand is in the repertoire, you have a lot of scope to gain ground by increasing the preference for your brand, so you have the greatest market share in the micro-economy that is your customer.

Become loyal

The next logical step is moving someone to total loyalty. This could be the home renovator that used to have a Smeg stove, but now has a brand-new kitchen with nothing but Smeg appliances. It could be the telecommunications sampler, who finally decides to bundle their cable, internet, and mobile services with one provider.

Not every category will evoke total loyalty. You could be loyal to one brand of car or toothpaste or toilet paper, but it's unlikely you are loyal to one brand of candy bar, financial services, or petrol station. Some categories of business go through this step in the cycle, others don't, hence the shortcut on the diagram. Whether they do or not, they can all get to the final step: Advocacy.

Advocate the brand

We are living in the age of advocacy. Years ago, people got their restaurant reviews from the newspaper, and got the lowdown on a new car model from a neighbour. Now, we've got social media, YouTube, blogs, and hundreds upon thousands of peer review sites, like Amazon, Yelp, and TripAdvisor, where anyone can give their two cents' worth on your brand.

There is nothing like peer endorsement to build a brand, because your customers can make a more compelling, authentic, credible case for your brand than you ever could with millions of dollars of advertising. They are creating the relevance for you. You just need to ensure they have something to talk about.

What does all of this have to do with sponsorship?
Plenty.

I know I've spent a lot of words describing the customer cycle, and you may be well familiar with it. Unfortunately, the lion's share of sponsorship seems to be completely disconnected with the most valuable parts of this cycle.

The typical sponsorship concentrates on visibility (awareness), may have some aspect of communicating a marketing message (understanding), and may have an incentive to try the brand or connect on social media (trial), and that's pretty much it. They concentrate on the people who have the least value to you, and do nothing to deepen your relationship with customers and increase their preference (repertoire), reward and value your loyal customers (loyalty), or deliver an experience worth recommending to anyone (advocacy).

Best-practice sponsorship works all the way around the cycle, and here's the kicker: It builds advocacy straight into the sponsorship. It doesn't get much better than that. Yet it does require a specific mindset and approach to make it happen.

> Best-practice sponsorship has advocacy built in.

Last Generation Sponsorship

"Last Generation Sponsorship" is a term I coined way back in 2003, and my oft-updated white paper of the same name has been downloaded hundreds of thousands of times. Before we get into what Last Generation Sponsorship is all about, it's worth outlining how we got here.

First generation: Pointless

The first generation of sponsorship was driven by gaining exposure and awareness, with a big dose of chief executive's choice thrown in for good measure. This was the norm throughout the '70s and early '80s. Unfortunately, it's still the norm for many corporate sponsors, particularly in less advanced sponsorship markets that still hold onto the notion that flashing their logo — in the company of dozens of other logos — in front of masses of cynical consumers, equals marketing return.

Second generation: Short-sighted

The second generation had its heyday from the mid-'80s to the early '90s. The focus was very clearly on sales, with immediate gains the driving force. Long-term benefits were rarely sought or even considered in this formula-based era, although some sponsorships undoubtedly achieved them as a side effect. Bargains were big news because results were measured in things like incremental sales, sales promotion participation, retail support, case

Examples: Win-win-win

There are many, many case studies showcasing the best-practice mindset in this book. Here are a few to whet your appetite!

Soccer fans in Mexico had a huge problem with pickpockets at games. As a result, many of them didn't bring a wallet or even their phone. **Corona** solved the problem (and sold more beer) by creating Corona Jersey Pay; RFID patches that can be sewn onto the jerseys the fans wear to games, allowing them to pay with the literal shirt on their back.

Jockey cross-pollinated two sponsorships and a retailer to save Kiwi men's lives. Working with Testicular Cancer New Zealand, NZ Rugby Union, and retailer **Farmers**, Jockey created "Remundies". Buy a pair of "Remundies", register it online, and your underpants will text you once a month to remind you to check your testicles for signs of cancer. The All Blacks were the, uh . . . face of the initiative, urging fans to be alert to the number-one cancer affecting young men.

When **Sharpie** wanted to demonstrate and build an understanding of their huge range of pens, particularly with mums of primary school age kids, they took up small sponsorships of many sports teams across the US, setting up free sign-making stations for fans. The kids (and parents) had a great time making and using their signs, while mums got familiar with their product range.

Mazda offered premium parking at rugby matches for people who drive Mazdas. It was so successful that a few university students spray-painted Mazda logos all over their old, beater, non-Mazda cars to get in on the parking deal. To Mazda's credit, they let these brand advocates use the premium parking as well!

commitments, profit margins, and sales conversions, as compared to the price of the sponsorship.

This generation has largely disappeared, with the exception of brands that sponsor primarily to gain vending rights or other guaranteed sales.

Third generation: Selfish

Third generation was a major step up from second, becoming popular in the early '90s, and is still used by a large proportion of sponsors today. Sponsorship moved from an ancillary activity to a piece of the marketing pie. Brand needs, multiple leverage activities, and the achievement of multiple marketing objectives are drivers of this generation, with the goals resting equally between the short and long terms. Skills are strong, processes are refined, and results well documented. It's creative and thorough, but it's also selfish, as their single-minded pursuit of brand goals is often intrusive and overbearing, carried out with precious little thought for the fan experience.

Last Generation: Selfless

This brings us to Last Generation Sponsorship. Why "Last" and not "fourth"? Because our industry has finally got the focal point in the right place: On the people — the fans, the customers, the staff, and the communities we serve. Last Generation Sponsorship is not ego-driven like first generation. It isn't short-sighted, like second generation. And it's not needy and self-centred, like third generation. Last Generation Sponsorship is, first and foremost, selfless.

Last Generation Sponsorship is about nurturing a brand's connection with a target market by putting their needs first. It isn't about how many times you can "get in front of" or "communicate with" your target market through a sponsorship, it's about how you can use the most emotional and personally relevant of all marketing media to improve your brand's relationship with a target market and, more importantly, their relationship to your brand. As much as those target markets change, and their needs change, and the world around them and their reaction to it changes, the basic building blocks of Last Generation Sponsorship will never change.

The new model of sponsorship

This has led to a very different model of sponsorship. In the past, sponsors have concentrated on creating bonds with properties, rather than with their target markets. An example would be an insurance company that decides it is in their best interests to be aligned with football. They spend a lot of time, effort, and money creating an indelible link between their brand and football — they put logos all over each other, the players appear in ads, and thank each other at end-of-year dinners — with the assumption that after all of this overt linking, the fans are just going to "get it", whatever that "it" may be.

Figure 2: Old model of sponsorship

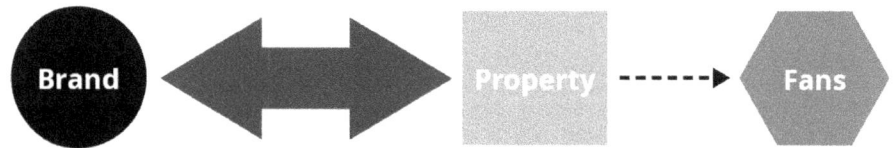

Unfortunately for all involved, it's just not happening. Signage is just wallpaper, and we don't bother with the convoluted mental gymnastics required to transfer our love from a property to a brand just because they're a sponsor (eg, "If that brand sponsors my team, and I love my team, I should love that brand!"). We have all become good at editing the few marketing messages that matter to us, from the hundreds that merely clutter our universe. If you find this hard to believe, ask yourself or a colleague or a friend these questions:

- What was the most recent major event you attended (in which you weren't involved)?
- How many logos would you have been exposed to on that day?
- How many can you name right now?
- Of those that you can name, did any of them change your perceptions of that brand or make you understand it better? Eg, your trust in their brand grew immeasurably, or you now understand how that product fits into your life, or you see that brand as "likeminded"?
- Did any of them change your behaviour? Eg, you ran right out and test drove a Ford, started to eat at KFC more often, or advocated that brand to others?
- As a result of seeing their logo, did you decide that any of those brands was the right brand for you?

I have asked these questions hundreds of times, and I'm guessing that they will remember being exposed to dozens of logos, will be able to name two to four of them, and none will have made them change their behaviour, perceptions, or alignment. If one did, it is probably because the brand leveraged it in such a way that it really resonated with them and added value to the fan experience. In that case, one out of dozens got it right.

Many would say that leverage is the key to maximising sponsorship returns, and it certainly is a critical factor, but even if a sponsorship is thoroughly leveraged using the old model, the focus of that leverage is football, not the fans. It may catch their attention, but it's unlikely to really matter to them. And to be an active part of the sponsorship, such as participating in promotions, the fans are required to make the lion's share of the effort, for probably no benefit at all to their fan experience. This brings us to the new model: The conduit.

Figure 3: New model of sponsorship

First, we have to ask ourselves, is it really an insurance company's job to "align with" football? Is it in the company mission statement to be "synonymous with" football? No. An insurance company's job is to sell more insurance by getting people to consider and try their brand, engendering loyalty to, and advocacy for, their brand, and getting the brokers who sell their insurance to promote it more than their competitors. Their job is to connect with target markets — internal, external, and intermediary. Sport doesn't buy the insurance; the fans buy the insurance. Football is simply a means to an end — a tool — and that's it. How we use that tool is what separates good from great sponsors.

Win-win-win

For years, good sponsorship was defined as being win-win; that is, the sponsor wins and the rightsholder wins, leaving out the most important part of the sponsorship equation: The target markets.

Best-practice sponsors realised long ago that their starting place with any fanbase is "interloper", and if they were to have any chance at all of meeting brand needs, they were going to need to meet fan needs first. Understanding, respecting, and adding value to the fan experience became the third "win" in win-win-win sponsorship. This sits in stark contrast to all of the previous generations, which grew more comprehensive and sophisticated over time, but were all too willing to sacrifice the fan experience in pursuit of their brand goals.

Given that the target markets are the pivot point for the wellbeing of both the brand and the rightsholder, it makes perfect sense to make the target markets' needs and wants part of the basic infrastructure of best-practice sponsorship. That third win is the very foundation of best-practice sponsorship.

Going back to the conduit, for the sponsor, the most important connection in the equation is the one between their brand and the target markets. The property is simply a conduit — a tool — through which the sponsor can strengthen that connection.

Herein lies the rub: The most important connection in the target markets' equation is their connection with the property. To those people, sponsors are extraneous and disposable, and frankly, they're right. Over the years, sponsors haven't exactly had a

> The property is the conduit.

> A sponsor's starting place is "interloper".

glorious track record of enhancing their fan experiences. This has improved over the past few years, but most properties are still an escalating battle between sponsors trying to draw people's attention to their brands, and people trying to ignore them, and those people are always going to win.

Want to make it work? Then knock it off. Ratchet back the hype, turn down the volume, and change the tone completely.

It's no longer:

"If you love the property, you should love our brand!"

Or worse:

"PAY ATTENTION TO US!!!"

Instead, it's:

"We know you love this property — we love it too! — and we've thought of a few ways to make it even better for you."

And that's the key. "Making it better" is the third win.

Win-win-win is an acknowledgement that achieving brand goals and valuing the fan experience are not mutually exclusive, and, in fact, delivering a sponsorship that makes the fan experience better will increase alignment to the brand, appreciation for the brand, and make it much more likely that the fans will cooperate in achieving brand goals. It's also an acknowledgement that if a sponsor makes the fan experience worse, they may get the attention of fans, but they will damage, not nurture, the relationship. In other words, if the fans lose, so does your brand.

For sponsors, the win-win-win approach is built around the provision of small, meaningful wins for all or most of the fans, customers, potential customers, employees, or anyone else in the target audience. Going into a draw where one person wins a giant prize isn't a win for anyone else, and neither is claiming that a fan is benefitting simply because a brand sponsors something that they love.

No, that third win will usually fall into one of three categories: Amplifying the best stuff around a fan experience; ameliorating the worst stuff; or amplifying fan passions or concerns. That means understanding the fan experience, and if the rightsholder doesn't provide that information, you'll need to work with them to get it.

Your new mantra

Understanding and using that third win leads naturally into what should be your new mantra: Don't sponsor the property, sponsor the fans.

Of course, you are technically sponsoring the property, but if you make that your focal point, you're leaving the all-important fans out of the equation. If you reframe your sponsorships as "sponsoring the fans", however, everything about the investment changes.

The way you vet potential sponsorship changes from "What do we get?" to "How can we use this to sponsor the fans?" You'll negotiate primarily for meaningful benefits that you

> Successful sponsors understand, respect, and add value to the fan experience.

> Use sponsorship to create small, meaningful wins for all or most of your target markets.

can pass through to fans, not cosmetic benefits that tie you more closely to the property. You'll see the fans as meaningful content creators, on par with the content you can create with the property. You'll elevate the fans, champion them, hero them. Most importantly of all, you'll realise that the fans aren't just the audience, they're not even just the lifeblood of the property, but the lifeblood of your sponsorship.

Examples: Win-win-win

NAB (National Australia Bank) used their sponsorship of the Australian Football League to make Australia's national sport accessible to everyone – even the estimated 25% of Aussies who were born overseas. They created a "Footify" website to teach those first-generation immigrants and other AFL newbies about the lingo (like calling it "footy"). They then went further, training their own bilingual staff to expertly commentate the game in a wide variety of languages, and creating an online "radio station" during the Australian Rules Grand Final, so even non-English speakers could enjoy the biggest game of the year live on TV, while listening to live commentary in their native languages. Inspired!

Canon used sponsorship of London Fashion Week to showcase their range and quality to pro photographers and consumers alike. Among their huge array of leverage activities, they provided product loans, servicing, and repairs to pro photographers at the event, ran Canon Studio – a studio where 5,000 attendees were photographed by a pro and prints provided to take away – and showcased their projection products in the Canon Cinema, projecting live fashion shows and on-demand fashion content. They also created short films, featuring fashion heavyweights.

If you're a **State Farm Insurance** customer and show your card, you can get parking at Atlanta Falcons games for half price in the State Farm Lot.

Global design phenom **Canva** worked with the Melbourne Victory soccer team to allow fans to design the team's new away jersey on their platform in a fan-driven leverage program called #DesignOurAwayKit.

In the UK, **Puma** answered the question, "What do you do when Valentine's Day falls on soccer match day?" with a video of the Hardchorus, a group of rough-looking soccer "hooligans", singing one of the world's most romantic love songs on your behalf. You could dedicate it to your loved one and send it via email or Facebook. Search "Puma Hardchorus" on YouTube and enjoy!

ANZ Bank customers who flashed their cards at the FINA World Swimming Championships got "Blue Lane" express entry and many other benefits.

> Don't sponsor the property, sponsor the fans.

Be respectful

Finally, if you are trying to connect with your target markets and add value to their experience, you need to respect the experience people are trying to have. Don't interrupt, don't get in their way, and don't put your needs above theirs. Above all, respect people's intelligence.

It doesn't take a PhD to be a savvy consumer, and if you think you can put one over on your target markets – or that even trying to is a good idea – you're kidding yourself. At best, they will ignore you. At worst, they will hate you.

Figure 4: Hate, ignore, or love

Hate	Ignore	Love
Disrespectful sponsors	**Most sponsors**	**Best practice**

Interrupting, or gratuitously intruding upon, a fan experience may get people's attention, but certainly isn't going to build affinity or alignment. And advocacy? I've never in my life seen someone post about how moving, blinking LED signage right next to the field during the play of game made the game a better experience for them.

Which generation sponsor are you?

The section on Last Generation Sponsorship may have already made it clear what generation your company is, or even that your company straddles a couple of generations. If not, these checklists should make it crystal clear.

First generation

If your sponsorship program has any of the following traits, you are operating in the first generation of sponsorship:

- A preoccupation with exposure, awareness, or branding.
- Little or no leverage activity, coupled with a belief that the sponsorship itself – the visibility, tickets, hospitality, etc. – will deliver your results.
- Measurement, if any, is of mechanisms, not results against overall marketing and business objectives.

You will never "put one over" your target markets.

Second generation

Your company has realised that you have to do something with – leverage – a sponsorship in order to get results, but what you do is very narrow.

Classically, this would be running a sales promotion anchored on the sponsorship and leaving it at that. But if you're only doing one leverage activity, and that activity is centred on only one very short-term goal, you fall into this category. Other examples of this one-dimensional, short-term thinking would be sponsoring a festival, with your sole goal to sell insurance to festival-goers at your booth, or sponsoring something strictly for the hospitality.

Third generation

Third generation is a big step up from second generation, with sponsors having the following traits – some good, some not so good:

- A range of brand objectives are driving your sponsorship program.
- You know that your results come from leverage, not the sponsorship itself.
- You're doing several creative leverage activities for each of your key sponsorship investments.
- Multiple departments/stakeholders are leveraging sponsorship across their objectives, often integrating them into already-budgeted activities.
- You're measuring results against objectives.
- Your leverage focus tends to be around on-site activities.
- Your leverage is strongly brand-centric.
- You want to be a "brand hero".
- You have been guilty of using sponsorship in a way that is intrusive on, or otherwise diminishes, the fan experience, in order to achieve your brand goals. Examples: Interruption signage, showing straight ads on the big screen at a game, making your presence and promotion overbearing. The list goes on and on . . .

Last Generation Sponsorship

- Your sponsorships are win-win-win; you win, the rightsholder wins, and the fans win.
- That third win comprises small, meaningful added-value activities, generally centred around improving the bad stuff around what you sponsor, or amplifying the best stuff.
- You know that aligning with the fan and your customers is more important than aligning with the property.
- You understand that meaning, relevance, and fan passion is more powerful for your brand than just getting in front of a lot of people.
- Your leverage activities take place across multiple objectives, target markets, departments, and channels.

- You welcome fan collaboration, with crowdsourcing, fan-generated content, customisable experiences and content being a centrepiece of your activity.
- You have moved away from being a brand hero, and instead use sponsorship to make your customers, the fans, or your staff the heroes.
- In addition to taking place within whatever you sponsor (at the game/event/whatever), you use the larger themes of the sponsorship to add value to your larger customer base.
- You sponsor the fans.

The trends driving best-practice sponsorship

Up to now, we've been concentrating on what best practice is, and why it's important to your brand and your results. Now, we're going to go through some of the big trends driving best-practice sponsorship.

Some of these trends are hotbeds for creativity. Some are edgy and occasionally controversial. Some trends have enormous potential for sponsors, some trends are (currently) expensive and impractical, and others need to be used with care.

Disruptive marketing

This trend is not so much driving best-practice sponsorship as validating it.

Over the past few years, disruptive marketing has been a big trend for brands around the world. There are whole books about disruptive marketing, but condensing it down to the bare-bones basics:

- Marketing should be customer-centric or people-centric (as opposed to brand-centric).
- Brands should be authentic.
- Brands should stand for something.
- Objectives have shifted from impressions and sales to sentiment and advocacy.
- Marketing sits at the intersection of analysis and creativity.

Disruptors focus on the target markets — what's important to them, their aspirations and disappointments, and, critically, how they connect with people and interact with the world. So, as people adopt new lifestyles, priorities, and technologies, disruptive marketers incorporate those changes in what they do.

The new currency of marketing

Dopamine – Reward, desire, happiness
Oxytocin – Bonding, trust, loyalty
Serotonin – Confidence, worthiness, belonging

Endocannabinoids – Bliss
Endorphins – Pain relief
Epinephrine – Adrenaline rush

The currency of marketing is no longer reach, exposure, influence, or even sales. It's dopamine, oxytocin, and serotonin. It's endocannabinoids, endorphins, and epinephrine. It's about emotions and connections and joy and self-worth. It's about identity, belonging, and feeling valued, and when a brand can evoke those things, people will align themselves with that brand in a way that will transcend any fleeting promotions a competitor may mount.

Does any of this sound familiar? Because it should. The basics of this huge trend in marketing mirror the basics of best-practice sponsorship almost exactly. That's right . . . with much fanfare, brand marketing has moved to where best-practice sponsorship has been for two decades.

The result of this trend is that sponsorship, which has often been viewed as the poor cousin of "real" marketing, is now being seen as a powerhouse for disruption, and smart sponsors are using these parallels to increase buy-in and integration across marketing channels. More on all of that — and exactly how to do it — later.

Moving up the influence pendulum

As marketers, we're trying to influence people – their perceptions, behaviours, and alignment. If we think of it like a pendulum, we're trying to swing it towards where we want these people to be.

In previous generations of sponsorship, it was about pushing the pendulum at the bottom; pushing for visibility, sales, and other shorter-term outcomes. With best practice, we've moved up the influence pendulum, evoking alignment to the brand and advocacy for the brand, with the understanding that if people align with the brand, and advocate for the brand, the sales and other objectives will come. Critically, a push at the top of the pendulum will create a lot more change than the same push at the bottom.

Figure 5: Influence pendulum

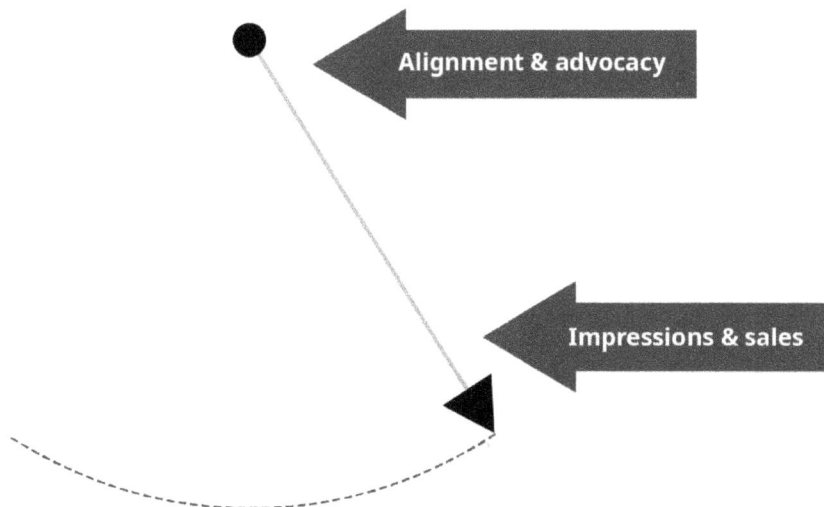

Alignment & advocacy

Impressions & sales

Remote fans

When you sponsor something, it's easy to fixate on the fans that attend; the people who rock up and experience it in person. These are the obvious targets, but usually just a small fraction of the people who care about what you sponsor and the broader theme.

Manchester United has a reported 1.1 billion fans around the world. That's billion, with a B. But how many of those have ever attended a game live? How many foodies who are into clean eating didn't get to that organic food expo? How many industry professionals want professional inspiration or development but couldn't make it to the conference? How many of your staff and customers are in this group?

These are the remote fans — the ones who care, but aren't there. They're still having a fan experience, it's just not on site.

Smart sponsors have seen the enormous value in remote fans since the early days of sponsorship, but it was brought into sharper relief during COVID restrictions, where remote fans were the *only* kind of fans. Sponsors suddenly had to get really good at understanding the remote fan experience and adding value to that.

When in-person events got back to normal, it would have been easy for sponsors to shift the focus back to the in-person fans, but many sponsors learned the lesson and didn't. They realised that remote fans are just as leveragable as they were during COVID, and can deliver huge results against objectives.

So, when you're working on a leverage plan and come up with a great idea for the in-person fans, always ask the question, "How can we make this work for remote fans?" When you're working on that leverage plan, come up with specific ideas for people having the remote fan experience. Lots more on that in Part 3: Leverage.

Emerging and improving technology

When discussing trends in sponsorship, talk invariably turns to the amazing technology now available for leverage.

I get it. It's amazing and easy to get excited about. Technology can deliver both messages and customer and fan experiences in ways we could only have dreamed about 10 years ago. But, it's also easy to go overboard and jump into using new tech just because it's the new cool thing. (Ahem . . . NFTs.)

But as cool as technology has become — and will continue to be — it's critical to remember that technology is just another mechanism to achieve your larger goals. That means adding value to the fan experience and engendering alignment. It still needs to be human-centric, providing real, meaningful, scalable value to actual people, and not all technology does that well.

The use of tech in sponsorship, with ideas, angles, and warnings, is fully explored in Chapter 13: The opportunities and traps of emerging technology.

Technology is just a mechanism to achieve your larger goals.

Standing for something

In the past, most brands stuck to sponsorships that were completely uncontroversial and apolitical — going for investments that would appeal to the broadest range of people. Over the past few years, however, people's expectations of the brands they use have risen. They want to use brands that align with issues that are important to them. This is the case across age groups, but is more pronounced with millennials and younger.

They do this because it aligned with their brand values — values they share with the majority of people in their markets. They knew they'd lose customers, but they also knew it would deepen alignment and brand love for many more of them.

Examples: Standing for something

For decades, soccer's global governing body, FIFA, was reviled by fans for their obvious corruption, and FIFA clearly wasn't listening. For a long time, the sponsors stayed out of it, preferring to concentrate their efforts around the World Cup. Until they didn't. The furore finally hit fever pitch in 2014, when sponsors including **Sony**, **Adidas**, **Visa**, and **Hyundai** decided to speak out, amplifying fan concerns and using their enormous financial investments to pressure FIFA into making changes. This has not only resulted in big changes with how FIFA operates, but has also given sponsors another angle for enhancing their bonds with soccer fans.

2018 marked the 30th anniversary of **Nike's** "Just do it" tagline. They celebrated by profiling some of their biggest stars, in a Dream Crazy campaign. The campaign included former NFL quarterback Colin Kaepernick, who left the league amidst controversy around his kneeling during the national anthem in a bid to bring attention to undue police brutality against black men. His photo was featured with this quote: "Believe in something. Even if it means sacrificing everything." Some Americans were outraged, burning their Nike shoes and apparel on social media, and calling for a boycott, but many more around the world deepened their brand love. Nike hit an all-time high after this controversy.

Also in 2018, **Levi's** partnered with American charity Everytown for Gun Control, even though there isn't much in the US more polarising than the gun control debate. They established a $1 million Safer Tomorrow Fund, matching employee donations, and compelled business leaders to come out for gun control, with over 220 signing a letter to the US Senate. The backlash was similar to Nike, and so was the result. Younger Americans, in particular – who had grown up doing active shooter drills – had been agnostic on denim brands, but this initiative gave them a good reason to consider, buy, and advocate for the brand.

> Brands are using sponsorship to make a statement about where they stand on issues.

If your brand stands for empowerment and giving people a hand up, don't shy away from organisations that help homeless people get back on their feet or domestic abuse victims rebuild their lives. If your brand is making big strides towards sustainability, ensure you're sponsoring organisations that share that commitment, and sponsor in a way that honours it. If equality is a big part of your corporate culture, sponsor LGBTQI+ organisations, or events and services in immigrant communities or the disability space, or make a big commitment to women's sport.

While I'm not advocating sponsoring something controversial just for the sake of it, if your brand stands for something, if your corporate culture stands for something, if your customers stand for something, you shouldn't be afraid of demonstrating that through sponsorship.

ESG and DEI

ESG stands for environmental, social, and governance. DEI stands for diversity, equity, and inclusion. While these high-level concepts have been around for some time, we've seen a big shift to an expectation that companies will be proactively embracing both in their forward planning and day-to-day operations.

Sponsorship can be an excellent way to support these initiatives, but the key is authenticity. Simply sponsoring something in the ESG or DEI space may give your organisation positive talking points, but it's not going to camouflage inconsistencies in the way you do business.

Examples could include sponsoring an environmental charity, while doing little to run the company in a sustainable way (AKA "greenwashing"), or sponsoring an LGBTQI+ organisation when the company isn't a reliably safe space for diverse people (AKA "pinkwashing").

Instead, look at sponsorship as an opportunity to bring ESG and DEI work to life. For example:

- Use sponsorships to provide expertise in policy development, culture change, and other areas that directly impact on the implementation of ESG/DEI initiatives.
- Use sponsorships to directly address and affect change around social issues in your communities.
- Decline to sponsor any property that is demonstrably bad for the environment.
- Decline to sponsor any property that doesn't actively support equity or inclusion (eg, a team that tolerates blatant bigotry by one or more players).
- Leverage in a sustainable manner across all of your sponsorships (eg, no throwaway plastic trinket giveaways).

Mindsets to let go

We're nearly at the end of this theory-heavy first chapter. But before we move on to how to make this all happen — the rest of the book! — there are a few mindsets that need to go. You may or may not have entertained these mindsets, but they can be pervasive in some corporate cultures. Unravelling them will be important to getting the most from sponsorship.

Fans appreciate sponsors

Some sponsors (and most rightsholders) try to make the argument that if you sponsor something the fans love, they'll love your brand for it. As previously noted, there is absolutely no evidence that this happens. If you pay attention to your own behaviour at events, sports, and the like, you'll know this is true — and you're paying more attention than most people because you're in this industry.

Here's the thing: Fans don't owe you anything. I don't care how much you've paid for the sponsorship, your brand is the one turning up uninvited to their fan experience. Brands have a long history of selfishly thrusting themselves upon fans, who wish they would just buzz off, so fans are rightly sceptical.

Example: Budweiser

Budweiser being at the vanguard of sponsorship for social good was not on my bingo card, but here we are, with two great examples:

Basketball is a huge community sport in Brazil. It doesn't take much space or equipment, but nonetheless, inner-city basketball courts were being torn up to build high-rise apartment buildings, removing these important community hubs. **Budweiser** used a little-known law that states that, "A place of public interest with artistic value is considered public heritage and cannot be demolished." They hired legit artists to paint basketball courts, creating large-scale art installations and saving many of them from demolition.

In 2019, **Budweiser** was one of three sponsors of the US National Women's Soccer League, while the Men's League had 24. This contributed to women players being paid 5% what the men were being paid. Budweiser addressed this disparity by creating a Future Official Sponsors of the NWSL campaign. Fronted by superstar Megan Rapinoe, they created fake "ads" for nine placeholder products, demonstrating how that sponsorship could look. Six new sponsors came on board for 2020, resulting in a salary cap increase of 20%.

Fans don't owe you anything.

This isn't difficult to overcome – this whole book is about using sponsorship to help people fall in love with your brand – but if your initial take is that fans will appreciate you just because you're there, you're wrong. A much better approach is that brands need to be loyal to customers and fans, not the other way around.

Sponsorship is a communications platform

I speak at a lot of conferences, including many with industry luminaries from around the world. And yet, so many of them consistently refer to sponsorship as a "communications platform". You might be thinking this is just semantics, but in context, it was clear that their primary interest in sponsorship was outbound communications aimed primarily at the properties' target markets.

If all you're doing with sponsorship is using it as a one-way communications platform, you're underutilising sponsorship to such an extent that you might as well not do it at all. Sponsorship is the most powerful tool in your marketing toolbox. It's driven by meaning and passion; it's flexible, powerful, and durable. If you understand how it works, you know that outbound messaging is just one tiny part of its potential for your brand.

I'm not knocking outbound communications, but if that's what you really want to do, use a media that's purpose built for it.

"Seen to be . . ."

> *"We want to be seen to be giving back to the community."*
> *"We want to be seen to be a friendly, helpful brand."*
> *"We want to be seen to be a big player."*

The implication is that either the sponsor expects their sponsorships to make them look like something they're not, or that the brand is more concerned with posturing than creating genuine connections and alignment with their target markets.

Don't say it. Seriously, don't. Instead, you should be saying, "How can we sponsor in a way that is consistent with our brand personality? That genuinely reflects the passions and interests of our customers and the fans?" The name of the game is authenticity, not posturing.

- Is your brand a positive part of the community? How can you leverage this sponsorship to benefit that community in a meaningful way?
- If your brand is friendly and helpful, how can you leverage the sponsorship in a way that is helpful to the fan experience?
- Want to be seen as a big player? Go all out on leverage execution – be bold, be innovative, and add big value to the fan experience.

"Proud sponsor of . . ."

I'm going to go out on a limb and say that these three words are among the most telling in sponsorship.

You don't see the great sponsors saying, "Proud sponsor of". They aren't doing social posts or running ads in programs or whatever, talking about how they're "proud sponsors of", because that doesn't say a single thing about the brand, except that they paid the money. It may as well read:

"Boring sponsor of . . ."
"Uninspired sponsor of . . ."
"Lazy sponsor of . . ."

I understand that sometimes it's all you can do. Maybe a sponsorship has been thrust upon you at the last minute. Maybe your CEO's pet project is so off-strategy that any amount of leverage would be pointless. Maybe you've simply got too many sponsorships to effectively leverage them individually. Maybe the sponsorship is stale, and you've still got time on the contract. Or maybe your company just lacks the vision or skills to make the most of a valuable marketing investment.

But that's exactly my point. If you're using throwaway words like "Proud sponsor of" with any regularity, it's a sign that something is fundamentally wrong with your sponsorship program.

Sponsorship is an expense

The C-suite, particularly finance, often sees sponsorship as an expense, not a marketing investment. In other words, the people who approve budgets and policies neither understand, nor value, the unique power of sponsorship. It is, in their minds, something that's nice to have but is ultimately expendable.

This can be tricky to address, but in the next chapter, I've got several strategies for making change in this area.

Being a "brand hero"

This is not so much an example of bad leverage as a mindset that poisons your entire sponsorship program.

You can do the best added-value activities in the world, but if your tone is self-congratulatory, you could undo all that good work. It's a bit like adding value to the fan experience, and then standing in the middle of the town square with a bullhorn announcing, "How good is all that stuff we're doing for you? Aren't we great?! Give it up for our brand!"

What you really want is for your target market to experience and appreciate your brand through the leverage activities you do, and to be saying those things themselves. Your goal is brand advocacy, not brand heroism. Your focal point should be on nurturing your connection and relevance with the target markets, and doing it in a way that says, "You're important to us" not, "Do you love us yet?"

If you want to create a hero, design leverage programs that make your customers or staff the heroes. This is a big trend and one that will see your brand basking in the reflected glow, not hogging the spotlight.

Hogging the spotlight is not good for your brand.

Sponsorship counter-arguments

Back when I wrote the first edition, the biggest argument against sponsorship was that it wasn't measurable. Not to put too fine a point on it, but that was wrong then, and it's still wrong now. This book has an entire section on measurement!

In the ensuing years, two other arguments have come to the fore, with marketers who really should know better espousing them in articles, interviews, and on stage at conferences. These arguments appear to stem from a complete lack of understanding of what sponsorship can do and how it works, so they're easy enough to debunk.

Given you're reading this book, you probably don't believe these counter-arguments. But in case you're dealing with sponsorship haters in your organisation, here's how to clap back.

Social media accomplishes the same thing as sponsorship

There is the argument that social media can accomplish much of what sponsorship can, and that is true to an extent. Social media allows you to put things into people's virtual paths and interact with them. The thing is, you need to have something relevant and interesting to say. If it's all about your brand, people will simply tune out. So, where does that shared relevance come from? If you're smart, a lot of it should come from sponsorship.

Don't get me wrong; I love, love, love most social media, and it is one of the most powerful tools for leveraging sponsorship, but they both work better when used in concert, and it's sponsorship that provides the relevance and passion.

Microtargeting accomplishes the same thing as sponsorship

Microtargeting campaigns allow a brand to target people not just based on demographics, but based on interests. That means it's possible for brands to target their ads to specific opera lovers, people interested in animal rescue, dodgeball fans, or whatever, without sponsoring anything.

But that's all it is: Ads. One-way advertising with some kind of call to action. It may target the same people as a sponsorship, but that's where any similarity ends.

This kind of campaign can work, just like any ad campaign can work, but it doesn't have any of the meaning, flexibility, authenticity, and integratability that sponsorship does. Positing that microtargeting can achieve the same things as sponsorship is only true if you think access to fans is the only benefit of sponsorship, which it's absolutely not.

Modern sponsorship is all about adding value to the fan experience, aligning with fans and customers, deepening relationships, and demonstrating shared values. It's collaborative, meaningful, and seeks to bring the fan further into the experience. The value for brands lies in that meaning, and its leveragability across channels and markets.

Trying to use microtargeted advertising to replace the power of sponsorship is doomed to failure. It's replacing a relationship with an ad, passion with an ad, an experience with an ad. It's like trying to replace a trip to Bora Bora with an ad for a trip to Bora Bora.

Brands can and should think about microtargeting, and it may be an efficient way to get your messages to the right people, but it's a replacement for less effective forms of advertising, not sponsorship.

It's like trying to replace a trip to Bora Bora with an ad for a trip to Bora Bora.

Chapter 2

Sponsorship framework

The first chapter gave you the right mindset. This chapter — and every chapter from here on — is about how to make best-practice sponsorship work for your brand.

This framework chapter covers sponsorship policy, creating and managing your stakeholder group, your frontline sponsorship team, equipping yourself for success, and using consultants and agencies.

I'll be addressing sponsorship strategy development in Chapter 3.

Sponsorship policy

Policy isn't fun. It's not sexy. But you won't get sponsorship right without one.

Teams create game plans before every game. They take into account strengths and weaknesses, home advantage and many other variables, so they have the best possible chance of winning. In sponsorship, your strategy is your game plan because it will be adaptable from one sponsorship, target market, or time period to another.

A sponsorship policy is not your game plan; it is the rules of the game, and just like in sports, the rules are the same for every game. Soccer isn't played on a triangular field in Asia. A soccer goal isn't worth four points in Canada. No, a soccer field is always the same shape and size, a goal is always one point and, just like soccer, your company's rules of sponsorship are consistent, no matter what you are sponsoring.

A short, sharp policy document is essential to create a consistent process and an adherence to your company's "rules" of sponsorship, instilling trust and confidence across your organisation because:

- It defines what sponsorship is and why you are doing it
- It defines the no-go zones
- It spells out the process
- It curbs sponsorship of pet projects

⮞ It reduces the perceived "risk" by spelling out the rigour applied to sponsorship decisions and management.

Below, I've outlined some sponsorship policy pitfalls, as well as the components of a strong sponsorship policy, along with some example wording.

Sponsorship policy pitfalls

A sponsorship policy is not a lot different than other policies, and many of the components will look familiar. A sponsorship policy also shares some of the pitfalls of policy, in general. Some of the things you need to avoid are outlined below.

Too general

Your sponsorship policy should be specific and tight, with a minimum of grey areas. Generalisations aren't helpful. Using generalisations in a sponsorship policy is like your local road rules being "Drive safe. Be nice."

Too specific

The flip side to being too general is a policy that is built around a predetermined "ideal" scenario, leaving little flexibility to explore different options. An example of this is indicating what property categories you sponsor.

Crossing into strategy territory

As some companies go through the policy development process, they start to include information that belongs in the strategy, such as plans for individual sponsorships, or how they intend to achieve marketing objectives through sponsorship. This needlessly complicates what should be a very straightforward document.

Full of meaningless corporate speak

This is a big one. If you want a policy that will be accepted and adopted by everyone from your regional sales teams to your senior executives, you have to say exactly what you mean, in plain English, with no room for interpretation. If you think that should be obvious, have a look at this sentence, found in the policy of a client of mine:

> *The outcomes we wish to achieve with sponsorship are to exploit synergies with outside partners to build on our core strengths in each of our product silos.*

This was supposed to be clarifying why the company was involved in sponsorship, but there were so many vague, overused buzzwords, it was anyone's guess what it actually meant. It makes my head hurt just reading it!

A sponsorship policy is not your game plan; it is the rules of the game.

Components of a sponsorship policy

Your sponsorship policy should include all of the following components. The goal is to address each of them thoroughly but concisely. Most sponsorship policies are only three to five pages long.

Situational analysis

In this section, you should briefly outline the current situation with both your brand and sponsorship portfolio. You should also include a paragraph or two that outlines the driving forces and principles behind your involvement in sponsorship, as it will provide some context for the rest of the document. An example:

> *We engage in sponsorship primarily to achieve marketing objectives, defined as changing or reinforcing the perceptions and behaviours of our target markets, and deepening their brand alignment. These target markets can be internal (staff), external (customers), or intermediary (our retailers).*
>
> *We use sponsorship to deepen our connection to target markets, demonstrate our understanding of them, and adding value to our relationships with them.*

Definitions

This is a short section that simply clarifies what you consider sponsorship and what you don't. This may seem obvious, but it may not be to some of the people you expect to adhere to this policy. For example:

> *Sponsorship is a marketing investment, entered into primarily to achieve multiple marketing objectives. It is leveragable across other marketing activities and usually involves a contractual relationship between the company and a rightsholder.*

If you are also involved with philanthropy, you may want to include additional wording, to delineate between these activities and sponsorship. For example:

> *We are also involved in philanthropy, which involves the donation or grant of funds to a registered charity, with no expectation of marketing or other commercial return. Philanthropic activities are covered under a separate policy, which is held in [department].*

Exclusions and exclusivity

It is a temptation to create all sorts of exclusions around things you can't imagine doing or probably wouldn't do. This is a mistake. A policy should be hard and fast, so only create rules or exclusions that are absolutes, because you never really know. You don't want to be in a situation where you have to knock back an amazing opportunity because of an overly arbitrary rule in your policy.

An example of this could be a winery that has an exclusion around sponsoring organisations that are focused on children. On the face of it, this seems reasonable — alcohol and kids aren't a great match. Then again, a children's charity may have an annual gala dinner that is perfect for a wine sponsor.

This doesn't mean that you will end up with a lot of investments that aren't right for your brand. On the contrary, your strategy and your selection criteria will shake out anything that isn't a great match for your brand or needs.

If you are going to exclude categories of sponsorship, be sure to include your rationale. An example:

> *In keeping with our strong sustainability credentials, we do not sponsor motorsport.*

Or:

> *As an alcoholic beverages company, it is inappropriate for us to sponsor with child-focused properties. We will only consider alcohol sponsorship for adult-focused fundraising events for these organisations.*

When it comes to exclusivity, you need to specify exactly which brand categories you are not willing to share and over what geographic area. Requiring category exclusivity means you won't consider sponsorship of a property if one of your competitors is already sponsoring. You will also require partners to honour that exclusivity and exclude those categories when seeking sponsorship. For example:

> *We require category exclusivity across all cable, wireless, and other telecommunications, cable television, streaming services, and broadband providers serving South Africa.*

Sponsorship process

This is no doubt the largest part of your policy document as it formalises the whole sponsorship process. To ensure it's clear that this is the process for all sponsorships — including those from senior executives — you should include some wording to this effect, such as:

> *While introductions to possible partners are welcomed from any area of the company, all opportunities will go through the following process, ensuring they are selected, negotiated, leveraged, managed, and measured in accordance with our strategic needs.*

Then, outline the processes under each of these headings:

- Selected
- Negotiated
- Formalised
- Leveraged
- Managed
- Measured

It does not go into what decisions will be made or why, simply the workflow, responsibilities, approvals, and documentation along the way.

Supporting tools

This section lists the tools and templates that are available to support the process and where they can be sourced. You will probably include many of the templates and tools from this book on this list.

Delegations

It is likely that there are levels of approval for sponsorship, and this is where you will outline those levels. I've provided an example below. Please take the dollar values as illustrative only. Every company will set these levels differently:

Regional marketing managers may approve sponsorships of up to $5,000 without sign-off from corporate. These expenditures will come out of the regional marketing budget.

The sponsorship stakeholder group, led by the sponsorship manager, may approve sponsorships of up to $500,000 per annum or $2 million over the contract duration.

The executive management committee must approve sponsorships valued at more than $500,000 per annum or $2 million over the contract duration. The marketing director will make the presentation and this must be supported by a recommendation from the sponsorship stakeholder group.

Contracts

As we will cover later in the book, all significant sponsorship investments must be formalised with an agreement. This is the section where you will set out what type of agreements are required at what levels. Again, take the dollar amounts in this example as illustrative only:

We will formalise all sponsorship investments valued at more than $5,000, cash or in-kind.

For investments between $5,000 and $100,000, cash or in-kind, we require a letter of agreement, with both parties addressing and executing all components of the relationship.

For investments of more than $100,000, cash or in-kind, we require a full contract.

Pro forma for both the letter agreement and full contract are available on the company intranet. Both agreements must be reviewed by legal prior to execution.

Note, some sponsors require all sponsorships to be formalised, while others are comfortable sponsoring at low amounts without a formal contract or letter agreement. Which approach is most appropriate for your company should be determined in consultation with your legal advisors.

Accountability and responsibility

This section lists the people or roles that are responsible for all of the process steps. This information can be integrated into the process section, kept separate, or you can integrate it and briefly restate it, which is my usual approach.

Review and evaluation

This section is not about the review and evaluation of your sponsorship portfolio (that will be outlined in your process steps) but the evaluation of the policy. You want this policy to be current and relevant, not languish out of date in the bottom of someone's drawer. For example:

The sponsorship manager will review this policy in January of every year, with suggested changes presented to the sponsorship stakeholder group for discussion and approval in the February meeting.

Sponsorship stakeholder group

Sponsorship doesn't work well in isolation. If one person or team is solely responsible for the selection, negotiation, leverage, management, and measurement of a sponsorship portfolio, you can be sure all or most of the following will be true:

- You'll be missing out on a huge opportunity to amplify your broader results because your sponsorships will lack integration across other marketing and business activities.
- You'll be spending way too much money because you will be creating leverage activities from scratch instead of integrating with existing marketing activities and channels.
- Your negotiations won't provide the specific benefits your broader stakeholders may need for sponsorship to work for them because you will not be getting their input before committing.

> Your measurement will be, *at best*, incomplete as you will not have access to all of the measurement metrics and benchmarks from across your company.
> Sponsorship will be seen as a luxury spend — expendable at the first sign of economic duress — because results will be restricted to one area, not spread across many key areas, amplifying the results.
> Your portfolio will be, at least partly, susceptible to the whims of senior management because who's going to say "no" to them? You?

The good news is that gaining the buy-in and participation you need to avoid this situation and create great, holistic results for your company isn't difficult, and the place to start is by creating a sponsorship stakeholder group.

What does a sponsorship stakeholder group do?

A sponsorship stakeholder group includes people from across your organisation, who come together periodically to:

> Assess shortlisted new sponsorship opportunities
> Develop negotiation strategies for new and renewing sponsorships
> Plan leverage activities
> Create and carry out measurement plans.

While the above list shows the most typical stakeholder group activities, they also provide two other critical functions.

First, having a sponsorship stakeholder group can mitigate senior executive micro-managing around sponsorship. You'll have a cadre of stakeholders signing off on highly strategic leverage and measurement plans, as well as making recommendations on whether to commit to various investments, and why. This has the dual role of gently educating the C-suite on best practice, while also demonstrating the degree of rigour and planning that goes into modern sponsorship.

Second, the other critical function is providing a brains trust of subject-matter experts. When facing issues or opportunities around a sponsorship — or the portfolio as a whole — their different perspectives can be instrumental to creating a positive outcome.

Who should be included?

This is a big question, and one that is wholly dependent on the structure of your company and your category of business.

Below is a sample list of departments, to get you started. Don't panic that this looks like it could be a lot of people. Not every member of the stakeholder group needs to be at every meeting, so you may end up with 15 or more members, but 8–10 in most meetings:

If you don't have buy-in, your sponsorships will underperform.

- Brand management
- Consumer/SME marketing
  - Customer retention/loyalty
  - Customer acquisition
- Major customer management (enterprise or institutional sales)
- Social media management/content creation
- Brand experience
- Marketing analytics and/or research
- Customer communications
- Events team
- HR (communications, recruitment, retention, corporate culture)
- Retail or branch management
- Customer service
- Regional marketing or sales managers
- External agencies or consultants (if pertinent)
- C-level manager, ideally, the CMO

The obvious follow-up question is, who do we target within each of these areas? Ideally, you want a decision-maker involved. Second best is a high-level decision-influencer. Anyone further down the hierarchy isn't going to have the juice to sell new ideas into their team.

That said, within each area, there will probably be one or more decision-makers or major decision-influencers who are a bit more creative and open to new ideas. Nurture one of those people to fly the sponsorship flag for you.

The importance of a senior executive champion

Best-practice sponsorship is often a big departure from the way it's always been done in a company. The goals will be different, the measures will be different, and that can make senior executives nervous.

The best way to counteract senior executive resistance to the new approach is to enlist one of them to be your champion. Your head of marketing is the obvious choice, but you could also work with the head of business development or a group brand manager.

In order to be a good champion, the senior executive doesn't need to be a sponsorship expert, but they do need to understand the basic mindset behind best practice. This will allow them to credibly promote best practice and the benefits to the company, and let you and your team get on with it. Suggesting that your champion read the first chapter of this book would give them a very good starting point.

Ideally, the champion will attend some of your sponsorship stakeholder group meetings — especially the first one. The goal is not to get them involved with implementation

You need a senior executive "champion".

but to introduce them to the new process and to get their input. There may be senior executive or big-picture issues that you won't be aware of without their help.

Of course, the champion needs to be kept apprised of any critical developments, milestones, and issues, so that the communication to these to senior executives is managed proactively.

Other advisors

There are a few other advisors and roles that are very useful for best-practice sponsorship.

Spokesperson

If there is any chance that the sponsorship itself may get media coverage, you need to have someone prepared to answer the questions. This is particularly true if the sponsorship, your leverage program, or the fact that you may be exiting a sponsorship, is controversial.

Whoever you choose to be the spokesperson, they must be credible and knowledgeable, and understand all of the elements in the case for your strategy and choices.

The spokesperson could also be fulfilling another role, such as sponsorship manager or champion.

Financial advisor

Financial management is another issue, and there is a lot of difference between how companies budget, acquit, and account for funds, so any specific advice I give would be woefully inadequate.

I will say, however, that sponsorship is more likely than most areas in your company to be accessing multiple budgets, as it is integrated across other activities. In addition, structuring your contractual payments, and acquitting any in-kind provided, can be quite complex, so it is important to have someone from finance involved from the outset. This will ensure that you know any protocols, that they understand what is going on, and that you have good and timely access to financial advice when you need it.

You also want to be sure that you are constantly taking the position that the more buy-in from business units and integration across media you have, the less incremental funding any given sponsorship will require. While this should be part of your initial sell-in, you need to keep saying it throughout the planning and implementation process as well.

Legal advisor

As with the financial advisor, your lawyer will be an on-call part of your sponsorship team. This should be a no-brainer – sponsorships are based on contracts that need to be structured, interpreted, and enforced. You can't do it yourself, unless you happen to be a lawyer!

You will need a lawyer to assist with the contract in the early stages of each sponsorship relationship. You will also need a lawyer if you get into strife. If things start to go pear-shaped, don't hesitate to involve your lawyer early. Even if it's just tweaking some wording in an email, so you don't unwittingly undermine your legal position, it is worth getting this advice.

The frontline sponsorship team

When I refer to the frontline sponsorship team, I'm talking about the people who make sponsorship happen. This could be a dedicated sponsorship team, or it could be a brand team with responsibility for delivering sponsorships.

Redefining the sponsorship role

Whether you work alone or in a team, the sponsorship role has changed a lot.

Historically, the sponsorship role used to revolve around three things:

1. Gatekeeping
2. Managing the rightsholder relationship
3. Admin

While the above tasks are still part of the job, there are many strategies for streamlining them, which I go through in Part 2: Sponsorship Selection, and Part 5: Management. This frees you up for the much more strategic, important parts of your role in modern sponsorship.

Strategist

Every company that invests significantly in sponsorship needs a formal sponsorship strategy, and while this should be a collaborative process, it needs to be spearheaded and formalised by the head of sponsorship. As a natural extension of the sponsorship strategy, the sponsorship manager will also manage the portfolio audit process.

The next chapter covers both of these functions in great detail.

Stakeholder group leader

Effectively leading the sponsorship stakeholder group will probably be the most testing part of your job. You must have exceptional sponsorship skills, with enough experience, authority, and charisma to lead a team of cross-departmental stakeholders, without being their boss.

As leader of this group, you'll be coordinating sponsorship assessments, negotiation planning, leverage planning, measurement, and more. You'll be facilitating brainstorms and building consensus. And you must have a strong, working understanding of every other marketing media because sponsorship needs to be integrated across all of it.

The sum total of this critical role puts you in a rare position, with a breadth of skills and expertise that's broader than anyone else in a mid-level marketing role. If you want to be chief marketing officer someday, you couldn't ask for a better proving ground.

Internal consultant

In my eyes, this is one of the most important — and overlooked — parts of the job.

Realistically, all of the people in your stakeholder group have other jobs. They are specialists in their own areas — social, sales, HR, retention, etc. — and while they may have a good, working knowledge of sponsorship, it is usually a minor portion of what they do, so when they have questions or challenges or need some inspiration, they need an expert to tap for advice.

Some stakeholders may also be selecting and managing sponsorships from their own areas. For instance, sales may drive trade show and trade association sponsorships, HR may sponsor properties specifically for recruitment and retention, and regions may be running their own sponsorship portfolios. But just because they're managing sponsorships doesn't mean they're experts, and they usually know it. Having someone they can work with on the trickiest parts of sponsorship can make a huge difference to their performance.

Typically, this means taking on tasks such as:

- Providing guidance on the sponsorship selection framework
- Working with stakeholders, so they can negotiate the most appropriate and leveragable benefits
- Facilitating their leverage and measurement planning process
- Issues management
- Providing advice on renewals, mid-term negotiations, and sponsorship reviews.

Information collator

As part of the internal consultant role, there is also the role of information collator, which is particularly important when it comes to measurement. Done correctly, a large portion of your sponsorship measurement will be done by members of your stakeholder group. They'll identify benchmarks, projections, and measure actual returns against objectives. Your job is to get that disparate information into a cohesive, digestible format, so it can be analysed and distributed.

Up-skiller

In addition to doing your job, day-to-day, it's also your responsibility to ensure that your skills, and those of your team, are up to date and reflect best practice. There are lots of ways to do this, including:

- Attending conferences and workshops
- In-house training
- Online training

> Internal consultant is one of the most important parts of the job.

- Certificate courses in sponsorship (CPD)
- Industry association membership
- Reviewing industry publications, as well as credible bloggers and podcasters.

Team structure

If you're a team of one, you can skip this part. But if you have a sponsorship team – or a brand team running a sponsorship portfolio – how you structure it is important to the effectiveness and efficiency of your department.

Below, I've outlined a basic team structure. Don't get too hung up on the job titles. While these are typical, they're by no means set in stone.

Sponsorship manager

As sponsorship manager, your job will include:

- Leading the sponsorship team
- Leading the sponsorship stakeholder group
- Spearheading sponsorship strategy development and sponsorship audits/reviews
- Being the primary internal consultant
- Overseeing measurement reports
- Assisting sponsorship specialists with negotiations, renewals, and issues management
- Heading up the largest sponsorship negotiations.

That's quite a hefty workload, and it doesn't leave a lot of time for managing individual sponsorships, which brings me to sponsorship specialists.

Sponsorship specialists

While the sponsorship manager job is big picture, sponsorship specialists head up the management of individual investments. Typically, this would include:

- Day-to-day management of rightsholder relationships
- Leading most new sponsorship negotiations
- Leading renewal negotiations
- Coordinating leverage planning and implementation
- Collating post-sponsorship measurement reports
- Some internal consulting, particularly around various stakeholders' involvement with a property they manage.

I often get questions about how to divide the workload between specialists. Some sponsors divide the portfolio by type; for example, one or two specialists handle the sports sponsorships, someone else handles culture and festivals, another specialist handles charitable sponsorships, and so on. This can work, but it's not ideal.

Instead, I favour specialists managing mixed portfolios. This encourages creative, resourceful thinking, and a broad portfolio requires a broader skillset, elevating all of the sponsorships. It also stops specialists from falling into the habit of leveraging and managing their homogeneous sponsorships in a homogenous way.

Finally, if you have a new or less experienced specialist, they can manage a mixed portfolio of smaller sponsorships, adding larger and more complex sponsorships as they gain experience and confidence.

Sponsorship administrator

Note that I haven't included admin in either of the job roles above. That's because it's a) not the best use of a manager or specialist's time; and b) there are professional admins that will do it better.

One of the best, most efficient hires a busy sponsorship team can make is a sponsorship administrator, who will take on tasks, such as:

- Ticketing and hospitality
- Managing merch, signage, and other collateral orders, production, and storage
- Shipping merch, signage, other collateral
- Shepherding IP approvals (both ways)
- Scheduling stakeholder group meetings and other general admin.

Size of the team

Getting the size of the sponsorship team right is driven by three factors:

1. Sponsorship has a high workload.
2. Unleveraged sponsorship is a total waste of money.
3. Team members need to manage no more sponsorships than they can effectively leverage and manage.

Can one person leverage and manage five sponsorships? Probably. Fifteen? Maybe. Forty (and I've seen that and worse)? Not a chance.

So, what do you do if you're more on the forty-per-staffer end of the spectrum? You've got a few options:

- Do a ruthless portfolio audit, culling all of the dead wood, and reducing the number of sponsorships.
- Structure efficiencies into the portfolio, making it easier to manage a larger slate of sponsorships (see Chapter 23: Structuring your portfolio).
- Hire more staff.

> One of the best hires a busy sponsorship team can make is a sponsorship administrator.

Before considering increasing the size of your team, I strongly recommend you undertake the first two strategies. In most cases, this will reduce the workload to a manageable level, *while increasing results across the portfolio.*

Another angle is to determine how much of your specialists' time is spent on admin tasks because the solution may not be another specialist, but bringing in a gun admin to look after that work.

Who should manage community sponsorship portfolios?

I've lost count of the number of sponsors I've worked with who managed their community sponsorship portfolio separately from their other sponsorships. In most cases, their "commercial" sponsorships were managed by the sponsorship or brand team, while their community sponsorships were managed by corporate relations (or similar). Different teams, different agendas, different KPIs.

This is so common, it could almost be called the norm, but that doesn't make it a good idea. In fact, by approaching sponsorship this way, you're doing a disservice to your brand, the power of sponsorship, and your communities.

Sponsorship is sponsorship

This approach usually stems from the misguided idea that some sponsorships are for achieving "real" objectives — ones that build the brand and sell stuff — and other sponsorships are for ticking the box. What box? The "social responsibility" box. The "giving back to the community box". The "halo" box.

But why are you really "giving back to the community"? It's not altruism. If it were true altruism, you wouldn't bother telling anyone about it. No, you're doing it for a reason, and that reason will always come back to the same three objectives as any other sponsorship:

1. Changing or reinforcing perceptions
2. Changing or reinforcing behaviours
3. Building alignment

While sponsors will use different types of sponsorship in different ways to achieve these goals, the process of pinpointing the meaning and relevance, leveraging, and measuring those sponsorships is exactly the same.

Your portfolio is already diverse

If you're still thinking that community sponsorships are different, have a good look at your current portfolio. Is a community sponsorship really that much of an outlier? Look at the professional sports, the solar race, and the multicultural festival you sponsor. Look at the industry events, the theatre company, and the fun run.

Whatever your portfolio looks like, it's already diverse. Including your community sponsorships is just a natural extension of that diversity.

Community sponsorships also need to be leveraged

Unfortunately, when community sponsorships are hived off from the rest of the sponsorship portfolio, leverage is often cursory, throwing back to the bad old days of doing a media release, some photo ops, a bit of "proud sponsor of" action on social media, and a photo in the annual report. Boom, done.

Community sponsorships can be extremely powerful marketing platforms, rife with all of the ingredients critical to making best-practice, disruptive sponsorship work. But making it work takes leverage — the same kind of leverage your other sponsorships enjoy — and if you're phoning it in, you're investing for virtually no return.

Meaning doesn't discriminate

People can be just as passionate about a community centre or recycling initiative as they are about a sport or major festival. Use that. Sponsor what's meaningful to your target markets, whatever that may be, then leverage the hell out of it.

Managing as a commercial sponsorship is better for those community organisations

Managing community sponsorships as the marketing powerhouses they are is also much better for your partners.

If a sponsorship is achieving multiple measurable objectives, it's worth more money. It could be the difference between providing a $5,000 token (AKA "go-away money") and making a $50,000 investment.

And even if the dollar figures are the same, if you asked any of those community partners whether they'd rather have $50,000, or $50,000 *plus* a sponsor proactively telling their stories, extending their market, using crowdsourcing and other strategies to get people interested in, and aligned with, what they're about, and making their people the heroes, they will clearly pick the latter.

Set up your social team like a fan

You will no doubt be embarking on substantial social media activities around your sponsorships, but the voice you use in socials can make or break its success.

Properties can be exciting, and people love them, so if one of your objectives is to build fan alignment, your voice needs to be that of a fan. Drop the bland, corporate speak — which builds a wall, not alignment — and become a fan.

> Post with enthusiasm, just like the fans.
> Hero the fans.
> Showcase staff and customers being fans.
> Reflect fan feelings — joy, frustration, awe, empathy, etc.

In addition, your social team needs to be responsive to things that are going on — great moments, wins, losses, emerging stories — on a timely basis. It's no good posting your excitement about a huge win if it's a week late because you had to run it through three layers of approvals.

Being responsive and timely is also about not getting too hung up on production values. Sometimes a scrappy, authentic response is exactly the answer.

Collaborative workspace

You may be lucky enough that your company has its own infrastructure for collaborative workspaces, and if so, it will be a great tool for managing the sponsorship process across all of the members of your sponsorship team. If not, there are many options for cheap or free collaboration systems.

In the absence of an in-house workspace, my collaboration and project-tracking tool of choice is Trello. (No, I'm not paid by them to say that.) Trello is a kanban-style organisation system, built around lists and cards. These are the lists I usually recommend to sponsors:

> Admin — Cards for major documents, like the contract, leverage plan, measurement plan, etc., so they're always easy to find and reference.
> Inbox — Cards for major tasks or categories of tasks that haven't been addressed yet. In each card, you can have multiple checklists for steps or sub-tasks of that task.
> Waiting — You're waiting for someone or something before you can start moving again.
> Doing — Cards for tasks that are underway.
> Done — Cards for tasks that are finished.

You can assign people to cards and tasks, put deadlines on cards and tasks, and add multiple attachments to cards. You can add labels, custom fields and buttons, and power-ups. You can also view all of your tasks in a list or calendar. The learning curve is easy, it can be integrated with your calendar, and you can follow and unfollow tasks. In addition, the flexibility is much greater than any purpose-built sponsorship management software that I've seen, and I've seen a lot of them!

Using consultants

I'm a sponsorship consultant — one of many around the world — and I've worked with a lot of corporate sponsors. Using the right consultant for your situation can make a huge difference to your results, if you're prepared to make the most of them.

Do you really need a consultant?

How do you know if you will benefit from a consultant? Here are some checklists that may help you to determine whether consulting is appropriate. For purposes of these lists, I'm limiting my advice to strategic sponsorship consulting, rather than sponsorship implementation, which I've addressed in the next section.

You probably don't need a sponsorship consultant if the following is true:

- Frontline sponsorship and marketing staff have a good, working understanding of best-practice sponsorship.
- You have a strong marketing plan for your brand.
- Your target markets are segmented primarily on psychographics (ideally, backed up by research).
- Your organisational culture is one of teamwork and cross-departmental cooperation.
- Senior executive influence on the sponsorship portfolio is minimal.
- You have at least one senior executive championing positive, strategic change in the approach to sponsorship.
- You are comfortable seeking out advice, ideas, training, templates and other supporting information from credible sources on the web and in books.

You would probably benefit from a strategic sponsorship consultant if the following is true:

- You or your team lack best-practice sponsorship experience (but want to learn).
- You and your team want to be engaged in the process.
- You have identified that elevating your approach to sponsorship is an organisational goal.
- Your main impediment to elevating your sponsorship approach is a lack of buy-in or understanding of sponsorship across your organisation and/or with senior executives.
- You are undertaking a major portfolio overhaul, which may include difficult or sensitive renegotiations and/or exits.
- Politics or senior executive choice drives many sponsorship decisions.
- Your sponsorships are largely regionalised and you want more cooperation and a uniform approach across regions.
- You have a large portfolio of brands, each managing their own sponsorship portfolio.

You will not fully benefit from a sponsorship consultant if the following is true:

- You do not have a marketing or brand plan in place. (It is possible to work with a consultant without a marketing or brand plan in place, but it's more work, requires more assumptions, and even really good work may lack credibility because it lacks some of the foundational elements.)
- Your senior executives and/or board have a stranglehold on sponsorship decisions and are unlikely to take advice.
- Your brand is changing so much that by the time the work is completed, it is outdated.

What kind of consultant do you need?

Sponsorship consultants have a number of different ways of working, and before you can hire someone, you need to know what you want. I've outlined some of the critical factors below.

Adding capacity vs building capacity

If you're trying to fill a gap in your team — whether that gap is time or expertise — you're looking to add capacity. You may be hiring someone who would define their business as "consulting", but the type of role you're trying to fill is more like a skilled contractor — an alternative to hiring another staff member. The role could be low- or high-level, full- or part-time, primarily in-house or not.

Building capacity, on the other hand, is where the consultant provides strategic advice and elevates the expertise, efficiency, and confidence of the team so that organisational capacity to do sponsorship well increases. There is often as much emphasis on education and support as on strategic advice.

Strategy vs implementation

Many sponsorship consultants, and particularly agencies, position themselves as "full service" — both strategists and implementers. In reality, most are primarily implementers; they work frontline and make things happen. They can be extraordinarily talented and indispensable when it comes to making a strategy come to life. Truth be told, though, most of the best implementers — the ones who can conjure an amazing fan or customer experience from thin air — aren't that great at pointy-end strategy. And when they do strategy development, it can tend to favour their strengths, rather than offering objective advice.

Then there are the strategists; the people who help to develop and sell-in the overarching strategies that spawn the leverage programs that need to be implemented. They can be very good at what they do, but will probably have little interest in being involved with — or even the expertise for — the nitty-gritty of making it happen.

If you know you need one or the other of these roles, hire a specialist consultant or

PART 1 / PREPARATION

agency. If you genuinely need both, consider hiring the two roles separately. If you are bound and determined to hire one agency to do it all, try to find one that has a dedicated strategist with some serious experience.

Project vs portfolio

This one is simple, and related to the preceding point. Is the consultancy centred on one, succinct project? Or does your whole portfolio need an overhaul?

If it is project based, you could need a strategist, implementer, or both. If it's portfolio based, you're probably looking for a strategist.

Expertise vs credibility (and expertise)

If you've got challenges and objectives and you don't know how to get there, you need strong, strategic expertise and a heavy dose of experience.

On the other hand, you may know exactly the way forward, but your organisation has a culture of valuing outside expertise more than internal. Or you may have complex politics to navigate. In that case, you're hiring for credibility and generating internal buy-in for a new strategy. You want someone that is not only experienced, but also has a strong bank of recognisable clients, and a reasonably high industry profile.

Hourly rate vs project fee vs retainer

Some companies prefer to hire on an hourly basis, but a lot of consultants just hate it because it's a pain in the bum to do all the admin. The other option is a project fee, where the proposal has a set fee to accomplish the brief. This will be more typical.

My opinion is that you get more value from a project fee as it is outcome based. That consultant is just going to keep working until the job is done, and that's really what it's all about. To get a good consultant, you're not hiring for X number of hours, you're hiring for their years of experience and talent, and people with experience and talent can crank through good work efficiently.

You may also elect to have a sponsorship consultant on retainer but understand there are three main reasons for doing so:

1. You have a very complex sponsorship situation, and you require high-level expertise on an as-needed basis.
2. You have a sharp, but inexperienced, team who need high-level advice to guide and develop them.
3. You have more work to do than you have people to do it, or you just want to outsource some of the more unpleasant work (like reviewing proposals).

In this last instance, you are looking more for a contractor with good skills than a high-level consultant. Don't pay for more than you need.

> You get more value from a project fee as it is outcome based.

How to brief a sponsorship consultant or agency

"Sponsorship. What can you do for me? Go."

That's the entire text of an email I received from someone looking for a sponsorship consultant. While it was a temptation to just delete it, I replied asking for more details. Never heard back.

If you want generic information about what a consultant does, check out their website. If you want a considered, customised proposal that addresses your specific needs, you need to provide a complete brief. You can provide this in writing, or you can book a meeting to discuss your needs. Either way, your brief should include:

- The specific outcomes you want to achieve, as a result of the consultancy
- Timeframe for achieving them
- The challenges you've identified that stand in the way (the consultant may identify more)
- The general approach and experience level of your team
- The size and structure of your portfolio, including the total value and the number of individual sponsorships — you can ballpark these figures — as this helps a consultant understand the scope of the project
- Potential political or budget issues
- Organisational culture around change
- Timeframe for the consulting project
- Timeframe and process for decision-making.

If required, get the potential consultant to sign a non-disclosure agreement, but you need to be upfront if you want to get a proposal that meets your needs.

What to look for in a sponsorship proposal

A good consultant will put together a proposal that makes it easy for you to make a decision. It doesn't have to be long but should include all of the following:

- The consultant's understanding of your situation and objectives
- Outline of overall approach
- Outline of outcomes and approach for each major component of the consultancy
- Exclusivity — Will the consultant be available to your competitors? If not, how long is the exclusivity period?
- Confidentiality — An undertaking to keep all materials and information confidential, whether an NDA is signed or not
- Information required — What background information do you need to provide to the consultant?
- Travel required

- Availability — An outline of any major issues with availability during the proposed timeframe, such as an office shutdown for the holidays, an extended vacation, or a major event
- Timeline
- Fees and other costs
- Terms, including when the offer expires

Unless you have some history with the consultant, or you found them via a trusted referral, you should definitely ask for references you can contact — and then contact them! Also good is to ask for two or three short case studies of where their advice made a difference to measurable sponsorship results.

Frameworks for large, decentralised, or diverse organisations

Up to now, this chapter has focused on companies with a reasonably concise, reasonably centralised collection of brands. But what if you're trying to achieve great, measurable, and consistent sponsorship results across a diverse portfolio of brands, regions, or even subsidiary companies? Organisational change around sponsorship is complex for big companies, and does require a commitment to actually do it, but it is doable. More than that, it is absolutely worth doing.

I've done this kind of work a lot, and if you're looking at embarking on organisational change around sponsorship, I have some recommendations.

Don't generalise

If the goal is a consistent, sophisticated approach to sponsorship — one that maximises results across your portfolio — you need to accept that this consistent approach will look different from one area of your company to another. And the larger and more diverse the company, the more tempting it will be to generalise with any capacity-building training or materials, but that won't do any of your brands any favours. Providing generic advice, like, "Leverage your sponsorship investments through all of your channels", or, "Select sponsorships that achieve multiple marketing objectives", falls into the category of being accurate, but not useful.

Channels, objectives, target markets, trends, and more could vary vastly from one brand and/or geographic region to another. If you actually want to increase your organisational capacity to do sponsorship well, and reap strong, measurable results from all of your investments, you have to be prepared to get specific and provide advice, examples, tools, and templates that suit each market and every major brand group.

Balance education and resources

If you want to maximise uptake of a more sophisticated approach, you need to ensure that you balance vision with how-to, theory with case studies, and recommendations with the tools to back them up.

Balance ownership and shortcuts

It's easy to go too far with providing shortcuts and how-to, and cross into the territory of telling stakeholders what to do, or giving them so little input in the creative process that they don't take any ownership, and uptake is half-hearted, at best.

In providing a platform to elevate your sophistication, the whole idea is to make great sponsorship — the theory, creativity, and implementation — achievable and doable. Your job is to provide the framework, tools, and inspiration so they get excited about it and can confidently make it their own. It's a fine line to walk, but if you don't do this, this whole exercise will fail.

Provide an expert safety net

Even if you do everything else perfectly, a big component of elevating sponsorship across a big organisation is creating confidence in the approach. For that reason, you should endeavour to have a resource who can provide support, particularly in the first year or so.

You could use a sponsorship consultant, but I usually try to position a person or small team internally who can fill the role of expert safety net. The role is about providing as-needed advice, coaching, and even some facilitation, until your various stakeholders are comfortable carrying on independently. In most companies, this would be the home office sponsorship team.

Don't skimp on the scope

If you've got a big company, this is a big job. Don't pretend it's not.

Make the commitment to do it properly. Don't be like most companies, who create some kind of generic guidebook with equally generic advice, refer people to their sponsorship policy and an agreement template, leave stakeholders to their own devices, and then wonder why nothing changes. Nothing changes because they skimped.

Emphasise credibility

If your corporate culture has a stronger focus on internal answers and in-house expertise, and you're confident in both your skills and capacity to do this, then there's no reason that a manager or team with a strong understanding of best-practice sponsorship can't develop these resources. You're going to need heavy senior executive backing for people to take it seriously across the company, and, ideally, sign-off from your executive committee or similar.

If you're not confident, don't have the capacity to develop all the resources and guidance required for your diverse brands or regions, you've got a lot of politics, or your company culture is one that values outside expertise more than internal, I strongly suggest that you hire a credible sponsorship consultant to spearhead this job for you.

This specific kind of sponsorship consulting – Sponsorship Systems Design – is a specialty of mine. If you want more information, see PowerSponsorship.com/sponsorship-systems-design/.

Chapter 3

Strategy development

Ahh, strategy. It's the pivot point where mindset meets action. Getting your strategy right is essential to transforming the opportunity you've got into the results you need.

I wish I could tell you what your strategy should be, but I can't. Every situation is different, so every strategy is different, and only you can determine what your sponsorship strategy is going to be. What I can do is share the process I go through to develop strategy for my clients, and give you a framework that makes both your intention and forward plan clear.

Without input, you have no outcomes

As covered in Chapter 1, one of the main tenets of best-practice sponsorship is that it can — and should — be integrated across multiple channels. This is a must if your sponsorship program is going to be both effective and efficient. The thing is, this approach requires a great degree of buy-in and participation from an array of departments and business units across your company.

When I start a consultancy, one of the first things I do is request a big list of these stakeholders and their contact details, so I can get feedback that will help me formulate a strategy. Part of this is about information gathering, and part of it is about unravelling politics and assessing skill level. A lot of it is about fostering a sense of collaboration. For many stakeholders, sponsorship has been either an abstraction they don't understand, or a royal pain in the arse.

Usually, it's the first time they've ever been asked about sponsorship, and they're delighted to be included. And the fact that I'm asking their opinion, and asking what they need from sponsorship, piques their interest. They stop seeing it as a distraction from the core business and start seeing it as something they can use to achieve their goals.

Do this exercise early on, ideally before you get your stakeholder group together for the first time. You may uncover issues or opportunities you didn't know about. You might find a political situation that needs to be managed. You may realise that you've got some strong creative thinkers on staff that you'd like to tap, or that an investment in some up-skilling might be in order.

This is also a great opportunity to get buy-in from people who are influential to the process of sponsorship but who may not be appropriate candidates for your stakeholder group. Examples might include senior executives or regional managers.

How to interview stakeholders

Here are the steps for interviewing stakeholders. I've followed these up with an interview template.

1. Make a list of decision-makers and decision-influencers from any part of your organisation that could benefit from sponsorship.
2. Add any consultants or agencies deemed pertinent.
3. If your company has regional management, add a selection of regional marketing or sales managers.
4. Make 30-minute appointments with as many of them as you can. It can be helpful if you have sign-off from your CMO (or similar) and use that in your request. In-person meetings are ideal, but Zoom meetings also work fine. If you do in-person meetings, it's a lot more efficient to book a meeting room for a day or two, and ask them to come to you. I strongly suggest you interview stakeholders individually, not in groups. You'll likely get more candid answers.
5. Create an interview template. I've included my basic template below. You can customise this to reflect your organisational structure and challenges. For instance, if you've recently gone through a restructure, you can ask stakeholders how that has impacted sponsorship in their area.
6. Start every interview by telling the stakeholder that anything they say will be held in the strictest confidence and none of their input will be attributed to them in any way, so they are free to be as open as they like. Also tell them that there are no wrong answers. It's not a test. You really want their opinions.
7. Ask the questions. Don't talk much. Take lots of notes. I prefer handwritten notes, simply because there may be answers that relate to each other, or side notes, and it's a lot easier to reflect these in handwriting than typing.
8. Never end a stakeholder interview without asking whether they'd like someone from their business area to represent them in a sponsorship stakeholder group. They always say "yes". Always. Hold them to it.

> Sponsorship is collaborative. It doesn't live in a vacuum.

◑ Stakeholder Interview Form

Name and title:

Department/unit:

What is your job role? What do you actually do?

How does that intersect with sponsorship (if at all)?

How would you categorise the current sponsorship portfolio? What's your opinion of it?

What are the biggest challenges sponsorship poses to you in your role?

Can you see any opportunities that are being missed?

Are there any sponsorship benefits that are/would be especially useful to achieving your goals?

How are you currently measuring results against objectives in your department or business unit?

Blue skies: If you could do anything, change anything sponsorship-related, or sponsor anything, what would it be?

Final question: Do you have any strategies, plans, reports, market segmentation, brand-tracking research, or other documentation that I should review to get a better understanding of your area?

Revisit your sponsorship strategy

With all of that information from all of those stakeholders, you're going to need to revisit your sponsorship strategy. And if you're starting a new strategy from scratch, don't do it until you've done your stakeholder interviews.

These stakeholder interviews will likely impact:

- The priorities for sponsorship selection and renewals
- The types of benefits you negotiate
- The whole process of leverage, measurement, and reporting
- Your leverage and measurement budgets
- The structure and role of the sponsorship team
- The tools and capacity-building required to support both the sponsorship team and stakeholders

There could be other areas of impact, such as competitive positioning, auditing and reworking the portfolio, new products and brand extensions, and more.

Get the stakeholders meaningfully involved in both planning and delivery

As soon as you've completed the interviews, schedule your first sponsorship stakeholder group meeting. Often, the easiest way to kick off is to create a leverage and measurement plan for an underperforming sponsorship. Try to get somewhere between 8–15 people in the room, from across the organisation. Bribe them with sandwiches, if you have to. You'll only have to do that once.

The leverage and measurement process will get their juices flowing, get them excited about the potential for sponsorship, and deepen the buy-in for doing sponsorship well across the organisation. Plus, it's a lot of fun. What you'll find is that everyone will leave with at least a couple of leverage ideas they know they can put in place, and possibly others that need some feasibility checking. You'll also have at least a draft idea of their objectives and how they'll measure results.

The whole process is outlined, step-by-step, in Part 3: Leverage.

Target markets

Another critical factor in your strategy development is your various target markets. You can't be market-driven without fully understanding the various target markets, who they are, what drives them, and how they factor in your success.

Different departments and business units could have very different target markets. These will fall into a number of buckets. Typically, these could include:

> Consumers
> SMEs
> Intermediary markets (retailers, dealerships, brokers, etc.)
> Major/enterprise customers
> Government customers
> Staff
> Future staff (recruitment)

Depending on your category of business and/or business model, you could add:

> Local communities that your operations directly impact (eg, where you manufacture, or where you are a dominant employer)
> Government decision-makers (lawmakers, regulators)
> Strategic partners
> Media

There are three components to target market segmentation:

1. Demographics
2. Psychographics
3. Behaviours

Demographics

As you are probably aware, demographics refers to the hard information about a person, such as age, gender, where they live, income level, family makeup, etc. Demographics are often the driving force behind sponsorship decisions, but this is a mistake.

Demographics are about what a person is, not who they are. Your mission is to become the natural choice for a person because you have created relevance and meaning around your brand that reflects who they are. You can't connect with who that person is, and influence their perceptions and behaviours, by using a blunt instrument like demographics. How do you connect with an 18–24-year-old female? Well, that would depend entirely on what kind of person she is, her priorities, motivations, needs, and self-definitions.

Demographics are most useful when it comes to defining who your target markets aren't. If you're selling $100,000 cars, chances are that people below a certain income will not be in your target market. That doesn't mean that people above that income threshold are going to buy your car just because they can afford it. To get the keys in their hands, you need to appeal to their psychographics. By the same token, a local government council might be targeting young mothers with a home support service, but they're not going to sign up simply because they fit the demographic of "young mother". No, the council needs to find the right emotional hot buttons to get them to sign up.

Using demographics as the driving force behind sponsorship decisions is a mistake.

Psychographics

Psychographics are all about who a person is, including their motivations, self-definitions, priorities, needs, wants, and the rest. It is nuanced and specific and, if you segment your target markets psychographically, you know exactly what hot buttons to push to influence their behaviours and perceptions, and exactly how to align your brand with them.

Psychographic segmentation is particularly important when it comes to sponsorship, supporting your role as a sponsor and giving you the information and insight you need to:

- Understand, value, and respect your target markets' fan experiences
- Add meaningful value to your target markets' fan experiences
- Demonstrate your brand's alignment with your target markets.

Let's say you are a bank and are sponsoring a boat show. Attendees will include members of several of your key psychographic segments. How you connect with and add value to the luxury-oriented, conspicuous consumers will be very different from how you connect with and add value to the saving-for-our-dream crowd, and different still from the adventure-seeker. Where would a 34-year-old man fit? I think you'll agree, he could be in any one of these groups, or none of them.

Your brand probably has some kind of psychographic segmentation. You may even have a set of personas or flagbearers – profiles distilling segment characteristics into the description of a single person. I recommend discussing those segments or personas with a decision-maker in the department that created them to determine what kinds of sponsorship and leverage will appeal to each of them.

> Psychographic segmentation is critical to great sponsorship.

Behaviours

This aspect of segmentation is second to psychographics in importance, and has to do with the behaviour of your target markets towards your brand or category of brands. The behaviour aspect of segmentation can further refine your market by identifying the current behaviours you'd like to influence, or behaviours that make them more or less valuable to you as customers.

As an example, if your company is a full-service airline, you wouldn't be concentrating on just filling your planes. Instead, you would be concentrating your efforts on your most profitable potential customers, such as full-fare economy and business class passengers, as well as your most loyal frequent flyers and club members. Even though you may sell *more* discounted economy class seats to tourists, they are probably not generating much profit, so would not be the marketing priority.

Brand and business plans

Another critical step before embarking on a sponsorship strategy is to review brand plans for any pertinent brands, as well as plans having to do with your corporate culture and purpose.

Brand plans

In some companies, brand plans incorporate target market segmentation. In others, these are separate documents. When reviewing the brand plans, what you are looking for is:

- Overall marketing objectives
- Current and future priorities — some objectives could be rolling out across multiple horizons
- Competitive situation
- Market challenges
- New or ongoing initiatives, such as rebranding, expansion into new markets, or brand extensions

What I have seen more times than I can count are astute brand marketers who develop "sponsorship objectives" based on a limited or outmoded understanding of what sponsorship can do. They understand sponsorship has value but don't understand the real reasons why and, as a result, connect it only tenuously to their "real" marketing plan.

There are others who retrofit a set of objectives to a specific sponsorship as post-justification for making the investment. The thinking is, "We've got it, now we've got to set some objectives." The sponsorships are driving the objectives, instead of the other way around.

Worst of the lot are sponsorship objectives that are about the sponsorship itself. They follow some kind of crazy, circular logic that goes something like this: The sponsor invests in a sponsorship with the primary goal being to get more people to say they are aware of the sponsorship this year than last year. In other words, the primary goal of the sponsorship — and the primary thing they're measuring — is whether people are aware of the sponsorship.

How exactly does this relate to brand goals? How does this change people's perceptions and behaviours, or build alignment? It doesn't. In fact, it totally misses the point.

Broader business plans

In the first edition of this book, I barely mentioned broader business plans. In the ensuing years, however, this has become a huge factor in many sponsorship portfolios, particularly in the area of corporate culture.

Many, if not most, large companies have created strategies, frameworks, or position papers around some or all of these overarching cultural themes:

- Diversity, equity, and inclusion (DEI)
- Environmental, social, and governance (ESG)
- Organisational purpose or mission
- People and culture

As mentioned in Chapter 1, sponsorship is an outstanding way to demonstrate any or all of these aspects of corporate culture. Understanding them can inform not only what you sponsor, but how you leverage those sponsorships.

Menu of measurable objectives

Building from your review of all of these plans, you should create a menu of measurable objectives. Every investment will relate back to a subset of those objectives, meaning that while each sponsorship may be accomplishing something different, every single one of those things has strategic meaning for your brand.

Below is a sample menu of measurable objectives. This sample menu is built around an FMCG brand:

- Increase the trust in our brand
- Increase preference, building loyalty
- Increase consideration and trial
- Encourage existing customers to purchase a broader range of our brand line
- Drive sales, particularly in our off-season (May–Sept)
- Increase advocacy
- Improve social sentiment
- Improve net promoter score
- Increase retail support – advertised specials, in-store displays, shelf space
- Increase retail case commitments
- Increase employee morale and retention
- Support brand extension launch in the second quarter
- Demonstrate our genuine commitment to the environment
- Demonstrate our commitment to DEI, particularly in the disability space

While your menu may be different, do try for this type of range. It will give you flexibility, strategic focus, and a head start on measurement.

When you do build a measurement plan around a sponsorship, you'll need to get more specific, noting the benchmark, target, target market, and measurement strategy. Example:

> *Increase the net promoter score from 7.8 to 9 among museum-goers in*
> *the Chicago metro, based on exit and membership surveys carried out in*
> *the fourth quarter.*

Sponsorship audits

You may call it an audit, or you may call it a review. Either way, getting real about your current situation — good and bad — is an important step for creating a sponsorship strategy that's going to work.

There are two main types of sponsorship audit. The first is a straight audit, looking at your current situation.

You should do this type of audit once you are totally clear about your situation, target markets, and overall marketing objectives. There is a line of thinking that you should do the straight audit after developing your strategy, but I'm not convinced. I believe you'll create a much more effective strategy if you take all factors into account, including the current state of sponsorship in your organisation.

On this type of audit, I recommend taking a two-pronged methodology:

1. Auditing your approach — Literally, how you do sponsorship, how effective it is, and how that stacks up to best practice.
2. Auditing your portfolio — Taking a bloodless look at all of your sponsorship investments, with the aim to create an effective, efficient portfolio.

The second type of audit — my favourite — is a zero-based audit. This would be comparably rare, but is at least as important as a straight audit. In many cases, more so. This type of audit is informed by your strategy, so should come a little later in the strategy development process.

All of this is outlined in detail below.

Auditing your approach

The first type of audit is auditing your approach to sponsorship. It's about whether your organisation has the mindset, expertise, infrastructure, resources, and capacity to do sponsorship well. It's not about your sponsorship portfolio, which we'll get to next.

Below, I've listed some of the questions you should address. Depending on your situation and structure, you may have additional questions, but these are the questions I address every time:

- How close is your organisational approach to best practice?
- Which key areas are performing, and which need work?
  - Selection
  - Negotiation
  - Leverage
  - Management
  - Measurement
- Are there differences in approach between your corporate office and regional offices? Between brand groups or business units?

➤ What is the expertise level of the frontline staff? Broader stakeholders?

➤ What kinds of sponsorship frameworks currently exist? Do you have a sponsorship policy? Sponsorship stakeholder group? Have you had a sponsorship strategy prior to this?

➤ Is the workload realistic? Do current frontline staff have the time and resources to make the most of every sponsorship?

➤ Are your timelines realistic? Are you committing to sponsorships with enough time to properly leverage them?

➤ How much visibility does the frontline sponsorship team have on sponsorship portfolios held by brands, business units (eg, sales), or regions? How much coordination is there?

➤ Do you have enough market intelligence or strategic insights to make good sponsorship decisions? If not, what's missing?

➤ What are the up- and down-sides to each of these assessments? How are they impacting results?

Auditing your portfolio

Now, it's time to look at your portfolio, and assess where you are with it right now.

I've lost track of the number of times clients have told me that only one or two, or maybe a handful, of their many sponsorships are actually delivering results; in fact, I hear that more often than not. It's sort of like the sponsorship version of the 80/20 rule, but it's unnecessary and wasteful.

The number-one priority for a portfolio audit is that it is objective. This is no time for sentiment. It also needs to be realistic, practical, saleable, and provide concrete recommendations. This kind of audit – a straight audit – is about assessing where you are now. Your strategy then becomes the roadmap – how do we get from here to there?

Your straight audit will look at both individual sponsorships and your portfolio as a whole, asking a number of hard questions and assigning sponsorships to categories.

For your individual investments, you want to review all of the information you have about the property's target markets, positioning (values, attributes, personality), the benefits provided, and any measurable results achieved. You will then compare that information to what you know about your target markets, objectives, and priorities, asking these questions:

➤ Is it relevant to key target market(s)?

➤ Is it a natural attribute/value fit with our brand?

➤ Does it offer opportunities for us to demonstrate brand or company values?

➤ Does it offer opportunities to build alignment with our target markets? Add meaningful value to our target markets?

- Does it provide the benefits we need to achieve our goals? Could the benefits be improved?
- Does it have buy-in from a range of internal stakeholders?

More subjectively, you should also note whether the partner is professional, responsive, demonstrates a good understanding of your brand needs, and has a track record of delivering on commitments.

These questions are explored in more detail in Part 2: Sponsorship Selection.

Once you've addressed your individual sponsorships, you want to look at your portfolio as a whole.

- Are there unnecessary overlaps or duplication? Holes?
- Are there geographic markets, objectives, or target market segments that aren't being served? Are there any that are being overdone?

As you go through the portfolio audit, you will categorise each investment based on their disposition. Below are the categories I have developed over the years.

No hope

These are sponsorships that are unredeemable. They may have been badly chosen from the start, or they may have worked in the past but are no longer a good fit, or are past their prime. Or, they may be perfectly good sponsorships that, for whatever reason, your stakeholder group just doesn't like and won't commit to leveraging (it happens).

For sponsorships in the "no hope" category, your action plan is simple:

- Create an exit strategy (more on that later in the book).
- Stop leveraging the sponsorship. Even if there is time left on the contract, don't waste the money or effort trying to make a dud sponsorship work. You need to concentrate on the investments with real value to your brand.

> If the sponsorship
> has no hope of
> working, stop
> leveraging.

Renegotiate

These sponsorships are generally a good fit, but the benefits are not ideal for your needs. Most sponsorships have standard benefits packages – some combination of logos and mentions, tickets to things, some kind of hospitality, and some kind of official designation. If that sounds familiar, and the sponsorship is not in the "no hope" category, chances are it needs renegotiation. You need benefits that are creative and specific to your needs if you want peak performing sponsorship.

For this category, your action plan is more involved than for the "no hopers" but will improve your results immediately:

- Work with your stakeholder group to create an ideal leverage plan.
- Negotiate with the partner to get the right benefits to support your best ideas.

Yes, there is a lot more to that process, but you will find full instructions for both leverage plan creation and renegotiation in their respective sections of this book.

Sponsorships in this category often languish because sponsors think they can't negotiate new benefits until renewal time. Not so! It is absolutely possible to renegotiate benefits during the contract term. I've done it more times than I can count and, as long as you follow some guidelines, everyone will be happier in the end.

Improve leverage

In this category, you are the weak link. You've got a good sponsorship and reasonably appropriate benefits, but you're just not making the most of it. In the lion's share of cases that is due primarily to a lack of stakeholder buy-in and involvement.

Although the situation is different than the "renegotiate" category, the action plan is exactly the same:

> Work with your stakeholder group to create an ideal leverage plan.
> If required, negotiate with the partner to fine-tune your benefits package to support your best ideas.

Umbrella

Through the audit process, you may realise you have many smaller, related sponsorships that could be roped together under one "umbrella" and leveraged as if they were one large sponsorship.

A typical scenario would be a company that has small sponsorships of dozens or hundreds of community non-profits. In that case, it would be a lot easier to create an umbrella program, where each small sponsorship becomes part of a much greater and more powerful whole, than to expect each investment to be perfect and deliver meaningful results against objectives on its own.

I've got a lot more about how to create and leverage an umbrella program, plus plenty of examples later in the book but, suffice to say, you may create some major efficiencies if you are open to this approach.

Working

The sponsorships in the category are strong matches to your brand and markets, as well as fully and creatively leveraged across many areas of your company. These sponsorships would not look out of place in your zero-based audit just as they are.

In my experience, companies will have no more than a handful that genuinely fall into this category. They are often newer, larger sponsorships that have prompted a more strategic approach. The performance of these sponsorships is often the driving force for improving the whole portfolio — "Hey, if we can achieve all of this with this one sponsorship,

Renegotiating benefits mid-term isn't that difficult.

imagine what we could do with the rest of our portfolio!"

The only warning I have about "working" sponsorships is to not let them stagnate. A leverage program that has worked for the past two years will be less effective as time goes by. You need to keep readdressing even your best performing sponsorships to ensure they remain fresh and relevant.

Final review

After you've developed your strategy, I suggest you revisit the audit as you may want to fine-tune your assessments in light of strategic recommendations. An example might be if you develop an interesting strategy to reach an under-serviced market. Upon review of your audit, you may see an opportunity to repurpose or reinvent one of your lower-performing sponsorships so that it fits with that strategy.

Sometimes, your strategic recommendations will impact on the audit and sometimes they won't. I end up tweaking the audit maybe 50% of the time. Either way, the review and fine-tuning process doesn't take very long.

There's more about structuring an efficient, effective portfolio in Chapter 23: Structuring your portfolio.

Zero-based audit

This is a process that allows you to take some time out from dealing with the administration of sponsorship and the improvement of sponsorship and, instead, dedicate yourself to the potential of sponsorship. The whole premise revolves around this one question:

> **If you had the same sponsorship budget but no commitments, what would the perfect sponsorship portfolio for your brand(s) and target markets look like?**

I do this for my corporate clients all the time. It's often one of the most powerful parts of my recommendation. Strip away the politics, sentiment, history, and headaches, and suddenly my clients can see the true potential of sponsorship. More often than not, a senior decision-maker will say, "Now, we know what our goal is!" Bingo.

That's your challenge. Whether your budget is $150,000 or $5 million or $50 million, leave the reality of your portfolio behind, work with your team, and ask yourselves these questions:

➤ What would you sponsor, if you could sponsor anything?
➤ At what level? What unique benefits would you want?
➤ Would you create any umbrella programs? Around what themes?
➤ Would you create and own any properties?
➤ How would you leverage your investments to meet brand needs?

> How would you integrate your investments across your other marketing and business activities?

> How would you involve your staff and customers in a meaningful way? Create a win for the people who are most critical to your success? Make them the heroes?

> How would you allocate your budget across rights fees, leverage, measurement, and contingency?

You can also do this if your sponsorship budget is changing. Use the new figure — whether higher or lower — as the basis for your zero-based audit.

The process is creative and strategic and fun, but the real moment of truth comes when you compare what you *could* be doing with your money with what you *are* doing with your money. Suddenly, settling for improving mediocre sponsorships will seem a lot less appealing, and the ambitious goal of an entire portfolio that operates at peak performance will seem a lot more attainable. Mark my words.

A word about defensive sponsorship

Defensive sponsorship happens when you sponsor something simply to keep your competition from sponsoring it.

Come on, people! Play your own game! Investing $100,000 in a property that is wrong for your brand, just to keep your competitors out, is a colossal waste. You may stop them from benefitting from that sponsorship, but they have literally thousands of other options, and you can't block them all.

Imagine, instead, that you could spend that $100,000 on something that was absolutely perfect for your brand, and that you created a fantastic leverage program around it. I can guarantee that the benefit to your brand will far, far outweigh any benefit your brand may enjoy by blocking your competition.

The exception to this is when you are really buying sales. If your sponsorship of the local lawn bowls club provides you with exclusive pouring rights for soft drinks, and the profit on the litres poured is more than the cost of the sponsorship, then you're not really blocking your competition. You're just buying sales.

The internal sell

I will say that whether you're doing a straight audit or a zero-based audit, selling that audit internally can be a political minefield. Everyone has their pet projects and agendas, and none of them want to hear that their favourite is not the bees' knees. You've really got two options.

Plan A is to manage the situation internally, which will take in all or most of the following strategies:

> Involve your broad stakeholder group in the audit process — both zero-based and straight audits. This takes more time, but will encourage your colleagues to think

Purely defensive sponsorship is always a bad idea.

objectively and strategically. They will also feel a lot more comfortable if they are part of the decisions, rather than having the decision forced upon them.

➤ Educate your stakeholders. If you've done your stakeholder interviews and found that their skills are pretty basic, it may be worth considering some education prior to embarking on the audit process. You could do a workshop, share articles or white papers, or find some pertinent case studies.

➤ Enlist a senior executive (ideally, your head of marketing) in the process, as they will be able to navigate the C-level politics better than you can. If you've got that support and a team with even a modicum of creativity, you're all set.

Plan B is to enlist outside help for your audit. For larger, more decentralised companies, as well as those with intractable politics, you are probably better off involving a consultant.

A good consultant will bring a lot of expertise and ideas to the table, but one of the biggest bonuses is that some companies trust and accept the objective viewpoint of an outsider more than someone internal. They can deliver unpopular news, out-of-the-box solutions, and, by virtue of their role, can present a reinvention on a scale that may be hard to accept if it came from inside.

Creating your sponsorship strategy

Eventually, it will come time to create a strategy document. You can choose to keep it lean and mean, or you can bulk it out with lots of rationale, procedures, and tools.

Some companies have a culture that favours one or the other approach, but given the degree of buy-in you need across your company, I strongly suggest that you at least include your rationale. That way, the document can travel around your organisation without you explaining why the recommendations were made. Procedures and tools can sit in separate documents.

Background

The background is a compilation of all the information and factors that went into the formulation of the strategy and will have a number of sections, including:

➤ Situational analysis

➤ Brand definitions/architecture (particularly if you're introducing or repositioning brands)

➤ Organisational mission or purpose, or corporate culture (if you're going to use sponsorship to support these things)

➤ Target market analysis

➤ Competitor analysis

➤ Economic or industry factors affecting the brand or consumer climate

When including material in the background section, it is important not to simply restate facts that are already understood and accepted in your company. Instead, you should be providing those facts in the context of sponsorship. You don't need to go into specifics, as those will be part of the recommendation, but if something will be impacting on the recommendation, you should be stating it.

In other words, don't provide generic information on your company; talk about how any recent changes impact how you should be using sponsorship to advance brand and company objectives. Don't just list your target markets; provide insights on how each target market is likely to respond to different types of sponsorship and leverage programs. Don't just list your competitors; give a rundown of the types of things they sponsor, and their general approach to sponsorship.

To demonstrate that the strategy wasn't developed in a vacuum, you also want to include sections on:

- The background documents reviewed prior to creating the strategy
- The stakeholders interviewed
- An overview of the stakeholder feedback

I include short stakeholder quotes, but I never put names to them. Being able to tell stakeholders that their feedback won't be tied back to them will make them more comfortable sharing information.

Review/audit of your approach and portfolio

I used to put the audit after the strategic recommendations, but I've now shifted it to right after the background section. I find that this analysis adds context and granularity to the current situation, leading naturally into marketing objectives and strategic recommendations.

I recommend handling the zero-based audit a bit differently, including it in your strategy recommendations.

If it's very comprehensive, you may not put the actual outline of what you would do, in a perfect world, into the body of the strategy recommendations. But you would address the zero-based audit, top-line it, and refer to the outline being found in its own major section.

Overall marketing objectives

As already canvassed, the objectives must reflect overall marketing and business objectives. Do not restate them in terms of sponsorship.

These objectives may come from people and documents from across your company, and some you may draw out via the interview process. Again (sick of this yet?), every marketing objective should fall into one of the following three categories:

1. Changing or reinforcing people's perceptions
2. Changing or reinforcing people's behaviours
3. Aligning with target markets

In my experience, the full list will usually number between 8 and 12 objectives, but it could be a few more or a few less.

Strategy recommendations

This section forms the core of your strategy document and is simply about how you are going to use the medium of sponsorship to achieve your stated objectives.

There is a temptation to try to line up the strategies under individual objectives but, in my experience, they are never going to be a perfect fit. Sometimes, one strategy will address three different objectives. Other times, it will take three strategies to achieve one objective, so keep the sections separate.

I can't tell you what strategies you should be recommending. I can, however, give you a list of some of the typical strategy categories:

> Changes to organisational approach to sponsorship – principles and processes
> Bringing sponsorship into line with broader strategic objectives, brand positioning, organisational culture, and/or purpose
> Shifting your portfolio towards the results of your zero-based audit
> Identifying meaningful focal points, unexplored or underused opportunities
> Finding financial and other efficiencies in the portfolio structure, leverage, and management
> Specific strategies for key target market segments, brands, regions, expansion markets, brand-tracking opportunities/issues, etc.
> Better engagement, buy-in, and participation by broader stakeholders from across your organisation
> Managing regional sponsorship management
> Measuring and reporting meaningful results against objectives
> Changes to staffing, job roles and responsibilities, and accountabilities
> Equipping stakeholders to do sponsorship well – resources, training, coaching, systems design

Zero-based audit

Depending on how comprehensive your zero-based audit is, you may want to include the outline of what the perfect portfolio would look like in its own section. That section belongs right after your strategy recommendations.

Keep your objectives and strategy recommendations sections separate.

Forward plan

Once you know what you have to do, you need to prioritise and put a timeline to it. Your forward plan will have two main components:

1. Next steps
2. Portfolio timeline

Your next step is essentially to make a to-do list, with timeframes and responsibilities. What do we need to do this month? Next month? By mid-year?

Your portfolio timeline shows what your portfolio looks like now, and how it will look over the next two to three years, as sponsorships end and new initiatives are entered into. I usually reflect this on a grid with the major investments listed down the side and the months of the year across the top.

One important thing to keep in mind is that the portfolio timeline will be speculative. It is more about creating a vision for how the portfolio could look rather than a commitment to how it will look.

When it comes down to it, you may know what you're going to drop over time, but there is no guarantee any given sponsorship is going to be available to you right when you have a gap in your portfolio and the budget to commit (or any time in the foreseeable future). Indicate, instead, categories of sponsorship, or other sponsorship-oriented initiatives that you will be investigating, and firm it up when you can.

Budget

The budget goes hand-in-hand with the forward plan. The main components will be:

- Rights fees – contracted amounts you pay to rightsholders.
- Leverage budget – incremental investment to bring the sponsorship to life
  - Does not include integration across existing channels
  - 10–35% of rights fees in most circumstances, IF you do smart, best-practice leverage (lots more on leverage and leverage funding in Part 3: Leverage)
  - Could be much higher for giant, often quadrennial-type events
- Audience research
  - Some can be incorporated into existing brand tracking
  - Will probably need to also do some sponsorship-specific research
  - More in Part 4: Measurement
- Capacity building – training, coaching, tools, templates, sponsorship systems design, other resources
- Contingency – 10–15%

Getting approval for your sponsorship strategy

I strongly suggest you get the strategy signed off by senior management. In most organisations, this would be the chief marketing officer, group brand manager, or similar.

That senior manager may recommend — and if they do, that's a good thing — that a short version of the strategy be presented to your executive committee. I do a lot of these presentations, as part of my strategy work, and it goes a long way to getting buy-in and support for the new approach. If that senior executive team understands the underlying rationale, and the rigour that has gone into the strategy, they're also a lot less likely to ~~meddle~~ make counterproductive suggestions.

Chapter 4

Sponsorship in financially challenging times

I didn't specifically address this issue in the first edition of this book. The reason is that best-practice basics will go a long way to getting your sponsorship program through an economic crisis. That said, there are a few key points to keep in mind. All of these are better implemented – or at least planned – when or before an economic downturn is being forecast, not after it has hit.

These strategies are also effective if your company or industry is going through a rough patch.

Fastest impact vs smartest impact

Our industry is particularly susceptible to knee-jerk recession decisions. You and I (and most people working in sponsorship) know the unique value of this powerful marketing tool, but there are still people – including plenty in the C-suite and finance – who view sponsorship as a frivolous luxury spend. To them, it's an expendable cost, not a crucial marketing investment, and as such, anything at or nearing renewal is indiscriminately disposable, with no real ramifications for the brand.

They're wrong, of course, as not all sponsorship investments are created equal. It's true that most sponsorship portfolios include some dead wood, but most sponsorship portfolios also include brand workhorses that deliver great results against objectives every year.

The tension ends up between the fastest budget impact and the smartest budget impact, and it's going to be on sponsorship and brand management to make the case for smart budget cuts, not just convenient ones.

This strategy goes back to the previous chapter. You need your senior executive team to buy into your approach and trust your recommendations. If you've done that, they're much less likely to insist on panic exits.

Do a ruthless audit

You already know that I'm a big fan of audits, but if you haven't done one, and you're staring down a recession or other economic challenge, you need to do one straightaway. You don't want dead wood in your portfolio when you're trying to economise.

Don't invest incremental resources if the property is weak

Shifting to a lean and shrewdly leveraged portfolio means making every leverage dollar, and all of your team's strategic effort, count.

As noted in the previous chapter, if you've done an audit and identified properties that aren't performing and you want to exit, but you've still got time to run on the contracts, stop throwing good money after bad.

Don't overbudget for leverage

I've been a sponsorship strategist for a long time, and I've worked with many sponsors in their quest to lower the sponsorship budget, whether driven by an economic downturn or other budgetary pressures. When I review the financials, many of them have huge leverage budgets, and I can often get them to their goal — and do it quickly — by addressing that.

For more on how much you should be budgeting for sponsorship leverage, see Chapter 12: Leverage funding.

Rethink experiential and on-site activations

I don't hate experiential sponsorship leverage, nor do I hate on-site leverage activities. They just tend to be extremely expensive and effort-intensive for the impact they deliver.

What you're doing may be cool as hell, but when you really parse the cost vs impact of experiential and on-site activations, the maths are often a lot less cool.

Clearly, it's not fun to cut back on these on-site activities, which people enjoy and deliver instant gratification to your brand — all those smiling fan photos you put in reports! — but when your budgets are being squeezed, you need to be pragmatic. I'm not telling you to give up on-site activities forever. In fact, there may be some much more cost-effective options to keep doing stuff on-site. But I do really want you to think through the opportunity cost before committing because chances are, you could be doing a lot more — for a lot more meaningful impact — with that money.

Remember that the fans are feeling it, too

If your region — or the entire world — goes into recession, your markets will be feeling it, and so will the fans of whatever you're sponsoring.

Their motivations around the property may shift. Their finances may limit access to the property. They may be looking for cheap or free options around the properties you're sponsoring. They may be feeling under stress and looking for things that bring them joy.

> It's true that most sponsorship portfolios include some dead wood.

This needs to factor into your leverage calculations, so when you're developing empathy for that fan experience — understanding what they want, what the best and worst things are, etc. — be sure you're addressing the financial and stress angles, alongside the other meaningful things around the property.

Temper your opportunism

If you need to cut the budget, and a property just isn't good enough to hang onto, by all means, exit. These are unpleasant choices, impacted by real commercial realities.

What you shouldn't do is bully rightsholders into giving you gigantic discounts, just because they're under financial stress, and you can. It's terrible sponsor karma, and you'll end up in a bad relationship. Unfortunately, there are still a lot of jerks who won't hesitate to use an economic downturn as a stick to hit rightsholders with.

If a sponsorship is worth keeping in an economic downturn, then pay a fair fee and work collaboratively on leveraging it. If it's not worth keeping at a fair price, it's not worth keeping.

Create and socialise a recession strategy now

You want to be analysing and making moves before a crisis. This doesn't mean just going through the steps above; it means creating and socialising a recession strategy. This strategy will include:

> Things you're doing now
> Things you'll do if a recession starts to bite
> Things to be added — and in what order — once a recession starts to ease
> Any resources, support, sign-offs you need in order to do the above

Be clear that this strategy is pre-emptive, and that parts of it may not be needed, but it's been created to ensure that there's a plan in place, just in case.

If a sponsorship isn't worth keeping at a fair price, it's not worth keeping.

Part **2**

SPONSORSHIP SELECTION

Chapter 5

Finding the right partners

Before I can provide any specific strategies for selecting the right investments, it is important to connect this process back into the overall best-practice mindset. It is easy to be dazzled by numbers and flash, and forget why you're really doing it. Too many times, I've seen sponsors talk a good game then make terrible choices in what and how they sponsor. I don't want that to be you.

As a best-practice sponsor, you have three priorities when selecting and negotiating sponsorship. They are:

1. Target market needs
2. Internal buy-in
3. Brand needs

"Hold up!", I hear you saying, "Brand needs are third?!" Yes, and for good reason: You won't meet your brand needs effectively if the other two priorities aren't met first.

Target market needs

Meaning is a recurring theme across best-practice sponsorship. The more meaningful a property is to the fans — the more passionate and motivated they are — the more leveragable and valuable the property is to you. Answering questions like the following is all about gauging relevance, meaning, and passion:

- What proportion of the property's fans (in-person and remote) are legitimately in our sphere of interest?
- What proportion of our customers and potential customers care about this property, or its major themes? Eg, your major market of foodies may not care about a specific food festival but might still love some of the content that comes out of it.
- Why do people care about the property? What motivates them? What has meaning?

- How much do they care? How passionate are they? How involved do they get? Does it mean enough for them to influence others?
- How powerful are the larger themes around the property? Why do people care? Is it a passion point or a passing interest?

One other thing that will come out of this process is the realisation that the relevance of a property is more important than its size. If a lot of people love a property and/or the larger themes around that property, it will have tremendous potential for meaningful, multifaceted leverage, even if the property itself isn't huge. You don't have to sponsor a national organisation to leverage it nationally. You don't have to limit yourself to a few weeks of leverage around a two-day event if the relevance is strong enough to leverage year-round.

On the other hand, a major property may have broad reach, but if the fans aren't passionate — if they're agnostic or fair-weather fans — your leverage will likely underperform.

Internal buy-in

The fact that sponsorship is the most emotional and meaningful of all marketing media isn't limited to the outside world. Internally, sponsorship can be both a powerful tool and a battleground. Everyone has their own perceptions about it as a medium, everyone has their own favourite sports, charities, and events, and a lot of them let those perceptions and pet projects rule their decisions about whether and how effectively they will integrate a sponsorship.

There is far more to say about integration and leverage that I will address later. For now, I will go so far as to say that there are three truths of sponsorship integration that many sponsors ignore:

1. Sponsorship is the most integratable of all marketing media.
2. If a sponsorship isn't well integrated across at least a few marketing media, it won't work.
3. You can't force integration to happen. Your peers have to want it.

The long and the short of it is that centralising sponsorship in your marketing portfolio, and achieving buy-in from a range of internal stakeholders, and commitment from them to use the sponsorship in a meaningful way, is a now a *prerequisite* to committing to a sponsorship.

The fact that this is taking place before a sponsorship commitment is made is the key here. Anyone who has tried to sell a sponsorship into uninvolved colleagues after the fact will certainly agree, and the result is a sponsorship that is more costly and far less effectively leveraged.

Figure 6: Sponsorship catalyst

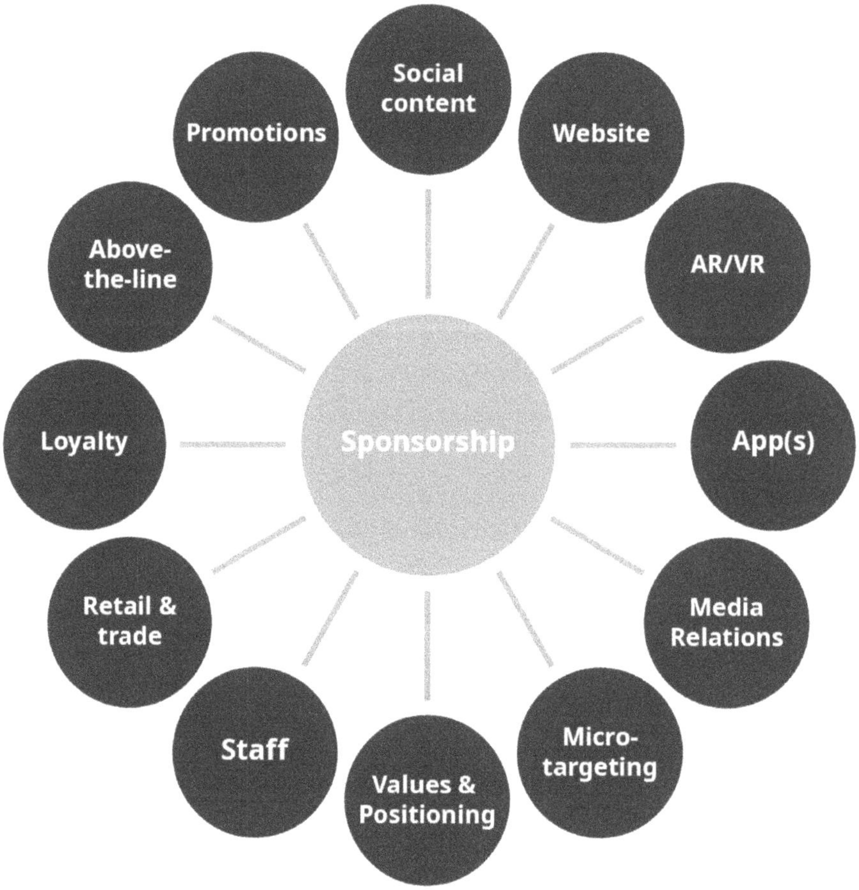

Brand needs

The good news about gaining internal buy-in prior to investing in a sponsorship is that you will also gain a far more comprehensive understanding of brand and business needs than you would if this information was coming solely from the brand group. One flows from the other, making brand needs sit comfortably as the third, yet still very important, priority.

Importance of authenticity

If we wind back the sponsorship clock by a couple of decades, the big buzzwords were "image transfer", and the concept has stubbornly refused to die.

The basic idea is that if you sponsor something, the property will "transfer" attributes onto your brand that it doesn't already have. A sponsorship can make junk food seem healthier, a discount retailer more stylish, and primary industries greener — all without changing who they are or what they do. Sounds good, doesn't it? Too bad it absolutely does not work.

People are cynical. We've all been fed so many lines of marketing bull in our lives that our ability to sniff out dodgy claims is finely honed. Brands can't buy credibility, and if you try, they will only succeed in making people think you're being deceptive and untrustworthy.

There has to be a natural fit between your brand and the property you sponsor. That sponsorship can highlight existing brand attributes and values, or underpin genuine new ones, but it cannot give your brand positive attributes it doesn't already have.

Understanding fans, their passion, and the culture

When esports exploded onto the sponsorship scene, a lot of money started flooding into the sport in some combination of trying to "reach a coveted demographic" and me-tooism. And many of those sponsors are failing. Why? Because esports fans know crap, inauthentic sponsorship when they see it. Fan backlash has been vicious, dispatching them from the arena as fast as they flooded in.

How are they getting it so wrong? Esports isn't just a sport. It's a culture, a community, an entire ecosystem, both enjoyed and created by its fans. Their fan experience is multi-platform, infinitely customisable, and they've got direct channels to the teams and stars that were unheard of not long ago. This makes esports different from all other kinds of sponsorship, and more difficult for sponsors to get right.

Actually, that's not true at all.

Virtually all fan experiences — charity, culture, sport, event, or otherwise — are multi-platform, infinitely customisable, with direct channels to the movers and shakers. All fan experiences have a tribal, community component. They all have their own cultures. They're all driven by passion. The difference is that in more established categories, fans just ignore terrible sponsorship, while esports fans actively work against it. Let that sink in.

The way to avoid this — whatever you sponsor — is to put the effort in and get the focal point in the right place. Immerse yourself in the culture before committing to any new sponsorships — particularly in categories you haven't sponsored before. That understanding will not only help you avoid missteps, but will be crucial to creating a powerful, effective, and efficient leverage strategy.

A sponsor's best friend: The multi-tool

If I had to hazard a guess, I'd say almost all of us have at least one multi-tool. I've got a much-loved, 20-year old Gerber that lives in the house and is pressed into duty anytime I can't be arsed going outside and unlocking the tool shed . . . which is a lot. I've done and fixed all manner of things with that one tool, and am constantly figuring out new ways to use it. If I could only have one tool, my Gerber would be it.

Consider how you can apply that thinking to sponsorship, and start identifying

> Sponsorship can't buy you credibility.

properties that can provide the same kind of flexibility and broad-ranging usefulness as your trusty multi-tool. There are specific hallmarks and management techniques for sponsorship multi-tools, which I've outlined below, but once you start thinking about your opportunities this way, you'll find it to be an absolute essential for portfolio management.

A sponsorship multi-tool is sponsorship that can be leveraged:

> In many different ways
> By many different departments or business units
> Over a long period of time, if not perpetually
> Across geographic regions
> Across multiple target markets, which could include end-users, internal markets, intermediary markets, enterprise/VIP markets, and others
> Differently across years
> To create durable content

Just like we still own other tools — tools that do specific jobs — there is no reason you can't have other sponsorships for specific objectives, markets, timeframes, or even departments. Plus, once you adopt a multi-tool mindset, you may see multi-tool potential in many of your current investments.

> Identify properties that can provide the same kind of flexibility and broad-ranging usefulness as your trusty multi-tool.

Attracting fewer, better proposals

If you're like most sponsors, you receive piles of unsolicited proposals, and your voicemail is overflowing with people following up on their usually crappy submissions.

Your goal should be to attract fewer, better proposals. The way you do that is not to insulate yourself, but to be more open with your potential partners.

Avoiding gatekeepers

If you're staring down an inbox overflowing with sponsorship proposals, there is definitely a temptation to implement one or more "gatekeepers" between those rightsholders and your team. Tempting as it is, this whole train of thought is unproductive.

There is an easy solution, but first we're going to address those gatekeepers.

Online sponsorship submission forms

I'm really not a fan of the sponsorship submission form. While the intent is usually for it to be a gatekeeper, the effect is usually one of a gate firmly shut. The forms may be effective in minimising admin time, but they simply don't have the scope to allow the great opportunities to shine.

Because the forms are so limiting, good rightsholders are going to ignore them. That means you're really getting nothing but junk proposals through your form. They can be so consistently bad that sponsors just stop reviewing them at all. I've had clients that only review submissions through the online form "maybe once a year . . . if we're lucky".

Agencies

Tasking an agency or consultant with vetting your proposals would seem like a reasonable idea and it can work. But most of the time, it doesn't.

The main issue is that the goal is to create an authentic, strategic partnership, and insulating yourself from these potential partners is simply a bad way to start that kind of relationship.

Then, there is the question of how well these agencies are representing your company. They may have all the good intentions in the world but be too heavy-handed or obtuse in their approach. Some agencies still see sponsorship as a threat to their core capabilities, and use the role of gatekeeper to shore up their own position. Smaller agencies can let this newfound power go to their heads. I would like to say these situations are rare, but they are not nearly rare enough.

Attrition

While attrition is not technically a gatekeeper, the result is the same. If you leave the proposal unread for long enough and ignore the voicemails long enough, every rightsholder will eventually go away, and you will miss what might have been great opportunities because you're overwhelmed by the workload of assessing them all.

Never ask for a generic proposal

"Just send me something."

We've all said this to a rightsholder. We've all answered the phone and regretted it, or been cornered at a function with a rapid-fire pitch, and we've blurted this out just to make it end. You may think this is saving you time, but it's not because you will spend the next four months fielding voicemails and emails chasing it up.

If you don't have any interest in the property or in working with that organisation, just tell them it's not a good fit and you don't want them to waste their time. Period.

Great rightsholders want to dazzle you. They want to demonstrate their understanding of your brand, your markets, and your goals. They want to showcase how you can use the investment to achieve your objectives. And they want to show you that they put in the work to be really good partners.

They know that the first impression is important, and that you'll start making your decision on whatever hits your desk first. Asking for a generic proposal, or some kind of "top-line one-pager" doesn't allow them to put their best foot forward. It's like asking a fashion designer to start their show with the sweatpants.

Instead, if you think there's any potential with this rightsholder at all, spend 5–10 minutes

> Just tell them it's not a good fit and you don't want them to waste their time. Period.

on the phone with them to discuss your objectives, target markets, and priorities, so they can create a fully customised proposal. Even easier, send them your sponsorship guidelines (see below), with a covering note on the specific priorities you'd like the proposal to address. Either one of those strategies will get you a much better proposal.

Sponsorship guidelines

If your real goal is to get fewer proposals and to improve the quality of the proposals you are getting, then you're far better off creating a set of sponsorship guidelines that set out your objectives and target markets, provide insights into your brand(s) and clearly articulate what you're expecting from a partner and what you need in the proposal. Set the bar high because, frankly, you're not going to invest in a mediocre sponsorship anyway.

What you do next is post those guidelines on your website and refer to them on your voicemail, using wording something like this:

> *Please note, we only consider proposals that meet our requirements as outlined in our sponsorship guidelines. They are available on fakesponsor. com/sponsorshipguidelines.*

If you really want to save a lot of time (and be a badarse), you can add:

> *If you submit a proposal that doesn't meet those requirements, we will not review it, and you will not receive a response from us.*

You also want to ensure all brand managers have a copy, and that your switchboard knows to refer anyone who calls asking for "whoever handles sponsorship" to your website for guidelines. You should definitely provide them to your senior executives and regional management (all of whom probably get hit up for sponsorship all the time). Finally, if you've got a sponsorship@ email address for proposal submissions – and you should – create an autoresponder with the same wording I recommended above.

Anecdotal (but consistent) feedback is that using a tight set of guidelines cuts the number of sponsorship approaches by 60–75%, and the quality of offers skyrockets. The idea is that if you are open about your needs, rightsholders will quickly work out whether they meet your needs, or aren't up to the task of working with a sponsor with such high expectations. They don't want to waste their time any more than you want them wasting yours.

Generally, I am a proponent for sharing information. If you tell potential partners exactly what you need, they will either rise to the occasion or realise it would be a wasted effort. Keeping rightsholders in the dark is counterproductive. Enlighten them, instead.

⟳ Sponsorship Guidelines Template

[Note: These guidelines are built around a fake electricity provider. Any resemblance to real brands is coincidental.]

PowerTown receives thousands of sponsorship proposals every year, most of which we reject because they do not adequately meet our needs.

We have developed this document to make our requirements clear to potential partners and to encourage the presentation of proposals that meet those needs. We will not consider *or respond to* any sponsorship opportunities that don't meet these guidelines.

> Tell rightsholders
> what you're after.

General

➣ We will consider proposals in all categories except:
  • Organisations that are political or religious in nature
  • Organisations that are controversial or divisive.
➣ We require sponsorship exclusivity in the category of electricity providers and solar/battery installation.
➣ We generally need a minimum of six months lead time to effectively plan and implement our leverage activities.
➣ Logo and/or name exposure is considered a bonus but is far from the primary goal of sponsorship.
➣ We prefer to invest in sponsorships that carry out audience research during and/or after the event, including questions relating to our industry and provide results to PowerTown.

PowerTown

PowerTown is currently the third largest electricity retailer serving the eastern half of Canada.

We want to work with organisations in our communities in a meaningful way. We don't just want to put our logo on things. To that end, we want to create an understanding of our brand and markets.

PowerTown masterbrand

Our goal is to partner with organisations and properties that are a strong, natural match to at least some aspects of our overarching brand positioning. More is better.

➣ Empowering
➣ Supportive and reflective of the diverse communities we serve
➣ Innovative and future-focused
➣ Helpful, caring

We are also heavily focused on demonstrating our purpose through sponsorship. Our purpose is as follows: Lighting the way to a better future.

PowerTown product lines

PowerTown has a number of product lines, with different target markets. While we do sponsor some properties on a company-wide basis, we are more likely to commit to sponsorships that are attached to one or more specific product lines.

- **Consumer electricity** — In most of our markets, customers have a choice of electricity retailer. Our target market for this is homeowners. Our goals are two-fold:
  - Driving new customer sales by providing competitive packages, increasing alignment with our communities, and increasing consideration, intent, and sales to homeowners.
  - Driving loyalty from current customers by providing excellent value and service, adding value to our relationships, aligning with customers, and proactively championing our customers.
- **SME electricity** (employing less than 500 staff) — The goals and drivers are virtually identical to the consumer market, but targeting ownership and/or senior management.
- **PowerTown Green** — Our 100% green power (solar, wind), moderately premium-priced option is aimed at middle- to higher-net worth households looking for low-involvement ways to be greener.
- **PowerTown Solar** — Our consumer solar and battery installation product competes with independent installers, except that we can package the cost into the electricity supply contract. Targets a similar market to PowerTown Green, except that they also tend to fit into one or both of the following categories:
  - More proactive about sustainability. Multiple green/sustainable practices in place around the home or small business.
  - High home/SME electricity users, looking to mitigate use of grid power.
- **Enterprise customers** — Maintaining and enhancing relationships with these large industrial and manufacturing customers is a key goal.

Sponsorship requirements

Sponsorships valued at $5,000 or more per annum must provide at least six of the following. Sponsorships valued at under $5,000 per annum must provide at least three of the following. All prospective partners must provide at least two of the items marked with an asterisk (*):

[Note: I usually use a cut-off figure between $2,000 and $5,000 per annum.]

- A natural link with PowerTown's brand positioning and/or purpose (see above).
- Provision of exclusive and meaningful content for social media and other communications.*

➤ Licence to create exclusive content for social media and other communications.*

➤ Access to what-money-can't-buy experiences to anchor promotions.*

➤ Access to what-money-can't-buy experiences (inner sanctum, day in the life, etc.) for use in VIP hospitality.

➤ Direct, face-to-face access to your fans (attendees, members, etc.).

➤ Space at the event for on-site activations.

➤ Opportunities to showcase property, fan, and community stories.

➤ Opportunities to showcase the creativity, ideas, volunteerism, or other contributions of our customers or staff.*

➤ Opportunities to provide our products and/or emerging technology for your organisation, creating content around it.*

➤ Access to industry leaders and/or innovators, particularly for the creation of exclusive content, and possibly VIP meet-and-greets.

➤ Other benefits that we can pass along to many of our customers and/or your fans. Feel free to use your imagination. Note: The PowerTown app has the ability to generate a scannable barcode for redemptions.*

➤ Promote switching to PowerTown to your fans/members, with a bonus or donation to you (as applicable) for every new customer.*

➤ Advertising, advertorial, or other distribution of our marketing materials to your target markets.

➤ Ability for PowerTown staff to participate in a meaningful way.*

To be considered, proposals must include:

➤ Key details of the opportunity

➤ Outline of your target markets, particularly psychographic

➤ Overview of your marketing plan, including what is and is not confirmed

➤ List of sponsors who have committed to date

➤ Comprehensive list of benefits, including how they relate to PowerTown, our brands, and our customers

➤ Creative ideas as to how we can use this sponsorship – leverage it – and those benefits to connect with our target markets

➤ Timeline, including important deadlines

Process for consideration

➤ All proposals are reviewed by the sponsorship team to assess suitability, feasibility and resources required (human and monetary). Shortlisted opportunities are further reviewed by a broader sponsorship stakeholder group.

➤ You will be notified of the disposition of the proposal within [X] weeks.

Submit proposal to:

[Insert full contact details, including an email address. A sponsorship@ email address is good.]

Proactively approaching rightsholders

If you've identified a property or category of property that you'd like to consider for sponsorship, don't wait for an unsolicited proposal to make it to you. Get proactive!

Requesting a proposal doesn't commit you to anything except reviewing it when you receive it. That said, don't request proposals willy-nilly. It takes a rightsholder a long time to create a customised proposal. If you're not seriously considering a sponsorship in their category, don't waste their time.

I've created a short rightsholder approach email template. The first paragraph is where you'll outline any specific angles or markets you're interested in. For instance, if you are approaching a major sporting club, you could specify that you're particularly interested in the women's team, as well as their business club. If you're approaching a home renovation expo, you could specify that your core target market is DIYers, and that you'd like to be heavily involved with the how-to clinics.

Make it clear that you've done some research, and that the proposal is a starting point for discussions. This should mitigate the risk of getting an immediate phone call with a heavy-handed, generic pitch.

⏻ Rightsholder Approach Email

Hello [Rightsholder] –

We are interested in exploring a sponsorship with your organisation, particularly around [specific property] and [specific markets]. We've done some research, and it appears this may be a good match for our needs.

To give us a starting point for discussions, we'd like to request a proposal from you. We're not interested in a generic proposal – and we're sure you don't want to submit one. To that end, we've attached our comprehensive sponsorship guidelines, which should provide enough background for you to create a compelling offer.

If the fit is as strong as we hope, we'll work with you to fine-tune from there.

I'm very happy to schedule a short Zoom meeting to answer any questions or clarify our needs.

[The Sponsor]

We're not currently investing

Even if you're not acquiring any new sponsorship at the moment, you can still use sponsorship guidelines and openness to your advantage. This is an instance where a lot of sponsors elect to post a sponsorship submission form and then send a form letter to the applicants at some point far into the future. But, wouldn't it be better if you posted this online instead?

We are not currently investing in any new sponsorship. When this changes, we will let you know on this page.

In the meantime, please feel free to review our sponsorship guidelines to familiarise yourself with our needs and expectations. If you think that your property might be right for one of our brands at some time in the future, you are welcome to submit a proposal, but please understand that it will be filed for future reference.

Chapter 6

Evaluating offers

We've covered a number of strategies to lower the number of proposals you get and improve the quality. Now, you've got to evaluate the ones you have.

What not to do

There are two very common, but very unhelpful approaches to proposal evaluation, and we need to cover those before we get into how it should be done, and the mediocre middle.

Looking at the back page first

If you've ever started evaluating a proposal by looking at price, you may have done yourself a big disservice. This approach is seated in a bargain mentality, but looking for something that's cheap doesn't mean it is right for you.

The bargain mentality is like buying a pair of fabulous designer shoes on clearance, even though they don't fit properly. The likelihood of you enjoying those shoes and getting good use out of them is about the same as a sponsor getting a top result out of a sponsorship purchased because it looked like a bargain.

Instead, you want to think of investing in sponsorship like investment dressing. That $2,000 bespoke suit will be worth every penny if it exudes the image you desire, and you look and feel great every single time you wear it. By the same token, if a sponsorship is perfect for your brand and your target market, you should be willing to pay a fair price for it. Not in the budget? There are lots of options for finding the money. More on that later.

> A bargain mentality is not helpful in sponsorship.

Using a scorecard

There are companies all over the world using a scorecard system for rating the proposals they receive. It goes something like this...

You have a list of "desirable" aspects of a sponsorship offer. They are usually a mix of strategic factors, old-school benefits (like exposure), and other sponsorship mechanisms. They are often weighted, so that some of the factors count more than others. Then, you score each factor on a scale of one to ten, do the multiplication and voilà, you've got some kind of numeric score. If the score is high enough, you pursue the sponsorship.

Does that sound extremely arbitrary to you? Because it sounds awfully arbitrary to me. Who's to say your weighting is appropriate, that the factors themselves are appropriate, or that every investment needs to fit the same priorities? And the scoring? It's nothing more than a wild guess. The end result is a finite number based on nothing more than conjecture.

The approach I recommend leaves all those arbitrary numbers behind and concentrates on analysing the offer, the presentation, the benefits, the audience, and many nuances directly against your needs. I don't believe you need to assign numbers when you can make direct comparisons simply by asking the right questions.

Three-way fit

Our industry talks a lot about finding a sponsorship "fit". There are actually three ways that a sponsor can fit with a property:

1. Target market fit
2. Attribute fit
3. Objective fit

You have an astounding number of choices for sponsorship. There's no excuse for committing to a sponsorship that doesn't have this three-way fit.

Figure 7: Three-way fit

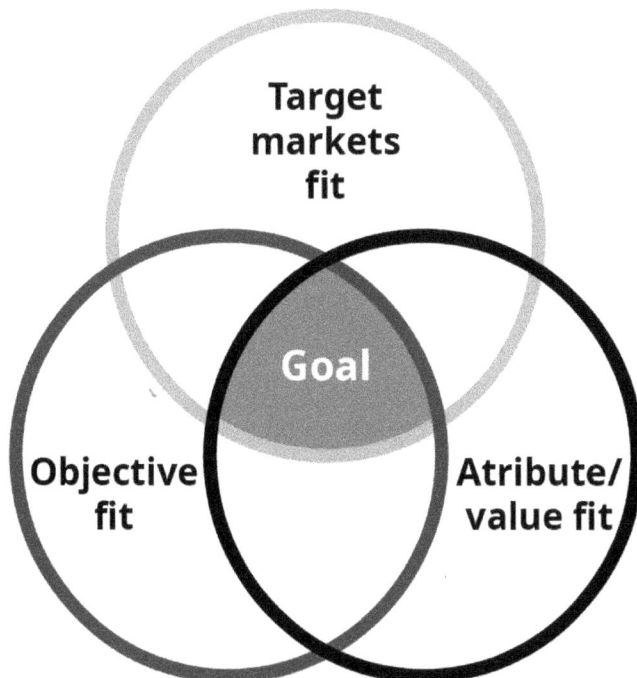

Target market fit

It doesn't matter how creative you are or how well the other aspects are matched, if the event or program isn't relevant and meaningful to at least one of your target markets, it won't work.

Attribute/value fit

The attribute fit will provide interest around your leverage program and underpin the relevance of your brand to the target market.

Assuming you have some kind of brand definition – often in the form of a brand bullseye or brand architecture – you will have a broad range of attributes that contribute to the personality of your brand. *Any* of them can form an authentic match with a property. You have two options for matching.

Attribute = attribute

Your attribute matches an attribute of the property. An example is the attribute "fast" – a broadband provider could underpin the speediness of their offering by sponsoring a motorsports team.

Attribute solves attribute

Your attribute solves an attribute of the property. An example is the attribute "dirty" – washing powder solves the dirt (and smell!) inherent in a fishing competition.

This type of matching is easy, but I do have one warning: Don't match on ubiquitous attributes. Attributes that your brand shares with many, many other brands are not going to be great for matching. Some of these include "excellent", "family", "fun", and "community".

This type of attribute falls into the category of accurate but not useful. It would be like asking you to pick my brother up from the airport and describing him as a "male wearing blue jeans". That may be accurate, but it isn't useful. Instead, concentrate on the attributes that are more unique and specific to your brand.

Objective fit

When you look for objective fit, what you're really looking for is scope and flexibility. If you have that, you have a platform you can leverage to meet any number of objectives.

Meeting your own objectives is clearly not negotiable. You have to do that, and your potential partner needs to be prepared to help you. Where sponsorship really comes into its own, however, is when the objectives met are mutual.

Look for opportunities to help a potential partner to achieve their objectives. Ask what their goals are over the next 12–24 months and, when possible, build a relationship that supports their broader objectives, not just their financial targets. Examples are introducing a charity to new markets, building relevance among kids for an emerging sport, or promoting the next Wiggles tour on-pack.

The implementation of this will take place as part of your leverage plan, but the question about their larger objectives needs to be asked during negotiations.

Shifting to process-driven sponsorship

For most sponsors, decisions to invest in or renew a sponsorship are based primarily on analysis against a set of criteria. This may seem sensible, and bean counters love this approach, but it doesn't actually work well with sponsorship. I'll go so far as to say that using analysis to drive your decisions is consigning your results to mediocrity, and the only way to achieve truly outstanding sponsorship is if the decisions around it are primarily process driven.

> Help your partner to achieve their objectives, and you will achieve more.

Example: Objective mutuality

When **Kellogg's** Australia took up a major sponsorship of charity Kids Help Line, they both needed each other. Kellogg's was facing a lack of brand identity – as a masterbrand, it didn't mean anything to the mums who bought the groceries. Kids Help Line had a fantastic service supporting the youth of Australia but lacked funding for sufficient infrastructure or marketing to reach kids and let them know they existed.

By working closely with Kids Help Line and fully understanding their needs, Kellogg's were able to create a multifaceted leverage program that benefitted both, including:

> Cents-per-purchase donation across a range of Kellogg's products.
> Kids Help Line logo, contact details, and information about what they provided on the side of Kellogg's cereal boxes.
> Coping skills for kids on the back of Kellogg's cereal boxes. The box with "how to deal with a schoolyard bully" sold 700,000 *extra* boxes of cereal (in a country of 21 million, at the time).
> Creating a television ad for Kids Help Line and using the bonus spots they received from television networks to educate Australia's kids about what the help line offers.

Sadly, a management change eventually scuttled this sponsorship.

Analysis-driven sponsorship

For new sponsorship investments, there is a predictable analytic track:

- Is the target market a match?
- Is it an attribute match?
- Does it duplicate an existing investment?
- Does it fit into our annual or seasonal calendar of sponsorships?
- Do we have enough lead time?
- Are the benefits appropriate?
- Is the price appropriate for the benefits?
- How does the price stack up against other options?
- Are the terms realistic?
- Is the offer/organiser credible?

I'm not saying that there isn't a role for analysis in sponsorship decisions. The thing is, making your decisions based on analysing the offer is inherently flawed and counterproductive because it has nothing to do with what makes a sponsorship great. Instead, consider analysis to be about threshold needs; telling you more about whether you shouldn't do something than whether you should.

Using analysis to drive your decisions is consigning your results to mediocrity.

Process-driven sponsorship

Process-driven sponsorship takes an entirely different approach to making decisions, drawing out the most important factors that go into top-performing sponsorship:

- Is this property meaningful to at least one of our core target markets? Why do they love it? How does it fit into their lives and who they are?
- How can we use this property to demonstrate our alignment with the passions of customers, staff, and fans?
- How can we use this to deepen our relationship with customers, staff, and fans?
- Do we have a vision for how we can use this to achieve our larger marketing or business objectives?
- Is there broad buy-in and a shared vision across our stakeholders?
- Are those stakeholders ready to commit to using this sponsorship across their channels?
- How can our stakeholders from across the company — sales, HR, social team, regional management, customer retention, etc. — use this to add value to our target markets?
- Can we use the larger themes of the property to transcend geography and timeframe issues?
- Can we use the larger themes to find relevance for additional target markets?
- Is it most appropriate to sponsor big? Or can we sponsor small and work it hard?
- Are there political or logistical issues for/with any of our stakeholders?

> What objectives do our internal stakeholders believe they can achieve? How will they measure results, and from what benchmarks?
> What benefits do we need to accomplish all of this?
> If we can accomplish all of this, what is an appropriate fee? What's the opportunity cost?

These are not factors that fit into checkboxes or some kind of matrix. This is about organisational belief and commitment, and the only way you'll know if you've got that is if you follow a collaborative process to build vision, commitment, and consensus. And if the investment isn't right for you, that process will shake out all of the strategic reasons you need to say "no".

So, what's the process?

This evaluation process is one of the most important things you can do with your sponsorship stakeholder group. But, importantly, you shouldn't bog that group down with every offer that comes your way because most of them will be terrible, and not worth their time or effort.

Instead, do a quick, first-pass analysis. This will get rid of the obvious losers. (See . . . there is a role for analysis.) I've outlined the steps for that below.

Only when you've identified an opportunity with real potential should you put it in front of your stakeholder group. The process for that is found in Chapter 14: Finding the big leverage ideas. Why is it in *that* chapter? Because what you're going to do is work through leveraging the sponsorship before you commit, starting with, "What can we do with it to achieve our goals?" and working backwards to, "What benefits do we need?" and, "What's it worth?"

How to read a proposal

Both the structure and content of a proposal will tell you a lot about whether, and to what degree, the offer is worth consideration. Good sponsors evaluate sponsorship proposals on these factors, in roughly this order, starting with the deal-breakers, progressing through some red flags, and then onto the proposal aspects that they love to see and which will really build vision with stakeholders.

Doing it in this order is also handy as you can stop assessing and do a rejection as soon as the offer appears untenable.

Is it actually a proposal?

Rightsholders often think they can send you anything, and you'll consider it. Newsflash: You shouldn't. So, the first question is, is this actually a proposal? Most of the offers you receive are not proposals, falling into one of two categories:

1. Letter of request — Literally, a letter requesting money, sometimes offering a few benefits in return, but often not.
2. Prospectus — A brochure or other generic document that provides a laundry list of sponsorship opportunities, usually with set benefits packages and prices.

You should be looking for a proposal that makes a complete business case — something you can use to sell the opportunity internally. Neither of these fits that bill.

Is the entire premise untenable?

From requests to sponsor someone's dream wedding or gap year, to requests to fund someone's idea for a "totally amazing, never-before-seen event concept", some approaches are just ridiculous on their face.

No one should be asking you to underwrite their wedding, dream trip, or anything similar. No one should be asking you to pay them to develop an idea. You should be looking for fully formed, leveragable marketing platforms, not undeveloped concepts with overdeveloped hype.

And if a rightsholder is looking for sponsorship, they'd better have significant skin in the game. With very few exceptions — primarily corporate VC — you shouldn't be underwriting the development of a concept.

Is the offer structured as gold-silver-bronze (or similar)?

Once you've determined that what you've got at least looks like a proposal, and that the basic premise seems sound, look at the back pages. Don't worry too much about the price right now, as an offer that seems like a lot of money at the outset might be fantastic value once you dig right into it.

No, what you're looking for at the back of the proposal is whether they've provided set packages in some gold-silver-bronze-style hierarchy. If they have, it should be a huge red flag.

This is one of the fastest ways you can tell if a rightsholder has done their homework, understands your brand, and created something custom for you, because if they've done any of those things, the back pages of the proposal would be fully customised to your needs, not gold-silver-bronze. It will also tell you that the rightsholder lacks sophistication, which will make it more difficult for you to collaborate with them for a good result.

Has the rightsholder thought laterally about the benefits offered?

Still at the back of the proposal, have a look at the benefits offered. You should be looking for some creativity and strategic thinking. If the rightsholder has loaded up the offer with commodity benefits (also known as hygiene benefits), and not much else, you're not giving

> You should be looking for fully formed, leveragable marketing platforms.

them much to work with. Gold-silver-bronze-type offers are virtually always made up of commodity (or hygiene) benefits.

Commodity benefits are:

- Logos on things and/or social mentions
- Tickets
- Hospitality
- Official designation
- Display or activation space, or speaking spot (as applicable)

There will certainly be some of these in any sponsorship proposal, but if the rightsholder is anchoring the offer on them, they've showcased a big lack of sophistication.

Is it a search-and-replace job?

Rightsholders seem to think they can do a search-and-replace proposal, and you won't know, but of course, you do. Even if they do some light customisation by brand category — eg, their proposal for banks will be different than their proposal for SaaS — you'll be able to pick it.

Is it full of bad language?

No, not swear words . . . although that would also be counterproductive. I'm talking about terminology that gives away how the rightsholder really sees sponsorship.

First, there's donation language, such as:

- "Support"
- "Assist"
- "Help"
- "Underwrite the cost of . . ."
- "Donate a prize worth . . ."

Using terminology like this indicates that the rightsholder sees it as more-or-less free money — a donation with a few benefits in return. It also implies that the rightsholder thinks sponsorship should be provided because they're deserving, not a commercial opportunity that you need to use to achieve brand and business objectives.

And then there's the closely related infrastructure language, such as:

- "So we can buy . . ."
- "So we can build . . ."
- "Capital project"

This is basically telling you that they need something, and they want you to buy it for them. But your goal isn't about underwriting their hard costs. They need to offer real marketing value and build a business case.

Have they offered anything that is totally unconfirmed

> *"We are looking into starting a new tour in Asia."*
>
> *"Streaming rights are in negotiation."*
>
> *"We are exploring alliances with associations in every state."*

Hype. Hype. Hype.

These things may or may not happen, but for the purposes of making a decision about a sponsorship right now, you have to assume they won't.

Has the rightsholder done their homework?

This is a place where rightsholders can really shine. A rightsholder that demonstrates that they've spent some time researching your brand will put themselves head and shoulders above probably 90% or more of the approaches you get.

How much of the proposal is about your brand, markets, and objectives?

Doing that homework is great, but if you don't see it until you've slogged through 14 pages about how great the property is, they're prioritising their needs, not yours.

The proposal shouldn't be primarily about the rightsholder, but about your brand and your target markets. Of course, they need to provide some context about what they do, but if it devolves into one page after another about irrelevant minutiae, their focus is in the wrong place.

On the other hand, if they get the focus in the right place, that's a good sign that they have an approach that's conducive to a good relationship.

Has the rightsholder included creative ideas for how you can leverage the sponsorship?

This section of a proposal is sadly rare. "Sadly" because it's this factor, more than anything else, that will help you and your stakeholders to get a vision for what this sponsorship can do for the brand. It makes it infinitely easier to sell-in to your colleagues, and can save you a lot of time when it comes to leverage planning.

You're looking for strong leverage ideas — ideas that showcase an understanding of your brand and objectives, ideas that work over time and geographies. Even if they aren't on target with an idea or two, if most of the ideas provided are solid, you can work with the rightsholder on some better ideas.

Has the rightsholder considered non-attendees?

Rightsholders spend months or years living and breathing whatever event or season or program they're trying to deliver, and this can breed a bit of myopia on sponsorship. But just because rightsholders need to focus so hard on the people that actually show up, that doesn't mean these are the only, or even the most important, people for your brand.

These non-attendees can include:

- Remote fans
- Fans of the larger themes of the property
- Your customers and potential customers
- Your staff
- Intermediary markets (retailers, brokers, resellers, dealers, etc)

Does it make a business case?

The primary role of a sponsorship proposal isn't to sell to you, but so you can sell it internally. You're looking for a strong, cohesive business case, and that business case needs to be laid out in a sensible way, building from one section to the next.

What if it's terrible?

If you know the proposal is going to be terrible and you just don't want to deal with it, there is a much better option than letting it die a death in your inbox. It doesn't take much review to know whether a proposal is going to be any good. As soon as you spot the signs, do one of these three things:

Delete it

Seriously, just delete it. If you've got sponsorship guidelines on your website, and you've included my recommended wording on your website and autoresponder, including the badarse bit at the end, you've already told them they'll only hear from you if they've followed instructions.

This will account for most of the unsolicited proposals you receive, and save you a lot of time.

Reject and provide feedback

If they've put in some effort, but it's just not right for you, you can reject the offer and provide some feedback. That feedback is really helpful for rightsholders to understand where they're going wrong. This is also an option if you don't have the stomach to just delete bad proposals.

I've provided an email template below.

Ask them to try again

If you see some potential in the sponsorship, but the proposal isn't great, you have the option of asking them to try again. I suggest wording like this:

> The primary role of a sponsorship proposal isn't to sell to you, but so you can sell it internally.

Thank you for submitting a proposal.

Unfortunately, this proposal doesn't provide the type or amount of information we need in order to make a decision, and on that basis, we will not consider the offer. I am attaching a copy of our sponsorship guidelines. Feel free to resubmit a proposal based on these guidelines for reconsideration.

This is also a good strategy if you've got politics to deal with. For instance, if your CEO sends a proposal from a friend down the line, but it's awful, you can use this approach as a way to get a better proposal from them, which you can properly consider.

You shouldn't do this a lot, but it is an option.

Lead time: The most overlooked selection factor

If you've created comprehensive sponsorship guidelines, you will have already outlined your minimum lead time for opportunities. Six months is pretty common, but there's no reason you can't make that timeframe longer or (a little) shorter.

Remember, lead time is the time you have to make a decision, plan leverage, and implement that leverage, before the property kicks off. How long that actually takes is entirely dependent on the size and scope of the property, and the size and scope of your leverage program.

Effective leverage of a festival may require only three to four months' lead time. Leverage of a professional sports league would more likely be in the range of six to eight months' lead time. If you are considering sponsoring the Olympics or a World Cup, your lead time could run into years.

Even if it's the best sponsorship in the world, if you don't have enough lead time, you're not going to be able to do much with it. It's usually best to respond something like this:

Thank you for submitting a proposal.

While the opportunity is interesting, there simply isn't enough lead time for us to leverage it properly before you kick off. For that reason, we're going to decline for this year. We would like to explore sponsorship for next year, however. Please drop me a line to make a time to discuss.

Very occasionally, it will be worth jumping into a sponsorship with a short lead time, but only do it if:

- It's a multi-year deal, so you can realise the benefits from full leverage in future years.
- Your stakeholder team is willing and able to make a Herculean effort to put together at least some kind of meaningful leverage for the first year.

Using preliminary evaluation criteria for the first pass

Below, I've provided a preliminary evaluation criteria template. Once you've deleted, or otherwise got rid of, the obvious "nos", use this form to do your first pass.

The basic idea is that it asks the right questions in the right order, so you get a good understanding of the offer's potential. This process will result in one of the following:

- Deletion (if it's way worse than you initially thought)
- Rejection with feedback
- Request for a better proposal
- Bringing the offer to the sponsorship stakeholder group

⏻ Preliminary Evaluation Criteria

Rightsholder: ....

Property: ....

Contact name: ....

Email: ....

Phone: .... Date submitted: ....

Basics

- What is the annual fee for the sponsorship, as presented? ....

- What is the term of the sponsorship, as presented? ....

- Is there enough lead time to make a decision, plan, and implement leverage?
  - ❑ Yes, we have over six months
  - ❑ Yes, we have over three months and are capable of accelerating our planning
  - ❑ No – If "no", you need to pass

- Do we have the expertise and capacity on staff to manage a sponsorship of this scope?
  - ❑ Yes
  - ❑ No, but we have an agency/consultant that can assist
  - ❑ No, but we have budget for an agency/consultant/contractor to assist
  - ❑ No – If "no", you need to pass

Professionalism

➤ Was the proposal prepared based on our published sponsorship guidelines?

❏ Yes

❏ No – If "no", delete or reject proposal and provide with a copy of the sponsorship guidelines

➤ Was the sponsorship opportunity professionally presented?

❏ Yes

❏ No

➤ Does the proposal include all information necessary to make an investment decision?

❏ Yes

❏ No – If "no", delete or request proposal is resubmitted to include all information required in the sponsorship guidelines

Strategic fit

All sponsorships under consideration for investment by [sponsor] must meet the following criteria. It should be noted that most proposals will not make it through this phase.

➤ Does this property fit within the [umbrella name] umbrella framework? [Only use if your organisation runs one or more umbrella sponsorship portfolios.]

❏ Yes

❏ No, but the rightsholder has another property that does (in this case, request a new proposal around the better fitting property)

❏ No, it must be considered as a stand-alone investment

➤ Must be a fit with at least one of our core target markets. Tick all that apply.

❏ [List core target markets, keep it primarily psychographic]

➤ Must provide exclusivity in the category of [category or categories].

❏ Yes, [category 1]

❏ Yes, [category 2, if applicable]

❏ No – please explain mitigating factor(s) ....

➤ Must be a natural value and/or attribute fit with the [brand] brand. List matching attributes/values from brand architecture below:

❏ ....

❏ ....

❏ ....

- ❏ ....
- ❏ ....

➢ Must either provide or provide for us to create exclusive and desirable content.
   - ❏ Will provide exclusive content
   - ❏ Will provide exclusive IP for us to create content
   - ❏ Will provide permission for us to create content related to the property

➢ Must provide at least one benefit that we can directly pass through to our target markets. List benefits that can be used to add value to our target market relationships below:

- ❏ ....
- ❏ ....
- ❏ ....
- ❏ ....
- ❏ ....

➢ Must not contravene our exclusions. Check to confirm that this proposal does NOT fall into the following categories. [Below are typical, but feel free to customise, as required.]
   - ❏ Political, social, or religious causes
   - ❏ Alcohol, tobacco
   - ❏ Firearms/weapons, fireworks
   - ❏ Pornography
   - ❏ Gambling/lottery

Disposition (choose one)
   - ❏ Reject/delete
   - ❏ Provide with sponsorship guidelines and request a stronger proposal or more information
   - ❏ Present to stakeholder group for determining buy-in, establishing scope (leverage planning), and making a determination

Preliminary evaluation carried out by:

Date:

⟁ Rejection Email Template

Feel free to add or adjust bullet points on this template. When using, delete all of the bullet points that aren't applicable to a particular offer.

Hello [name] –

Thank you for the sponsorship proposal for [property].

We will not be taking you up on this offer this time. This decision was based on the following reason(s):

- Your proposal was not prepared as required by our sponsorship guidelines. Here is a link to those guidelines: fakecompany.com/sponsorshipguidelines.
- Your proposal is generic and does not address our objectives or target markets in any meaningful way.
- You have not provided a complete business case for why we should invest marketing funds in this sponsorship.
- We need an absolute minimum of six months' lead time, so we have time to plan and implement our leverage activities.
- We require exclusivity in the category of [category].
- Your offer duplicates another sponsorship in our portfolio.
- Your offer was priced unrealistically for the opportunity provided.

If you are able to address the above, we are happy to revisit.

[name]

Due diligence

Sponsorship is an investment, and like any other substantial investment, some due diligence is required to ensure that the organisation you are considering sponsoring is viable, professional, and delivers on their promises.

There are dozens of things you can check, but these are the two I find most useful:

1. Call at least a couple of their other sponsors and get their feedback before you invest any money. No, you don't need the rightsholder's permission to do this.
2. Do a quick web search on the organisation and property. Do another couple of searches, adding terms like "scandal" or "cancellation". There is no shame in anyone having a failure or two under their belt — we've all been there — but if there is something worrisome or a pattern, you need to know about it.

These two simple steps can save you years of heartache, or they can confirm that you're making a sound decision to invest in a credible, hardworking partner. Either way, you need to know.

The dark side of a buyers' market

In a buyers' market, there are a lot of organisations that are really hurting for funds, and they are willing to do almost anything just to get some money in the door. On one hand, that's good for any sponsor on a budget. On the other, taking advantage of their desperation is unlikely to be a good move, in the longer term.

As with any marketplace, there are buyers' and sellers' markets, and there are two traps that sponsors can fall into with a buyers' market.

Bargain fever

A buyers' market depresses sponsorship fees, and for some sponsors, there is a temptation to buy without the kind of rigour that would normally go into sponsorship decisions. It's a bit like those frightening people who line up outside department stores at 5:00 am waiting for the big January sales to start, then buying things they don't need, or that don't fit, just because they're cheap.

Financial bully

While buying up sponsorships that don't work, on the cheap, is a bad idea, the only party it hurts is the sponsor. That's not the case with a financial bully. These are sponsors that take advantage of a rightsholder's desperation, offering a pittance for a sponsorship just because they can.

Not only is this terrible sponsor karma, but you'll end up with a disgruntled partner, and that's unlikely to end well.

My advice is to not let a buyers' market change how you do business in any significant way. Ensure every potential sponsorship goes through all of the rigour you normally would, and if it's a good fit for you, be fair on pricing.

> Never, ever bully a rightsholder.

Chapter 7

Negotiation

You've done the evaluation. You've got your buy-in and leverage plan. And you've done your due diligence. It's now time to negotiate!

Win-win-win negotiation

Let's face it, it's been instilled in most of us that negotiation is an adversarial process. This attitude is rarely productive, and it is never productive when negotiating sponsorship. Instead, we should be negotiating for win-win-win sponsorship because the reality is, if any of the three parties lose, everyone's going to lose.

Win #1 – Your brand

When you negotiate you are trying to create a leveragable marketing platform. It needs to be right for your brand and provide both flexibility and scope.

It is unlikely you will need exactly what the rightsholder has included in their proposal, and you shouldn't be afraid to counteroffer to get what you need. (There's lots of advice on counteroffers later in this chapter.) If the rightsholder won't negotiate so you get what you need, I'd think long and hard before investing.

Win #2 – The rightsholder

While it's important to get what you need for your brand, it is equally important that you treat the rightsholder with respect, and be willing to honour their needs. You should never propose benefits (or leverage activities) that hurt the rightsholder or undermine the success of the property. In fact, you will reap many added-value benefits if you ensure they are just as happy with the partnership as you are.

And again, don't squeeze the rightsholder down on price just because you can. I'm not saying you should pay an over-inflated fee, but if their price is fair, make your decision based on that. Bullying a potential partner on price is just not a good way to start a relationship.

Win #3 – The target market

The most important win of all is the win that the target market gets. You will not influence perceptions or behaviours in a positive way, or build alignment, if you don't protect and advance their interests first.

The target markets are the most important party to this relationship, but they don't have representation in negotiations, so you need to be prepared to represent their best interests.

You want to negotiate for benefits that you can pass through to your target markets. There are hundreds of options, but some examples are: Ways to enhance their experience; exclusive content or behind-the-scenes information you provide; or ways they can be more involved or provide more input. There's lots on the kinds of benefits that are great for target markets later in this chapter.

You also want to ensure that you don't propose or agree to anything that diminishes or disrespects the target markets' fan experience, even if it's the rightsholder's idea.

Leverage before you negotiate

As noted in the previous chapter, it's critical that you develop a leverage plan with your sponsorship stakeholder group before you negotiate. I don't care how much of a genius brand or sponsorship manager you may be, you won't get top results if you commit to a sponsorship without collaboration.

Right-sizing the sponsorship

As part of your pre-negotiation leverage planning, you will understand what you *need* to make a sponsorship work for you. Stick with that. Don't go bigger. Don't let your corporate ego get the better of you.

While there are plenty of good reasons to take up principal or naming rights sponsorship, it should not be your default position. Being thorough and creative, and focusing on the connection with the target market rather than the property, can create huge results — much bigger than your typical naming rights sponsor, who concentrates on visibility, not creating real returns for the brand.

Investing over the right timeframe

If your goal is to change your target markets' perceptions and behaviours around your brand, and their alignment to the brand, in the long term, you need to make investments that have some consistency over time. You can get decent results in one year, but if you're working the sponsorship well, you'll be getting even better results in years two and three.

> Don't make naming rights your default position.

You want investments that will create lasting effects — building your brand for the long term (growth) — while providing a platform for shorter-term and tactical benefits (dividends).

On the other hand, if you are sponsoring to support a new product launch, IPO, or other short-term need, then you're looking for a big return on a short timeframe. Either only sponsor for one year or cycle, or build a benefits adjustment into the contract for future years when your brand is more mature and your needs will be different. This is not the time to sign a 30-year deal for stadium naming rights.

Knowing your benefits

Many, many sponsors are in a rut. They negotiate the same types of sponsorship, and for the same boring benefits, over and over again. They buy logos and mentions and tickets and stock-standard hospitality, with the overriding assumption — and point of comparison — that it's largely a commodity business and more is better.

WRONG!

Go ahead and negotiate some of those commodity benefits, but understand that's not where your real marketing opportunity lies. Instead, concentrate your efforts on getting the type of benefit that can be:

- Used in multiple ways
- Used over a longer period of time
- Used to add value to the fan or customer experience
- Used to make fans, customers, or your staff the heroes

There's a rundown of examples below, and there are examples of great benefits in the case studies throughout the book.

Sponsorship benefits you should want

These are a few of my favourite sponsorship benefits, ticking all of the above boxes. Deals featuring a lot of these benefits are the true workhorses of your portfolio, as they're leveragable in many ways, with many markets, over a lot of time.

Value-adds that can be passed through to fans and customers

Some of the most important and powerful benefits you can negotiate are those that can be passed through to fans and customers. These are small, meaningful benefits that can comprise the third win in a win-win-win sponsorship.

It could be . . .

> A bag check at a festival
> Preferred parking for your customers, or for fans with kids under six
> Sign-making stations in the stadium
> A VIP lounge for your platinum card holders
> Childcare at a weekend trade show
> Express lane entry for customers
> Luxury restrooms for retirees

These examples are pretty basic, and the list could go on and on, but this kind of benefit is generally comprised of either amplifying the best stuff or ameliorating the worst stuff around a fan experience. Negotiate for, and deliver, these benefits to your customers and fans, and your brand becomes a welcome part of the experience. That's a lot more than signage will ever get you.

Control that can be passed through to the fans

If fans love an experience, they love it even more if they've had some influence on it. Try to find something that your brand can take control of, and then hand that control to customers and fans.

Can you crowdsource the programming of a stage? Do a people's choice award? Let people nominate the charity or program a donation will go to? There are so many options!

Not only will this enhance the experience for fans – that third win – but it will open up your promotional period, as you could be running the voting/crowdsourcing for months before an event, season, or program kicks off. You could also use this to make your sponsorship look bigger and more impactful than it "should". While bigger sponsors are being super-loud and visible, you're doing something meaningful for fans during a big run-up to the property.

Durable, exclusive content

Content is king. We've all heard that before. And durable content is even better; that is, content that is relevant and lives on well after the property that generated it. Make it episodic video, and you've hit the jackpot! The bonus for brands that sponsorship is a mother lode of content.

There is the property itself – the festival, the game, the cause, the museum, etc. – and plenty of information about that, but that's usually easy for people to access. What's much more desirable is access to exclusive content – the stuff people don't generally see or know. You can negotiate access to it, or you can create it – such as doing a YouTube series providing tips for curating an artistic home from a gallery curator.

Personally, I'm a big fan of creating content, as you can be more creative and responsive to what your target markets and fans want to know or see. But this still often requires access to the right people, which brings me to . . .

Appearances

When we think of athlete or celebrity appearances, we generally think of the big, name-brand people doing meet-and-greets or high-production ads. That's all well and good, but it's also been done to death. It's time to think about appearances more broadly.

- Could that appearance be used to generate content for thousands or millions of people, not just meet a few hundred?
- Could you use that time to do a video? And what could you do with it — YouTube? Virtual reality? Creating a game or app? Something personalised for fans?
- Could you do face mapping for AI-driven content creation?
- Does it really have to be the biggest star? Could it be a support player? Or someone who is usually behind the scenes? A rookie or a larrikin?
- Could you do something funny or unexpected?
- Could you ask the fans for suggestions on how to use one or more of the appearances?

In addition, don't just think about sportspeople. Lots of rightsholders have access to experts, visionaries, and people with super-cool jobs, and you can work with them to create really interesting content. This extends to curators, scientists, trainers and nutritionists, and so many more.

> Think broadly about who could do appearances, and how you can use them.

Customisable and/or experiential content

This is all about getting access to information, images and videos, stats, advice, or any other intellectual property that might be interesting to fans, so that it can be turned into content that genuinely adds to the fan experience.

Make it customisable — whether in a choose-your-own-adventure sense or simply about the fan — and that's a huge win. Doing this definitely doesn't *require* AI, but AI's capabilities expand customisation options.

Behind-the-scenes access

Getting access to inner-sanctum-type experiences, places, or people can be effective for a lot of reasons. Could you:

- Use it for amazing, one-of-a-kind hospitality?
- Create exclusive, durable content?
- Do a virtual-reality tour?
- Deliver messages from the fans right to the stars?

The access you need will depend on what you want to do with it, but you should be negotiating for at least some of this.

What-money-can't-buy experiences

This has been part of a negotiation package for a long time, but generally consists of some huge prize — backstage at a concert, for instance — that anchors a sales promotion where lots of people enter, but only one person wins. Bo-ringggg.

The trend now is to use that one what-money-can't-buy experience as the pivot point for something much bigger.

- How can you make the process of the winner being chosen more inclusive, participative, and fun? Could people upload something — photo, video, poem, song, haiku, etc. — in order to enter? Could fans nominate a shortlist or vote for the winner? Could there be some kind of audition process that could be captured and shared?
- How long can this whole process be stretched out? Months?
- How about the prize itself? Could that what-money-can't-buy experience be captured — videos, blogging, live tweeting, etc. — and shared, as unique and exclusive content?

It's no longer, "SMS to win a backstage pass to every mainstage band at Lollapalooza." Instead, you could get people to submit two-minute videos of themselves interviewing a (fake) band. These are shared in your social media, with a shortlist chosen based on social media feedback of the best, funniest, most insightful, etc. The winner(s) would be chosen by a vote, and then would be charged with conducting two-minute video interviews with all of the bands as soon as they come off stage, creating content that could live on for years.

Examples: Using one (or a few) what-money-can't-buy experiences to create lots of wins

DHL has created Fast-Track Sessions, providing three artists from around the world the opportunity to win a three-day recording session at Abbey Road Studios, a big-name record producer, mentorship by an established band, a feature article in *NME*, and more. Artists/ bands enter by posting a short video of an original song to Instagram Reels, tagging DHL and using their hashtag. Critically, music fans will be treated to a mini-documentary and filmed live performance by each band. Wins for everyone!

Years ago, **ANZ Bank** sponsored the first Australian tour of *Wicked*. One of the many things they did was offer one person the opportunity to win a walk-on role for one night of *Wicked*. Anyone could audition, and auditions were conducted by videos uploaded to ANZ socials. The shortlist was then crowdsourced by customers and fans (lots of wins!). When the shortlisted people were flown to Melbourne for their proper auditions, it turned into a generator for tons of exclusive, behind-the-scenes, durable content (more wins!).

Finding the right experience to anchor this approach is important. Getting the best seats at the opera is not a what-money-can't-buy experience. Being in costume and on stage is.

Special hospitality

Beers in the skybox . . . yada yada yada. Everyone and their dog has had beers in some corporate suite at one time or another. You can do it, and I'm not saying you shouldn't, but let's face it, it's not that special.

If you have clients that really deserve or expect something special, you need to think more creatively about how you can deliver it. For example:

- Could you give them a day-in-the-life experience? Top-level training in a sport?
- Could you have a super-special dinner in some behind-the-scenes or generally off-limits venue?
- Could you do something amazing for their kids or grandkids?
- Could you arrange a volunteer day with a charity, and invite your clients? (Note: This is a trend.)

These days, hospitality isn't necessarily about a luxury experience, it's about a special experience — something very few people will ever do. That could happen at a major concert sound check or in a soup kitchen. Again, the key word is "special".

> Everyone and their dog has had beers in some corporate suite at one time or another.

Least powerful benefits

The benefits listed below are some of the most common, but least powerful, sponsorship benefits on offer. Collectively, they go by the terms "commodity benefits" or "hygiene benefits", because everybody offers them, and they're basically interchangeable.

These benefits lack meaning to the people you're trying to connect with, and when meaning is the basic foundation from which a strong sponsorship is built, that's not good. These are the benefits you should be willing to minimise or forego in order to get more of the powerhouse benefits, listed above. And if you do get some of these commodity benefits, don't fixate on them as they're not where your results are going to come from.

Official designation or endorsement

No one thinks a sponsor is higher quality (or whatever) because they've got some official designation.

Think of your own fan experiences. Do you think an insurance company is better or more trustworthy because they're the official insurance of a 10km race? Of course you don't. All that designation says is that they paid the money.

This is another one of those things that you may receive as part of a package, but understand — like the fans do — that this benefit has extremely limited value.

Non-VIP tickets

If you accept the idea of win-win-win, the lack of power in non-VIP tickets is apparent.

You're not going to get enough of them to create a win for many people. Even if you get a couple of hundred tickets, or a couple of thousand over a season, that's a drop in the bucket when compared to how many fans, customers, or potential customers you're targeting. And in a lot of cases, it's not all that expensive to attend and it's not sold out, so the perceived value is low.

If you get a ticket allocation that you can't trade out for something more useful, often the best option is to do something for staff. If there's any left, give them away to one or more charities.

Naming rights or presenting sponsorship of something no one cares about

As part of sponsorship packages, some sponsors are offered naming rights to sub-events, specific days or areas of an event, or some other inconsequential component. I went to a Christmas festival last year and saw, "Santa's Elves, presented by . . ."

The inanest one I can recall is a sponsor who took up naming rights to the foyer of a theatre, solely because their competitor was naming rights sponsor of a big arts festival, and people would have to walk through their foyer to buy tickets. It wasn't leveragable as a sponsorship, nor was it effective as an ambush because no one cared.

I'm not saying it's a bad thing to have some kind of epicentre for leverage activities, but the designation itself isn't powerful, and, unleveraged, won't deliver any results.

Ho-hum hospitality

As noted above, most hospitality is essentially interchangeable. The decision-makers targeted by one sponsor are also being targeted by other sponsors, all of whom offer the same experience. This substantially reduces its power as a relationship-building tool.

Signage and other exposure

The fact that signage can cost a lot of money doesn't mean it's powerful, and there is study after study that shows logo exposure doesn't contribute to changing perceptions, behaviours, and alignment around a brand — in other words, "marketing".

Sure, there are still sponsors that haven't seen the light. Some senior executives can be far too preoccupied with corporate ego. And still other sponsors know signage does nothing for them, but are too lazy to actually change anything.

In any case, there's no need to get your undies in a bundle. You can still have signage; you can still get your logos on stuff. Just understand that this is not where results are going to come from. It's window dressing. That's it.

Interruption signage

Thinking that signage is powerful is wrong, but it's not actually detrimental to the fan experience. Interruption signage is.

Interruption signage is specifically designed to take a fan's attention away from the experience they are trying to have. Ever been annoyed by moving, lit-up signage right next to the field or court at a game? That's interruption signage, and the annoyance you felt at the sponsors who are making the game harder to watch is the annoyance all fans feel. That's not good for your brand.

Sponsor speeches

Like interruption signage, sponsor speeches are not only low value, they're also almost always counterproductive.

People hate it when sponsors speak at events. Hate. It. And, frankly, you know that because you don't like it either. You don't like it when sponsors interrupt the festivities of an industry awards dinner to waffle on about how they're, "So proud to sponsor an awards program that showcases the kind of excellence our company is known for. From the day we opened our first office in Columbus, Ohio . . ." Kill me now.

You don't feel like your $1,600 conference registration fee was totally worth every penny after you've sat through a tone-deaf, 45-minute pitch for some sponsor's brand, disguised as an educational session.

You may or may not be able to get your senior executives and/or sales division to stop doing these things, but at the very least, understand that sponsor speeches are not powerful brand drivers.

⏻ Negotiation Checklist

What follows is a negotiation checklist. This was initially developed for rightsholders to take inventory of all of the benefits they could offer. But it also works really well for sponsors, broadening the understanding of the benefit options available, and allowing for customisation and prioritisation.

The types of benefits that are typically most valuable to smart sponsors that take a best-practice approach to connecting with their target markets — the blue-chip benefits that most sponsors should be looking for — are marked with an asterisk (*). This is not to say that the other benefits should be ignored or minimised, but that you should endeavour to include at least some blue-chip benefits in every sponsorship contract.

Sponsorship types

> Naming rights sponsorship
> Presenting sponsorship

> People hate it when sponsors speak at events. Hate. It.

- Naming rights or presenting sponsorship of a section, area, entry, or team
- Naming rights or presenting sponsorship of a day, weekend, or week at the event
- Naming rights or presenting sponsorship of an event-driven award, trophy, or scholarship
- Naming rights or presenting sponsorship of a related or subordinated event
- Major sponsorship
- Supporting sponsorship
- Official product status
- Preferred supplier status

- ....

- ....

- ....

Exclusivity

- Category exclusivity among property sponsors at any level
- Category exclusivity among property sponsors, exhibitors, speakers, and/or other brand participation mechanisms
- Category exclusivity across an overarching property, and all subordinate properties as well, such as a league sponsor getting exclusivity across teams (this is generally reserved for only the largest sponsors of an overarching property)
- Category exclusivity as a supplier to the property, or as a vendor (eg, exclusive beer pouring rights)

- ....

- ....

- ....

Licence & endorsements*

- Licence to use rightsholder or property logo(s), images, and/or trademark(s) for content, promotion, advertising, or other leverage activities
- Licence to use other rightsholder or property intellectual property for content, promotion, advertising, or other leverage activities
- Merchandising rights (the right to create co-branded merchandise to sell or give away)
- Product or brand endorsement

- ....

> ....

> ....

Contracts

> Discounts for multi-year contracts

> First right of refusal for renewal at conclusion of contract

> Last right of refusal for renewal at conclusion of contract (not recommended)

> Performance incentives

> ....

> ....

> ....

On-site

> Dedicated space to carry out on-site leverage activities

> Speaking opportunity

> Sampling opportunities

> Demonstration/display opportunities

> Exhibition space

> Opportunity to sell product on-site (exclusive or non-exclusive)

> Coupon, information, or premium distribution

> ....

> ....

> ....

Exclusive content*

> Provision or facilitation of content for leverage activities (eg, weekly health tips, star athlete's training diary, pertinent articles, podcasts, other exclusive downloadable content, etc.)

> Provision or facilitation of online "events" (eg, online chat with a star, webcast, webinar)

> Access to venue, athletes, celebrities, artist, curator, etc. for creation of new, exclusive, "ownable" content

> Access to background information, statistics, photos, video clips, autographs, Q&As, etc. for creation of new, exclusive, "ownable" content

> ....

> ....

> ....

Other online*

> Promotion of relevant sponsor leverage activities through rightsholder's social media, app, newsletter, and/or website

> Promotion of sponsor through rightsholder's social media activities, app, newsletter, and/or website

> Ability for sponsor to add value to rightsholder fans/followers via rightsholder-controlled social media or app*

> Advertising on rightsholder or property website, app, and/or newsletter

> Promotion or contest on rightsholder social media, app, newsletter, and/or website

> Links to sponsor website from rightsholder or property website

> Sponsor profile on rightsholder or property website

> ....

> ....

> ....

Customer added value*

This section is about benefits that you can pass on to your target markets in order to reinforce your customer relationships:

> Access to events, parking, or merchandise discounts for customers or a specific customer group (eg, frequent flyers, Gold Card holders)

> Access to events, parking or merchandise discounts, or other perks for customers

> Exclusive access to an event, area, contest/prize, service, celebrity, or experience for all or a specific group of customers

> Early access to tickets (before they go on sale to the general public)

> Block of tickets, parking, etc. that the sponsor can provide to loyal customers. Can be provided with or without naming rights to that section (eg, the Acme Energy Best Seats in the House)

> Discount admission for customers

> Discount or free parking for customers

> Free premium item for customers (eg, people can scan app barcode for a free program)

> Access to or creation of what-money-can't-buy experiences to anchor leverage activity*

> ....

> ....

> ....

Signage

> Venue signage (full, partial, or non-broadcast view)
> Inclusion in on-site property signage (exclusive or non-exclusive)
> Inclusion on pre-event street banners, flags, etc.
> Press conference signage
> Vehicle signage
> Participant uniforms (eg, on marathon race numbers)
> Event staff shirts/caps/uniforms

> ....

> ....

> ....

Hospitality

> Tickets to the event (luxury boxes, preferred seating, reserved seating, or general admission)
> VIP tickets/passes (backstage, sideline, pit passes, press box, or other inner sanctum)
> Celebrity/participant meet-and-greets
> Access to or creation of what-money-can't-buy experiences for hospitality*
> Development of customised hospitality events to suit the interests of the target market (high-end, adventurous, behind the scenes, for their families or kids, etc.)*

> ....

> ....

> ....

Venue

> Input in venue, route, and/or timing
> Use of sponsor venue for launch, main event, or supporting event

➤ ....

➤ ....

➤ ....

Database marketing

➤ Unlimited access to event-generated database(s), such as member lists, for direct marketing follow-up (be careful not to breach privacy laws, which vary from country to country)

➤ Opportunity to provide content for rightsholder mailings or EDMs

➤ Rental/loan of rightsholder database for one-off communication with people who have opted into third-party promotions

➤ Opportunity to run database-generating activities on-site

➤ Opportunity to generate databases through other leverage activities

➤ ....

➤ ....

➤ ....

Employees*

➤ Participation in the property by employees

➤ Access to discounts, merchandise, or other sponsorship-oriented perks

➤ "Ownership" of part of the event by employees (eg, creating an employee-built and run water station as part of a marathon sponsorship)

➤ Provision of a celebrity or spokesperson for meet-and-greets or employee motivation

➤ Creation of an event, day, or program specifically for employees

➤ Creation of an employee donation or volunteer program

➤ Opportunity to set up an employee recruitment station at your event

➤ Distribution of employee recruitment information

➤ ....

➤ ....

➤ ....

Public relations

➤ Inclusion in all press releases and other media activities

➤ Inclusion in sponsor-related and media activities

➤ Public relations campaign designed for sponsor's market (consumer or trade)

➤ ....

➤ ....

➤ ....

Ancillary or supporting events

➤ Tickets or invitations to ancillary parties, receptions, shows, launches, etc.

➤ Signage, sampling, and other benefits at ancillary parties, receptions, shows, launches, etc.

➤ ....

➤ ....

➤ ....

Other promotional opportunities

➤ Custom design of a new event, program, award, or other activity that meets the sponsor's specific needs

➤ Securing and administration of entertainment, celebrity appearances, etc. to appear on sponsors' behalf

➤ Provision by sponsor of spokesperson/people, celebrity appearances, costumed characters, etc. for sponsored event

➤ Opportunity to provide prizes for rightsholder-driven promotions

➤ ....

➤ ....

➤ ....

Media profile

➤ Inclusion in all print, outdoor, and/or broadcast advertising (logo or name)

➤ Inclusion on event promotional pieces (posters, flyers, brochures, apparel, etc. – logo or name)

➤ Ad time during televised event

➤ Inclusion in outdoor (billboards, vehicle, public transport)

➢ Ad space in event program, catalogue, etc.

➢ ....

➢ ....

➢ ....

Research

➢ Access to pre- and/or post-event research

➢ Opportunity to provide a selection of brand-tracking or industry-oriented questions on property's audience research

➢ ....

➢ ....

➢ ....

Pass-through rights

➢ Right for sponsor to on-sell sponsorship benefits to another organisation (this is always pending rightsholder approval). An example would be a telecommunications company on-selling part of a sponsorship to Samsung. They would then usually leverage the sponsorship jointly

➢ Right for retailer sponsor to on-sell sponsorship benefits to vendors in specific product categories

➢ Right for retailer sponsor to involve vendors in sponsorship-driven in-store promotions, sales promotions, and social media

➢ ....

➢ ....

Contra/in-kind

➢ Opportunity for sponsor to provide equipment, services, technology, expertise, or personnel useful to the success of the event in trade for part of sponsorship fee

➢ Opportunity for sponsor to provide media value, in-store/in-house promotion in trade for part of sponsorship fee

➢ Opportunity for sponsor to provide access to discounted media, travel, printing, or other products or services in trade for part of sponsorship fee

> ....

> ....

> ....

Production

> Design and/or production of key sponsor events (hospitality, awards, etc.)
> Hiring and/or administration of temporary or contract personnel, services, and vendors for above
> Logistical assistance, including technical or creative expertise

> ....

> ....

> ....

Cause tie-in

> Opportunity to involve sponsor's preferred charitable organisation or cause
> Donation of a percentage of ticket or product sales to charity

> ....

> ....

☝ Inventory of Assets

This is a menu of the non-cash benefits you could provide to a rightsholder. If a benefit offsets an actual cash cost, you may be able to negotiate a commensurate discount on your cash investment. Otherwise, these benefits may simply be part of a multifaceted deal, where you work collaboratively to achieve each organisation's objectives.

This is a starting point only. You may have access to more, fewer, or different assets.

Products and services

Note: These should be things that are on the rightsholder's budget, and must be valued at what the rightsholder would have to pay for them.

> Provision of product that the rightsholder needs (in their budget)
> Provision of services that the rightsholder needs (in their budget)
> Provision of significant discounts on the above

Promotion

- Promotion of the property through your brand marketing channels
- Promotion of the property on/in-pack, or at retail
- Inclusion of one or more brand ambassadors in leverage activities

Media buy

- Access to heavily discounted media rates through your media deals or media buyer

People/services

- Secondment of employee for fixed-term assignment (full- or part-time for a set number of weeks/months)
- Access to in-house experts (creative, production, analytics, etc.)
- Mentorship
- Access to staff professional development (eg, in-house executive development)

Infrastructure

- Use of office, conference, function, or other spaces
- Use of spaces to which you have access, such as through other sponsorships
- Event equipment or services
- Access to your distribution network
- Access to discounted subcontractor deals (printing, mailing, travel, etc.)

If the rightsholder is a charity

- Cause-related marketing (donation with purchase)
- Opt-in donation with bill (eg, add $1 donation to your phone bill)
- Round up donation at retail (round up purchase to the nearest dollar, donate the difference)
- Inclusion in employee giving program
- Facilitating fundraising events, auctions, etc.
- Facilitating donations (eg, at retail, at bank branches, at dealerships, etc.)

Counteroffers

Even if a proposal has a lot of potential for your brand, you should always consider it simply a starting place. On occasions, a proposal will be bang on target, requiring no fine-tuning. Most of the time, however, you will need to fine-tune — or even totally overhaul — the offer. This is particularly the case if you leverage before negotiation, as that will likely identify both benefits that you want that aren't in the offer, as well as benefits that have little value to you, and you're happy to forego.

There are two issues that can be addressed with a counteroffer:

1.   The benefits are not right for your needs.
2.   The pricing is unrealistic for what they are offering.

Asking for what you really need

Creating a counteroffer may seem daunting, but it's actually straightforward, and you'd be surprised how willing rightsholders are to negotiate when they realise you're serious.

There are three main steps to creating a counteroffer, which I have outlined below.

Be both specific and flexible

A counteroffer is not a request for the rightsholder to go away and come back with something better. On the contrary, it is a request for very specific changes to the offer. I suggest using wording similar to this:

> *Our sponsorship stakeholder group has discussed your offer and come up with some ideas that could make it work well for our brand. Those ideas will require significant adjustment in the benefits currently on offer. As a starting point, we have outlined some of the benefits that have limited value to us and we'd be willing to forego, as well as the benefits we'd like to have.*

Following that wording, you would list the benefits that you don't need, or don't need in the quantity offered, as well as the specific benefits your stakeholder group want for support of their leverage plan.

I recommend that you also leave the door open for the rightsholder to get creative. For example:

> *Now that we've made our brand needs clear, you may have some other ideas or benefits that you believe would be appropriate for us. We are very open to discussing other options or creative ideas.*

Be realistic

Unless you are prepared to pay a lot more than the initial offer, you need to accept that in order to get the benefits you want, you will have to give up some other benefits.

This is a hard pill for some sponsors to swallow. They want the strategic benefits but have a hard time letting go of lower-value, commodity benefits. Reasons range from senior executive expectations of what a sponsorship "should" look like, to a belief that negotiation is primarily about getting more for less, so why would you ever give something up?

In my experience, proposals tend to be full of low-value fluff — commodity benefits that have little bearing on the potential returns of the sponsorship. These are the easiest to get rid of, and because they are in limited supply, the rightsholder is often delighted to get them back, so they can sell them to someone else, giving you a strong position to get benefits of real value.

These are a few of the low-value benefits I typically advise my clients to get rid of:

> A proportion of the proposed signage – Do you really need 14 major logo hits at the event? Is there any major downside to only having 8?
> Tickets – Some events provide hundreds of free tickets as part of their offer. If you don't need tickets to make your leverage plan work, let some or most of them go.
> A proportion of the proposed hospitality package – Do you really need a client cocktail party for every ballet performance of the season? What if you only had cocktail functions on Friday and Saturday nights?

Although these are obviously just examples, they are reflective of the kinds of hard questions you need to ask yourself about the benefits on offer. That way, you will keep what you need and, by letting go of what you realistically don't, will put yourself in a strong negotiating position.

Be clear how the counteroffer will benefit the rightsholder

Some rightsholders will enthusiastically welcome your counteroffer. Others will be concerned that, because you're veering off the well-worn path of their standard benefits package, you may be a difficult sponsor.

To assuage their reticence, I suggest you tell them both how you intend to use these newly proposed benefits and how those leverage activities will benefit them. You don't need to go into a lot of detail. Simply include their wellbeing in your rationale. For example:

> *We want to use the proposed parking area to allow parents with children under five to park near the front entrance of the event. This allows us to add value to our core target market of young, active families, and it benefits the event by alleviating the increasingly difficult parking situation for some of your most inconvenienced customers.*

The collaboration option

Another option is not to go back and forth trying to fine-tune the offer, but to work together to achieve a result that works for both parties.

You may want to consider inviting the rightsholder into your stakeholder group brainstorm, where you're discussing leverage plans and developing a negotiation strategy. That way, they can respond to questions about what is and isn't possible in real time, and will also get a sense of the commitment level of your team, and how much the leverage plan will benefit them.

> Unless you want to pay more, you will have to give up lower-value benefits to get the benefits you need.

Putting your cards on the table doesn't always work. Sometimes your stakeholder group will be concerned about having an outsider involved in a planning meeting, as they may inadvertently disclose something that is commercial-in-confidence. Or, your potential partner may be stuck in an old-school, package mindset and uninterested in working with you to do anything creative. Neither of these situations is particularly common, yet they do happen.

Calling out unrealistic pricing

Some rightsholders have absolutely no idea how to price what they offer. In their defence, sponsorship pricing isn't easy — especially when creating highly customised offers. Plus, while *you* look at dozens or hundreds of proposals in any given month, so have some understanding of the market and benchmarks, there is every chance that their own proposals are the only ones they've ever seen. What I'm saying is that when you get a proposal and the price is way too high for what they're offering, it's often less likely to do with greed than with simply not knowing what the market value is.

Clearly, you're not going to pay an inflated rate — even for a really great opportunity — but you don't have to be nasty about it, either. For example:

> *We are very interested in discussing the sponsorship of your association and annual conference. We are concerned, however, about the pricing. We are current sponsors of two associations that are similar in scope and offer a similar complement of benefits. We also see a lot of proposals in this vein. Given that perspective, you should know that the fee you are proposing is around 35% higher than its market value. It would be unrealistic for us to pay that kind of premium.*
>
> *We would like to work with you to develop a tailored offer, but we can only go down that track if the price is reflective of market value. Please advise if you would like to take this further.*

Unrealistic pricing is not necessarily a deal killer.

If you don't hear from them, or they indicate they are unwilling to drop the price, don't sweat it. There are always more opportunities to reach a particular target market. You don't need to pay an unrealistic price to do it, and it's never good to work with an unrealistic, inflexible partner.

Valuing contra vs cash sponsorship

How to value contra, otherwise known as in-kind, sponsorship is a question I get almost every day. What is most interesting is how differently sponsors and rightsholders view contra, with both overcomplicating what is really quite a simple equation.

Rightsholders tend to take contra for granted. The attitude is, "Those airline seats would be empty anyway, so why do we have to put a value on them?" Of course, if they didn't get those seats through contra, they would have to pay someone for them, so they do have value.

Sponsors, on the other hand, tend to value what they offer at full price, whether that's what a rightsholder would have to pay for those goods or services on the open market or not. Media sponsors are among the biggest offenders, valuing every spot in a contra deal — no matter how crappy — at rack rates, even to rightsholders who would normally get a significant discount on media deals with them (eg, local governments). But non-media sponsors can be just as bad, pricing everything based on the recommended retail price, even though nobody actually pays that price.

What's it worth?

So, with sponsors overvaluing contra and rightsholders undervaluing it, what is the answer? It all comes down to one thing: Contra is worth what a rightsholder would have to pay for those goods or services. No more. No less.

If a rightsholder needs two new laptops, and has a maximum budget of $3,000 for them, even if a sponsor offers two top-of-the-line units worth twice that much, the contra value is only $3,000. Air tickets are worth what a rightsholder would have to pay for them. A media package is worth what the rightsholder would have to pay for the same package.

The words "have to" are important. If the goods or services are not in the rightsholder's budget, the contra has no value. I once had a sponsor offer to pay for a sponsorship with $25,000 worth of socks. I kid you not . . . socks. Those socks had value to somebody, but not to me, so the offer was roundly knocked back.

Does sponsor leverage count as contra?

This is a question I really hate. Don't get me wrong, it's a valid question, but I hate that it needs to be asked at all.

Sponsors, listen to me very carefully: What you do to leverage your sponsorships is developed specifically to reach *your* goals, add value to the fan experience of *your* markets, nurture relationships with *your* staff and customers, and create authentic, meaningful content for *your* channels. If that also benefits the rightsholder, good. Mutuality is what being a partner is all about.

At every stage of sponsorship, you need to keep foremost in your mind that the fans love this property — if people didn't have passion for it, you wouldn't be sponsoring it, right? — and if you're so short-sighted that you can't see the benefit to your brand of being fair to the rightsholder, then you can expect your results to suffer.

Negotiation issues

There are a number of negotiation issues that can affect both the success and the cost of your sponsorship.

> Contra is worth what a rightsholder would have to pay for those goods or services. No more. No less.

Exclusivity

Category exclusivity is a good thing, and you want to have it. That said, how you define that exclusivity can have a big impact on the price you pay. The more exclusivity you demand, the more you are going to pay.

Let's say, for example, that the Coca-Cola brand wants to sponsor a festival and have both sponsorship and vending (selling on-site) exclusivity in their category. If they define their category as brown-coloured, carbonated soft drinks, they will pay relatively little for the sponsorship, because the rightsholder is free to secure other sponsors in the beverages category, as long as they don't contravene the brown, fizzy category.

On the other end of the spectrum, Coca-Cola could demand exclusivity across all non-alcoholic beverages, including soft drinks, juices, plain and flavoured waters, energy and sport drinks, sport shakes, powdered drink mixes, and flavoured milk. Because this amount of exclusivity cuts off many potential sources of sponsorship revenues for the festival, it is entirely fair that the rightsholder charges more.

The most cost-effective option is usually to aim for somewhere in the middle of the spectrum — you get exclusivity across all of your direct competitors and possibly some indirect competitors but don't demand exclusivity in the fringe categories.

Payment structures

As with the rest of a proposal, you don't just have to accept whatever payment structure the rightsholder has put forth. You have a lot of options.

Instalments

For any significant investment, you should be able to pay for the sponsorship in instalments across a given year. There are as many different ways to do this as there are sponsorships, but I've provided a couple of typical examples below:

> Annual event — 30% upon execution or anniversary of the contract, 30% two to three months prior to the event, and 30% two to three weeks prior to the event.
> Ongoing sponsorship (eg, sponsorship of a museum) — Annual or semi-annual payments for the term of the sponsorship.

Payment upfront

If the rightsholder proposes instalments and they are a reputable organisation, you do have another option. You could offer to pay it in full, upon execution of the contract, in exchange for a small discount on the fee.

This doesn't fall into the category of strong-arming because the decision to take up the offer is left up to the rightsholder. They may well appreciate the cash flow and willingly part with 10% of the fee, for instance, to get the money sooner.

You should (and will) pay more for greater exclusivity.

Performance-based bonuses

Performance-based bonuses make their way into many sponsorship contracts. Frankly, your partner's responsibility to you is the same whether you incent them with money or not, but offering a cash bonus can be a good way to keep them focused on that task.

As an example, we'll use the fictitious Portland Polo Club, who is hosting a major international polo tournament. The local Mercedes dealership is interested in being involved and there has been talk of temporarily dumping some piles of dirt in a back paddock so that people can test-drive their newest luxury 4WD. The dealer is clear on their goals: They want at least 45 test drives by qualified prospects over the weekend; and they want to get at least 150 qualified prospects onto their database.

> Option 1: The dealership pays $20,000 to sponsor the event and get the benefits they need.
> Option 2: The dealership strikes a performance-based deal:

Sponsorship fee	$16,000
Bonus for more than 45 test drives	$4,000
Bonus for more than 150 qualified prospects on database	$4,000
Total	$24,000

As a sponsor, even though the second option will likely cost you more, you will probably prefer it. It may be easier for you to sell internally, and you will have more confidence that the rightsholder will be delivering what they promised and working on your behalf.

Do take note of what I've done here. I've discounted the fee by only 20% as I don't want to cut the guts out of the polo club's revenues. I have then added the 20% back on twice, linked to the achievement of two marketing objectives, providing a substantial incentive around two clear goals.

It's not fair to make a performance-based fee about sales.

Example: Payment structures

Recruitment company **Manpower** won the Swedish Sponsor of the Year Award with their sponsorship of various causes. Manpower's main investment is expertise, providing skills, such as management consulting and bookkeeping, to causes for a minimum of three months. They have provided many thousands of hours, so far, and have successfully demonstrated their service not only to the causes themselves, but to their other sponsors, board members, and associated organisations.

What you should never do is make performance-based fees about sales. Selling your product or service is your job, not the rightsholder's. Their job is to help you get the right people to have the right information, mindset, impetus, and opportunity, so that they will be most likely to buy your brand *if you do your job*. If your product is awful, or your price is too high, or your sales force is unmotivated and you don't sell anything, that's not their fault and you shouldn't penalise them for it. Make the bonus based on achieving milestones that should lead to sales, if you and your people do your job.

Multi-year deals

I see too many one-year proposals. Way too many. Some rightsholders seem to be under the impression that it will be easier for a sponsor to say "yes" to the lower commitment of a one-year deal. In reality, sponsors say "yes" to offers that fit their target markets and brand and offer creative ideas for leverage.

Of course, if what you're selling is only happening once, it makes perfect sense to do a short-term proposal, but the majority of opportunities out there don't fit into that category.

I also see way too many sponsors who commit to single years. On one hand, I can see how it might be appealing to try out a sponsorship for a year to see if it works for the brand. On the other hand . . . how do I put this nicely . . . how about just doing your bloody homework, picking investments that are great strategic fits, and leveraging them properly? Dabbling here and there is treating sponsorship like it's a risky proposition, when it's not — if you know what you're doing.

Creates consistency

Your brand has a personality and a voice. You may do different takes on that for different strategic and tactical reasons, but when it comes right down to it, you are striving for a degree of consistency over time to build and maintain your brand.

Having major turnover in your sponsorship portfolio undermines that proposition. It turns sponsorship into the schizophrenic cousin to your sensible, stable marketing plan.

Consistency is absolutely critical if you subscribe to the tenet of sponsorship being win-win-win. That third win is for the target markets, and adding real, meaningful value to a target market over time is going to have much more sustained impact than just making a gesture and moving on.

Results will build year-on-year

Like so many things, a sponsorship lifecycle works on a bell curve. Sure, you can do a great leverage program and get fantastic results in the first year, but if you tweak it and keep it fresh, you'll get even better results in years two and three.

Dabbling — especially if you're expecting the kind of results in year one that other sponsors are enjoying in year three — never allows the sponsorship to really hit its straps. In many cases, a successful first year will compel more of your internal stakeholders to get involved in future years, using the sponsorship as a catalyst to make money they're already spending go further.

Creates a bank of valuable content over time

One of the best ways you can extend the geographic reach and timeframe of a sponsorship is through content creation – content you've created, your fan-generated content, customer-generated content, and exclusive content provided by your partner.

Allows you to be responsive to research

You should be doing research, your partners should be doing research, and you should be using that research to hone and improve your sponsorships from one year to the next.

Multi-year deals can be more cost-effective

Committing for three or more years allows you to plan longer term and provides a nice, stable platform for leverage year-on-year. It also provides the rightsholder with stable cash flow over time, which is a great incentive for them to either sweeten the deal or lower the price. There are two structures that fit most circumstances:

1. If the property you're looking to sponsor is mature, attracting a strong audience every year, with very modest growth, you could propose a three-year offer, instead of the one-year offer, at a discount of 15–20% per year. So, if they have offered you a complement of benefits at $20,000 for one year, you could propose a three-year deal at $16,000–17,000 per year. The other option is that you could request additional strategic benefits to raise the value of the package by 15–20% if you sign on for three years.

2. If the property is on a growth trajectory, you could commit for three years at a set increase each year. That increase would be based on a conservative estimate of property growth and could save you from a potentially big jump in fees every year you're involved.

There is a third option, which is being a foundation sponsor. A foundation sponsor is one that commits when an event, program, or organisation is brand new. A foundation sponsor commits because they have a belief in the potential of the opportunity and often provide a bigger chunk of money – seed money – in the first year, to help it get off the ground. This is not common, but it does happen. In this instance, those foundation sponsors are often involved on the board or an advisory committee, providing expertise, advice, and often marketing power that the organisation doesn't have. It is a riskier way to sponsor, but the payoffs can be big.

> You could save 15-20% if you commit to a multi-year deal.

Negotiating and managing multi-brand sponsorship

Most sponsors have embraced brand sponsorship as the default position for investment. That is, they sponsor with one brand, not the whole portfolio.

There are, of course, a couple of exceptions. The first is when a sponsorship creates a platform that is large, relevant, and/or flexible enough that it can be leveraged across an entire portfolio of brands. An example would be if Kellogg's sponsored a World Cup. They could make that work across their brand portfolio and most, if not all, regions. Or maybe you have a strong commitment to a charity, or category of charities, and that works across brand lines. In these cases, the masterbrand (eg, Kellogg's) is the sponsor, and it's leveraged across brand lines.

The second exception is where you have two brands that are both strong fits for a sponsorship, and provided you keep a few strategies and tactics in mind, there is no reason you can't negotiate a sponsorship across both of them. This differs in that it's not about Kellogg's sponsoring, it's about two brands sponsoring, like Rice Bubbles and Pop-Tarts.

Ensure the brands don't compete

This is a big one. You don't want to go down this track if there is any chance of confusion, so try to keep the two brands in two different categories.

For instance, Procter & Gamble could easily sponsor a major tennis tournament with both the Gillette brand and Secret Antiperspirant brand. A bank could sponsor an investment expo with both their mortgage and retirement savings brands. On the other hand, a brewer would be ill-advised sponsoring a festival with two brands of lager, as they could present a confusing message and could cannibalise each other's effectiveness.

A useful way to think of it is, if you owned one of the two brands and another company owned the other, would you require exclusivity that blocked the other brand from being a sponsor alongside your brand? If so, don't consider sponsoring with both brands.

Get both brand teams involved in negotiation planning

When considering sponsorship by two brands, I strongly recommend that you undertake the pre-negotiation leverage planning for both brands at the same time. You may find that one brand sees a lot more scope than the other, so you may decide to negotiate a larger sponsorship for one and a smaller sponsorship for the other.

Be prepared to spend more, but not double

If you sponsor with two brands, you're going to pay more than if you sponsor with just one. Think about it. You're going to demand category exclusivity, so there are now two categories the rightsholder could have used to generate revenue that are committed, so you need to be reasonable.

What you shouldn't be doing is paying full price for both. There are financial and time economies of scale. The rightsholder will only have one relationship to manage, one contract to prepare, and probably only one complement of hospitality benefits to deliver.

Aim for minimal leverage cross-over

While I think it's a great idea to do leverage planning at the same time, you need to treat the brands as separate. If the brands don't compete against each other, it is unlikely that a similar leverage program will work for both of them anyway.

What you want to do is create the leverage program that's right for each brand, as though it was the only brand sponsoring. This will minimise leverage cross-over and any confusion or cannibalisation in marketing messages.

You may find a leverage idea or two where the brands can cooperate. If so, then do it. But do ask yourself whether you'd consider doing that cross-promotion if the second brand was owned by another company. If it isn't a good idea to do it with an independently owned brand, it's not going to be a good idea to do it with two of your brands.

Sponsoring just for the hospitality

If there is any requirement for local hospitality — eg, a marquee at a local grand final — but the sponsorship isn't a fit for your needs, buy the hospitality from the rightsholder à la carte. That is, buy the hospitality, not a sponsorship.

Games rightsholders play

I am not a proponent of playing games when negotiating. I don't believe it should be an adversarial process, and, if it turns into one, it could damage the potential of your sponsorship in the longer term.

That was the idealist in me talking. Realistically, there are a few negotiation games that rightsholders do play, and you need to know how to manage them. I'm not talking about subterfuge or brinksmanship, but elevating and professionalising the situation.

Threats to go to your competition

Every sponsor has heard this line: "If you don't sponsor us, Company X will."

That is a big, fat lie. They may have a proposal into that company, but if your competition were really ready to sign on the dotted line, the rightsholder wouldn't be talking to you.

If you choose to believe this, and rush your decision-making process, or, worse, commit to a sponsorship for defensive reasons (primarily so the competition doesn't get it), you are doing your brand a huge disservice. Make the decision in your own time, for your own reasons. Even if you do believe the competition is interested, you need to play your own game, get the planning and buy-in right, and sponsor what's right for your brand.

If the competition was close to signing, the rightsholder wouldn't be talking to you.

My advice is to call their bluff:

> *If you're close to signing with Company X, you should probably just go with them. We don't make rash sponsorship decisions and need to ensure we get the appropriate internal buy-in and planning in place before we're ready to commit. We're looking at another two to three weeks before we could give you a firm answer. If you're demanding an answer right now, then the answer will be "no".*

99% of the time they will tell you that they can probably hold off the other company for a couple of weeks because they would prefer to have you on board. (Watch how fast they can backpedal!) There is always the slight chance they weren't overstating their position, and you do lose out to the competition, but taking that risk is far better than investing without planning and due diligence.

Bidding wars

The bigger, uglier cousin of the competitor threat is the bidding war. This negotiation ploy is usually reserved for the largest, most desirable properties.

The basic premise is that, rather than the rightsholder making a business case for the sponsor, sponsors are required to pitch to the rightsholder; in essence, bidding for the right to be a sponsor. For those super-desirable events, teams, or whatever, they are in the enviable position of being able to choose amongst a number of potential sponsors in each category, so it makes sense for them to evaluate each potential partner based on the financial and marketing benefits they can provide.

Example: Bidding war

I was doing work for a brewery years ago, and they got involved in a bidding war for sponsorship of a stadium. The main benefit was exclusive and substantial pouring rights, but there were a few genuine sponsorship benefits. My client was the incumbent sponsor.

While I wasn't involved in the negotiation, I heard all about it. After a bit of back and forth, the price tag eventually rose to the equivalent of about US $12 for every litre of beer poured at the stadium. No brewer is going to make $12 of profit for every litre of beer wholesaled to a venue, and the other sponsorship benefits weren't anywhere near valuable enough to justify the overpayment.

Thankfully, my client lost that bidding war, and their competition was saddled with a sponsorship for which they'd massively overpaid. Don't be that guy.

Where it devolves into a bidding war is when, rather than making a decision on the offers put on the table, the rightsholder plays the sponsors off each other. They are asked in turn to better the previous offer until the sponsorship fee gets to be virtually untenable, at which point they award it to the highest bidder.

If you get involved in a bid process for sponsorship of a major property, your best strategy for avoiding a bidding war is to offer a fair price, but more than that, emphasise your creative leverage program and all the advantages it provides to the rightsholder and fans. Push the right buttons and all but the most short-sighted and selfish rightsholders will want to work with you.

If a bidding war does break out, feel free to get involved, as long as the numbers make sense. You really need to leave your ego out of it, know your bottom line — your walk-away number — and stick to it.

> The bigger, uglier cousin of the competitor threat is the bidding war.

Charging the sponsor a "leverage fee" on top of the sponsorship fee

First off, it is *your* job, not the rightsholder's, to leverage the sponsorship and pay for it. Second and most important, what this fee provides for has nothing to do with leverage. It is virtually always used to pay for some of the harder costs of what has already been promised in the proposal, such as the production of sponsor signage.

Don't fall for this. Tell the partner flat out that you will not be paying a leverage fee. Further, tell the rightsholder that if they want to revisit the sponsorship fee so that all benefit delivery costs are covered, they are free to do that, and you will re-evaluate your position once you've reviewed the new offer.

Plus, you have to sponsor our foundation

This is a special relative of charging a leverage fee.

I've worked with a number of corporate clients as they've been negotiating major partnerships with teams and sportspeople. They have all embarked on these sponsorships backed by strong strategy, and have been prepared to leverage the investments across their marketing and business channels.

Sounds good, right? On closer examination of the proposal, however, many of them required an additional investment in the six figures (sometimes well into the six figures) to sponsor the athlete's or sports organisation's community foundation. The rightsholders called it "leverage", but all they offered were a few logos on things, and not one was even remotely interested in customising the offer so it also delivered on the sponsor's community objectives.

I have no problem with teams putting funds into their community programs. Clearly, this is good for the team and the community, and the right thing to do. My problem is when teams and sportspeople provide a sponsorship proposal, get a sponsor on the hook, then try

Just because the rightsholder calls it "leverage" doesn't mean it is.

to bolt on this extra chunk of revenue, attempting to disguise it as a leverage opportunity. It's not. It's just a revenue grab — an attempt to get sponsors to fund a program that makes only the sports organisation look like a hero.

And let's not forget that if your company is big enough to be taking on a major sporting sponsorship, it's likely that you have your own community program — meeting the needs of your customers and communities in a way that is right for your brand. In that case, what's better, spending $350,000 for a bit of visibility on a team's community program, or spending $350,000 to extend and amplify your own community program? I know what I'd do.

For sponsors faced with this kind of proposal from an organisation you really want to sponsor, you can do two things:

1. Make your community agenda clear to the rightsholder, and try to work with them to develop a community angle to the sponsorship that works for both parties and your target markets.
2. If that doesn't work, you need to consider the community part of the investment as just a cost of doing business with that organisation. Stop trying to justify the cost against a feeble set of benefits that don't provide value. Instead, just add that figure to the overall sponsorship cost and make your decision about the sponsorship based on the total required investment. It's really all you can do.

Chapter 8

Contracts

Contracts are no fun. Leverage, negotiation, strategy development, and even measurement can be a lot of fun. But contracts? Yuck.

The plain truth of the matter is that without contracts, sponsorship wouldn't be possible. We're talking about creating complex relationships between very different parties, with a lot of rights, responsibilities, and money involved. These relationships do have to be formalised, not because your partner is the enemy, but because grey areas are the enemy.

It is only when both parties are very clear on their mutual accountabilities that we can get onto the creative, strategic, results-driven, fun stuff.

Types of contracts

There are four main types of contracts:

1. Handshake deal
2. "Yes, we'll take it" letter (or signed proposal)
3. Letter agreement
4. Full contract

Although a surprising amount of sponsorship is committed with only a handshake, a "Yes, we'll take it" email, or a signature at the bottom of a proposal, none of these offers the structure or accountability you need to protect your investments.

The more formal the agreement, the more likely it will be complete and legally binding. In order of desirability, these are the types of agreements you could have:

> Legal contract drawn up by a lawyer, bearing signatures from both organisations.
> Legal contract adapted from a template drawn up by a lawyer, bearing signatures from both organisations. Note:
  - In the Appendix, you will find a comprehensive Sponsorship Agreement Pro Forma that has been developed by sponsorship law guru Lionel Hogg, partner at Gadens Lawyers.
  - If your lawyer customises the template for your organisation and jurisdiction, and checks/adjusts any contracts before they're executed, it's just as good as a contract created from scratch. Possibly more so as your legal team may not be sponsorship experts.

> In sponsorship contracts, grey areas are the enemy.

> Letter of agreement outlining all the points of agreement, including benefits, communication and reporting, payments, and key dates, and signed by both organisations.

> Confirmation letter outlining the benefits and payment dates. Either the sponsor or the rightsholder could produce the letter. This is not desirable and should be avoided for all but the tiniest sponsorships, as it does not offer the structure and protections of a contract.

Typically, a company will use a letter of agreement for lower-level sponsorships, usually delineated by a dollar amount. At a given total value, which you should specify in your policy, a full, legal contract will be required.

That number varies considerably from one company to another. I've seen companies require full contracts if the value is more than $10,000, and other companies that don't require a full contract until the value is more than $100,000. Some companies will also use a confirmation letter for very small, rats-and-mice sponsorships (think sub-$1,000).

This contract is provided by . . .

It makes sense that any agreement will at least slightly favour the party that produces it. As the sponsor, you will know that all your needs will be addressed, and your legal team will be happy to be in control of the process. If possible, you want to produce the contract on bigger sponsorships.

The downside of creating the agreement is that it may take a long time for your legal team to create one from scratch, particularly if they're not sponsorship experts. On small- to mid-sized sponsorships, the slight benefit you may gain by producing the contract may not be worth the headaches of waiting on your lawyers to produce something. In that case, you've got two options:

1. Use the agreement produced by the rightsholder because allowing your legal team to provide input on a draft agreement will take a lot less time than writing one.
2. Use a sponsorship agreement pro forma as the starting point for contract development. Again, I have provided a great pro forma in the Appendix. More information about how to use the pro forma is included later in this chapter.

The contract delay conundrum

If your legal team has insisted on producing the agreement, and there has been a major delay in doing so, you may have an issue with releasing payment.

Most companies don't like releasing sponsorship fees unless an agreement is in place. While it makes sense in most situations, in the case of a contract process dragging on, this policy may do harm to the rightsholder, who could probably use the cash flow. While you're not under any legal obligation to pay anything until the deal is done, causing financial problems for your new partner is something you should try to avoid.

One option I've seen work is that the sponsor will authorise a refundable deposit equivalent to the first payment on the agreed schedule. The reason you make it refundable is that you're not making a concrete commitment without an agreement in place. Technically, it means you could back out of the contract and ask for your money back. Realistically, if you are simply waiting on lawyers to dot the i's and cross the t's, the deal is probably not going to fall to bits. Even in the highly unlikely situation where an agreement does fall to bits, the rightsholder will have had access to a no-interest loan from your company during their planning process.

The deposit itself will require a short agreement, outlining that the refundable deposit is made in good faith and in anticipation of a legally binding relationship. It also needs to state that if, for any reason, the agreement does not go ahead, the deposit will be fully and immediately refunded to your company. Again, you need a lawyer to help you with this, but we're only talking a one-page document, so it should be fast to produce.

Resolving issues

Sometimes, things just don't go as planned. Events can be like that. So can anything else you may sponsor. Problems may be swift and shocking, like a scandal or cancellation, or they may build slowly, like the annoyance of a partner that never delivers quite what was promised. Sponsors aren't immune to issues either.

Whatever the circumstances, once a sponsorship issue hits critical mass, passions fire and the rhetoric can turn ugly. The next step is calling in the lawyers and the expensive, difficult process of litigation. Even if you're the one feeling wronged, litigation is something you want to avoid if you can.

Rather than waiting until things get heated to decide how to resolve an issue, you should build problem resolution right into your agreement. That way, you are bound to a process that will likely see the situation resolved well before you get to the stage of litigation. It will also stop anyone from doing anything rash in the heat of the moment.

You should include a four-step resolution process. These are the steps and options:

1. Discussion — The first step is just as it sounds: Sit down and rationally discuss the issue(s) to see if you can find a resolution you can both live with. If not, you will move onto mediation.
2. Mediation — This involves directed discussion and problem-solving, with the assistance of a professional mediator. If emotions are still running high, this can be an effective way of distilling the facts and addressing them.
3. Arbitration — The next step is usually arbitration. This is when a professional arbiter,

Build problem resolution into the agreement.

or a panel of arbiters, hears both points of view and makes a decision. This is not as formal as going to court but does require preparation and it is easy to rack up legal fees. Or:

4. Binding mediation — An alternative to arbitration is binding mediation, which follows the collaborative mediation process, and, at the conclusion, the mediator will make a binding ruling on any outstanding issues.

If the problem is still unsolved, you may end up in court. This can be a long, expensive, stressful process. Avoid it if you can.

Rights of refusal

There are two "rights of refusal": First right of refusal and last right of refusal. These are both legal rights, but their meanings are very different.

Please note: I have defined these two terms because I want you to understand what they are all about, but they are legal terms, with complex ramifications. You should not commit to either of these without the advice of a qualified sponsorship lawyer.

First right of refusal

First right of refusal is a benefit you can negotiate with a rightsholder. It ensures that, as the incumbent, you have the legal right to renew an agreement before any negotiations take place with another company. This is usually about the rightsholder not entering discussions with one of your competitors, but it could also extend to negotiating with any other brand for your specific sponsorship designation, such as a naming rights or presenting sponsorship.

This right to renew could specify the terms of the renewal, including the price and sponsorship rights, or may involve extensive renegotiation of some or all of the key terms of the agreement.

Typically, a sponsor with first right of refusal will get a specified window to negotiate the new contract, before the rightsholder can put the opportunity onto the open market. When you negotiate first right of refusal, ensure that window is long enough for you to make a decision. You also want to ensure you give the rightsholder enough time to get into the market, in case the renewal doesn't work out. Technically, this isn't your issue, but you need to be fair.

Last right of refusal

This right ensures that, no matter what another company offers for a sponsorship, you will have the opportunity to match or better the offer. If they increase their offer again, it will come back to you to match or better it. Last right of refusal is common with top-tier sponsorships, and sponsorships involving a substantial sales component, like being the official soft drink supplier to a stadium.

I believe that last right of refusal is just a bidding war waiting to happen, and the only winner in a bidding war is the rightsholder. Even then, it's only short term, as they will need to see out a contract with a sponsor that knows they were played for maximum cash, and probably paid too much. I encourage my clients not to play that game, but to be such an outstanding, active partner that the rightsholder wouldn't want to lose them.

I'm a strategist, so I would think that way. A lawyer, on the other hand, would tell you that this is a great benefit to have and that it's better to have the option to have the last word in the fight than to risk losing a sponsorship you really wanted to maintain.

Surprise, surprise. Strategists and lawyers don't always agree.

> Strategists and
> lawyers don't
> always agree.

Force majeure

In a legal sense, one of the biggest changes to our industry, post-COVID, is the heightened focus on force majeure clauses in sponsorship contracts. Literally, this is the clause that protects parties in the case of some catastrophe that either cancels or renders what you're sponsoring moot.

Prior to COVID, these clauses were often cursory, boiling down to a sponsor having the right to end a contract, if the event, season, or whatever didn't go ahead as planned.

During COVID, our industry realised that there was a middle ground that most of us hadn't even thought about. What if a sports season goes ahead, but it's shorter, or has no in-person fans? What if an in-person conference turns into a virtual conference? And what's the recourse or plan of action if a sponsor is disadvantaged by a force majeure, but doesn't want to exit the property?

The result is that force majeure clauses have been made a) more robust; and b) more flexible. There are often more specifics on when a sponsor can exit. Is it only when something is cancelled altogether? Or partially cancelled? And what qualifies as "partially"? What if it's shortened or moved or postponed?

As for flexibility, the choice is often less binary. It's not just stay or exit, but often includes a number of options, such as:

- Providing benefits in lieu of the benefits that were supposed to be provided.
- Extending the contract for another year/season/event at no or minimal cost, so the sponsor still gets *some* sponsorship benefits, even if the main event doesn't go ahead in a specific timeframe.
- Pausing the contract until the property can be delivered again, as promised. This is similar to the above, but with no benefits flowing until the contract resumes.
- Shifting the sponsorship to another property owned by the rightsholder.
- Continuing the sponsorship, if the rightsholder can deliver the property substantially as planned, within a specified time period.

Of course, all of these options must be mutually acceptable.

How to keep major rightsholders from stealing your leverage ideas

If your company sponsors a major event or professional sporting organisation, there is every chance that the rightsholder will require you to submit your leverage plan for their approval, well in advance of the event or season. This seems reasonable enough. They are ensuring that sponsors are actually going to do something with their investments, and can run interference if two sponsors are planning very similar programs.

In the past few years, however, I've been seeing a new and sinister trend: Rightsholders stealing the best sponsor leverage ideas for their own marketing plans.

In one instance, a major sponsor of a top international team had submitted the leverage plan, as required. This was a client of mine, and I'd created the leverage plan. A few weeks later, they were invited to the launch of the team's marketing plan. Not one but three of the sponsor's best leverage ideas had been appropriated by the team and presented as part of their own marketing plan. The sponsor was blindsided. This rendered those ideas moot for the sponsor, and gave them little time to reinvent the leverage program. There were threats of legal action, and a compromise was reached, but this is only one of dozens of instances I've seen in the past few years.

So, how can sponsors preserve ownership of leverage ideas when approval to implement them is being put into the hands of another organisation? And what about the consultants or agencies who the brand has paid for a licence to the creative ideas, and then seen their strategies appropriated by an unrelated organisation? (Like me!)

I asked sponsorship law expert, friend, and trusted legal advisor Lionel Hogg, partner at Gadens Lawyers. His advice fell into the categories of best option and second-best option.

Best option

Without question, your best option is to include wording in your sponsorship contract, prohibiting the use by the rightsholder of any leverage ideas provided for their approval, without your explicit consent. This would appear in the section where you are compelled to provide your leverage plan for approval and, as always, you should consult your lawyer to ensure the wording is appropriate and will protect you in your jurisdiction.

Second-best option

If you are already under contract and you have to submit a leverage plan, include confidentiality wording on the front page. Lionel suggested this:

> **Confidentiality Notice**
>
> *This document is provided to you in strict confidence and only for the purpose of obtaining your consent to the proposals contained in it. Except to the extent necessary for that purpose, you must not distribute*

this document, or disclose its contents or the substance of any related discussions with us (Confidential Information), to any person. You must not use the Confidential Information for any other purpose without our prior written consent.

Copyright [name of Sponsor] [year]. All rights reserved.

This is an imperfect and far-from-watertight solution, but it at least serves as a warning that appropriating your ideas will be taken seriously.

This wording may not be appropriate in every circumstance, so you should consult a lawyer for specific wording and strategies that are applicable to, and most likely to protect you in, your situation.

◑ Agreement Checklist

Whether you are using a formal contract or a letter agreement, you need to ensure that it covers all aspects of the agreement, including responsibilities, indemnities, benefits, reporting, and payments. This agreement checklist has been developed to help you assess whether it is complete prior to executing the agreement.

The basics

❑ Is the agreement dated?

❑ Does it clearly state who the agreement is between?

❑ Have you ensured that the party with whom you are entering into an agreement controls the rights you are purchasing? (You would be surprised how often benefits are promised by a rightsholder that doesn't directly control them.)

❑ Over what period of time is the agreement valid?

❑ Have you ensured that the details of the sponsorship are confidential?

Benefits

❑ Is every benefit to both parties included within the contract?

❑ Are the categories and level of exclusivity included?

❑ Are naming rights or presenting rights artwork and agreed acknowledgement lines specified within the agreement?

❑ Are any additional costs for agreed benefits (eg, signage production, hospitality catering) outlined within the agreement?

❑ Are all costs associated with the purchase of extra benefits (eg, buying additional tickets) outlined in the agreement?

Reporting and evaluation

❑ Have you ensured that the timing, type, and frequency of reports are included in the agreement?

❑ Have you outlined the agreed schedule of in-person meetings (eg, bi-monthly) in the agreement?

Renewals

❑ Have you set a date or window for starting renewal negotiations?

❑ Have you set a cap on how much a sponsorship fee can rise at renewal (if applicable)?

❑ Have you included first right of refusal?

❑ Have you included last right of refusal (if applicable)?

Corporate/brand image

❑ Have you ensured that you have the right to proof all printed material, all media releases, and anything else that includes your name, acknowledgement, and logo? Note: For more off-the-cuff activities, such as social media, it will be more appropriate to agree to the overall tone and language than to pre-approve every posting.

❑ Do you have a clause ensuring that the sponsee agrees to use its best endeavours to present the sponsorship and your brand in a positive way within all communications and media opportunities?

Insurance

❑ Have you ensured that insurance responsibilities (event insurance, public liability, professional indemnity, workers compensation) are detailed in the agreement?

Transfer of contract benefits to a third party

❑ Can the rights of either party be transferred to a third party?

❑ Can benefits be on-sold to a third party?

❑ Are there limits to the types or amount of benefits that can be on-sold (eg, hospitality)?

❑ Are there limits to the types or organisation to which the contract or benefits can be on-sold or transferred?

Dispute resolution

❑ Have you ensured that a dispute resolution process is included in the agreement?

Payments

❑ What is the agreed fee for the sponsorship?

❑ When and how will it be paid?

❑ Is there contra involved? Detail the specifics.

❑ Have performance-based fees been agreed? Detail the specifics.

Sponsorship agreement pro forma

Included in the Appendix is a Sponsorship Agreement Pro Forma, which was developed for this book by Lionel Hogg, partner of Gadens Lawyers. The full agreement is also downloadable with the rest of the tools.

This sample agreement may be a useful starting point for a sponsorship agreement. It is very general, however, because it is impossible to draft a document that accounts for all situations or for legal differences in all countries.

Ideally, it should be used as a template that is completed by the sponsor, in conjunction with the rightsholder, and then given to a lawyer to check the drafting, change it to suit the law in the relevant location and better outline the rights of the parties. Starting from this template will make the process shorter and less costly than securing a lawyer to draft an agreement from scratch.

Warning

Lionel is a top lawyer and, as good lawyers do, has advised that I must very explicitly warn you against misusing the Sponsorship Agreement Pro Forma. So, here goes.

This document is provided as a sample only and is not a substitute for legal advice. You should seek the advice of a suitably qualified and experienced lawyer before using this document.

In particular, you or your lawyer should:

> Check the law in your jurisdiction — Make sure this agreement is appropriate wherever you are located.
> Check for changes to the law — Law and practice may have altered since this document was drafted or you last checked the situation.
> Modify wherever necessary — Review this document critically and never use it without first amending it to suit your needs, as each sponsorship is different.
> Beware of the limits of expertise — If you are not legally qualified, or are not familiar with this area of the law, do not use this document without first obtaining qualified legal advice about it.

How this agreement works

The agreement assumes that there are standard clauses that should be in every agreement, and special clauses needed for your sponsorship. The standard clauses that should apply all of the time are called the "Standard Conditions". The parts that relate to your specific sponsorship are the "Schedules" and the "Special Conditions".

The Schedules and Special Conditions have precedence over the Standard Conditions. In other words, what you insert is more important than what is already written. This is why it is vital to use a lawyer or know what you are doing.

Read the agreement

Before doing anything, read the agreement and see how it might apply to your situation. There may be Standard Conditions that are unsuitable. There may be new conditions that you need to add. Do not assume that the agreement is right for you.

The sample agreement is for an *exclusive* sponsorship in the relevant sponsorship category.

Complete the Schedules

You should complete each Schedule following the guidance notes in that Schedule.

For example, there is a Schedule called "Sponsor's termination events". The guidance note refers to a specific clause in the Standard Conditions. You should read that clause and understand the circumstances in which the sponsor has a right to terminate the agreement. You then insert into the Schedule any other circumstances peculiar to your sponsorship. For instance, you might want to terminate the agreement if the team being sponsored loses its licence to play in the major league, or if the contracted lead performers for the musical withdraw their services.

Add Special Conditions

The Special Conditions (at the end of the Schedules) enable you to insert other conditions that are not dealt with by this sample agreement.

Changing Standard Conditions

You should *not* change the Standard Conditions without consulting a lawyer. The agreement is drafted as a package, and changing the Standard Conditions might have an unintended, domino effect on other terms.

If you have to change the Standard Conditions, do so by adding a Special Condition, such as "Clause 18 of the Standard Conditions does not apply."

Sign the agreement

The parties sign and date the document on the last page. Make sure that the person with whom you do the deal is authorised to sign.

Finding a lawyer

You should consult a lawyer practising in your jurisdiction and experienced in sponsorship matters. If you don't have a good sponsorship lawyer, there are a number of sports law organisations around the world that can provide a referral, or you can contact Gadens Lawyers in Australia.

Although you may not be a sporting organisation, these associations will be a great source for referrals as sponsorship law skills are quite transferrable across sponsorship genres.

If you have questions about the pro forma agreement

If you or your lawyer has questions about the Sponsorship Agreement Pro Forma, you are welcome to contact its author:

Lionel Hogg, Partner
Gadens Lawyers
GPO Box 129
Brisbane QLD 4001 Australia
Phone: +61 7 3231 1518
Email: lhogg@qld.gadens.com.au

Chapter 9

Dealing with sponsorship brokers

Never negotiate a sponsorship unless a decision-maker from the rightsholder is in the room.

Financial advisors, brokers, and other middlemen are a feature of many of our big personal and business decisions. We trust them to have our best interests at heart, but forget that they don't actually work for us. Their job is selling, not delivering on the sometimes shaky promises of the institutions they represent.

Sponsorship brokers fall into the same category. They represent rightsholders in the sales process, and most of them do it professionally and completely above board. Unfortunately, there is a legion of unscrupulous brokers out there who will promise anything to earn a commission, including misrepresenting what a rightsholder can or will do.

That doesn't mean that you should avoid opportunities presented by brokers, because there are some great ones, but I do have one big piece of advice: Never negotiate a sponsorship unless a decision-maker from the property is in the room.

You need to be absolutely sure that they understand their responsibilities, and what your expectations are, before you sign any deal. At the end of the day, the broker is going to walk away, and these are the people you'll be dealing with, while trying to make the sponsorship work for your brand.

A good broker will have no problem including their client in the negotiations. If the broker balks, that is a big red flag, indicating that they may be playing fast and loose with the truth. In that case, contact the rightsholder directly and tell them you're ready to negotiate, but require them to be at the negotiation. It will happen.

Part 3

LEVERAGE

Chapter 10

Leverage vs activation

Before we get into how to do leverage, let's have a look at two terms: Leverage and activation.

Ten years ago, the terms were basically interchangeable, referring to the activities a sponsor undertakes around a sponsorship, to turn that opportunity into the results they need against objectives. Fast forward and the meaning of "activation" has, for many organisations, morphed into something completely different.

This isn't the case with all organisations, but I've had one after another client where the meaning of "activation" has narrowed so much that it's seriously affecting their results.

What is sponsorship leverage?

Leverage is everything that a sponsor does with a sponsorship to achieve marketing and business goals. It really is that broad.

These activities aren't tied to a specific location or timeframe, as creativity and the right strategic framework can make local sponsorships deliver on a national level, and turn a two-day festival into a platform that can be legitimately leveraged for many months or more.

What is sponsorship activation?

For some organisations, "activation" is still synonymous with "leverage", and the wide net that it casts. For those organisations, you're good. Just use whatever term works for you.

For others, however, the term has dramatically narrowed, over time, leading them to focus their efforts primarily on:

- Activities they do on-site at the property — in areas often designated as "activation spaces"
- Social media run in a tight timeframe around the property

How did this narrowing happen?

Sponsorship professionals get on stage at conferences and present about the amazing activations they do with their sponsorships. Industry media love case studies about often jaw-dropping on-site sponsorship activations, which then get liberally shared around sponsorship networks. Activation agencies, more often than not, are all about designing and manning the on-site "brand experience". Sponsorship proposals talk about activation ideas and activation spaces, focused almost exclusively on-site. There's nothing nefarious about it, but this multi-pronged focus on these sexy, high-touch, often high-tech activities have, over time, shifted what "activation" means.

To be clear, I have absolutely nothing against your brand doing super-cool things on-site, and in social media right around that timeframe, but if your focus has narrowed to the point where those are more or less the only ways you're leveraging, you're leaving an enormous amount of opportunity unrealised.

Why does it matter?

At risk of putting too fine a point on it, I'm going to canvas a few of the problems inherent to the above view of activation.

Activation ignores the remote fans

Nurturing relationships with those remote fans can be an extremely valuable exercise for sponsors, multiplying the impact of any given sponsorship. It's not even difficult if you've got a creative process in place that takes them into account. But if the focal point is on-site, it's not going to happen, and you've wasted the opportunity.

Activation can be inefficient

Creating on-site activities can be expensive. Manning those activities can be expensive. You can absolutely do these things, but if it's eating up your whole budget, you might want to think twice.

It's not actually either/or, though. You could do some great activity on-site, and create a relevant way for remote fans to get in on the action. The incremental cost of that would be minimal, and your efficiency would skyrocket.

Activation is playing in the most cluttered space there is

When your focal point for activities is activating on-site, you're like an elite marathoner volunteering to start from the back of the pack. You're going to have to fight your way through a crowd of other sponsors — who are just as committed and creative as you are — to get where you're trying to go. You can certainly do it, but don't forget you also have dozens of other channels and hundreds of other ways you can leverage a sponsorship.

What can you do about it?

I'm not saying you shouldn't be leveraging your sponsorships on-site at events or games or whatever. But if your brand's focal point for activity and budget is on-site activity — if that's the default starting point for your sponsorship plan — you've fallen into the activation trap. Thankfully, resetting isn't difficult.

Say something like, "We've got this on-site activation stuff nailed. Now, we need to concentrate our efforts on the broader leverage of this property." Use the term "broader leverage" liberally. Talk about activation as being a "component of a broader leverage strategy".

Ensure you're discussing how to add value to remote fans, fans of the larger themes around the sponsorship, your customers, staff, VIPs, and intermediary markets. If you come up with a sexy activation idea, immediately shift to, "Great idea. How can we scale it to involve more fans, remote fans, and other markets?"

The idea is that you're reframing what you do around sponsorship, removing the false limitations that the term "activation" may have engendered, and reclaiming both the breadth and depth of what sponsorship can do for your brand.

Talk about activation as being a "component of a broader leverage strategy".

Win-win-win leverage

As mentioned in the previous chapter, leverage is what a sponsor does with a sponsorship after the deal is done, and it's the most critical factor in getting a good result from an investment.

This chapter is all about providing the mindset and framework for doing leverage well, before we get into the nuts and bolts about exactly how to do it. I'm going to start with reminding you of your new mantra, from back in Chapter 1: Don't sponsor the property, sponsor the fans.

Sponsoring the fans

In the early days of sponsorship, the thinking went something like this:

> If we connect our brand strongly enough with this property we sponsor,
> all the people who love that property will transfer some of that love to us.

Yeah, that doesn't happen. There's no research that supports it, but we don't even need research. We're all fans of something, and we know as fans that we don't transfer our love like that, and as industry professionals, we're probably paying more attention to those sponsors than anyone else.

In more recent years, best-practice thinking has changed a lot. It's become fan- and target market-centric:

> How can we use our sponsorship of this property to deepen our
> relationships and alignment with the fans and our larger target markets?

That's sound thinking, exactly in line with the most important tenet of best-practice sponsorship: That sponsorship should be win-win-win, with the third win going to the target markets. But some companies still struggle to translate the sponsorship — with a contract and all the mutual accountabilities — into forging meaningful bonds with actual people.

In my experience, the trouble seems to stem from the starting place of, "How can we use our sponsorship of this property?"

Some companies just don't get past that relationship between their brand and the property to the important, meaty part of the statement. They create brand perks and incentives — let's give fans a coupon! Let's offer a sponsorship-driven prize for people who engage with us on Instagram! — but miss that the real benefit of the partnership to the brand is that you get the privilege of connecting with people through something they've already decided they care about.

Nowhere is "sponsoring the fans" more critical than in leverage planning. This thinking de-emphasises the property relationship and puts the emphasis where it belongs: On the relationship between your brand and the people who care about what you're sponsoring. If you and your team can embrace this mindset, everything else about sponsorship leverage becomes infinitely easier.

The three rules of leverage

There are three rules, or principles, that drive best-practice leverage:

1. When a sponsor invests in sponsorship, they are investing in opportunity. Leverage is what provides the results!
2. Brand needs are not the most important factor in best-practice sponsorship.
3. You will focus more energy leveraging in the areas that you measure.

Investing in opportunity

It is easy to believe that because you've made an investment and received something in return, you've purchased a *result* — that the benefits in which you've invested will provide a marketing result for your brand. I hate to break it to you, but that's just not how it works.

As an example, if you were to invest in a TOP Olympic sponsorship, it would likely cost well into the hundreds of millions of dollars. For that, you would receive two main benefits:

1. The right to call yourself a sponsor and use the rings (with lots of rules).
2. The right to purchase ticket, accommodation, and hospitality packages.

Let's say you purchased those rights and did nothing additional. What would the result be for your brand? A big fat zero. Olympic sponsors know that, and they create huge leverage programs, ranging from content development to consumer promotions to staff programs to amazing hospitality for their VIP customers, and more. The opportunity comes from the sponsorship, while their return comes from leverage.

Most of your sponsorships will offer more benefits, so you might think you will get a result from those benefits. In reality, you have just purchased a more comprehensive opportunity. You still need to leverage it to get a return.

Letting a sponsorship go unleveraged is an investment wasted.

Think of it like your overall marketing and business objectives are a bucket, which has some small balls in it, representing your sponsorships. If they're not leveraged, or minimally leveraged, they're never going to meet your objectives. But leverage is like inflating the size of the balls — bulking up their relevance and impact — so you easily meet all of your objectives.

Figure 8: Fully leveraged sponsorships

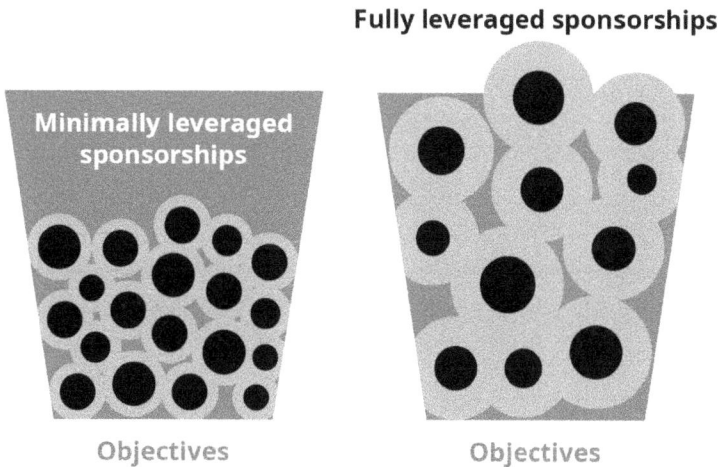

Fully leveraged sponsorships

Minimally leveraged sponsorships

Objectives

Objectives

As with so many things, there is an exception that makes the rule. In sponsorship, there are a few benefits that do provide a return with no leverage, such as exclusive vending rights. In that case, if all you're doing is trying to buy sales, you are free to just leave it at that. If you want to get a larger marketing return, however, you still need to leverage the opportunity.

Brand needs are not the most important

Corporate ego is a powerful thing. It is also an enemy to best-practice sponsorship. As a company — as a brand — you really need to get over yourself if you want to get the most from your sponsorship investments.

So, at this point, I'm going to remind you that brand needs are third on the list of priorities. Those priorities are:

1. Target market needs
2. Internal buy-in
3. Brand needs

I'm not saying that brand needs are unimportant, but there are two priorities you need to address before you will be able to achieve your brand needs. If you ignore, or worse yet,

> You must always put target market needs first.

disrespect your target market, they will not help you achieve your brand needs. If you don't have internal buy-in, your leverage program will be much less effective and cost a lot more.

The importance of measurement to leverage planning

You don't run a race without knowing where the finish line is, and it's crystal clear that your performance will be judged on your time and whether you broke any rules to achieve that time. In other words, you know how your success will be judged, not only before the starter fires their pistol, but before you start to train for that race.

Sponsorship is exactly the same.

For each and every investment, you should know what overall marketing and business objectives the sponsorship is aiming to achieve, how the success will be measured, and from what benchmarks. You need to know this before you embark on your leverage program or, even better, before you commit to a sponsorship. Commit to measuring effectively, and your leverage program will become immediately more effective.

As you move through this leverage section, I will address in detail how measurement integrates with the leverage-planning process. Part 4 of this book is specifically about measurement techniques.

Cast the net wide on leveragable markets

Most rightsholders don't understand leveragability. They don't understand all the markets, and all the ways that a sponsorship can be leveraged.

Instead, they concentrate on the markets they market to, and assume that's the sum total of the markets you're interested in. Their proposals concentrate on their on-site fans (or other direct customers, like donors), and the proportion of remote fans that follow them on social or sign up for EDMs, and leave out the myriad leveragable markets you have beyond that.

If you buy into that approach, thinking that all you have to leverage are the markets that have been sold to you by the rightsholder, you're wasting a ton of opportunity.

What I want you to do is cast the net much wider on leveragability. Yes, you can leverage to the on-site fans, but you can also leverage to all of the remote fans, whether they follow the property on social media or not. You can leverage to your customers and potential customers, whether they're B2C, B2B, or B2G. You can leverage to staff. If your company is a big factor in a local community, such as a power company having a large power generation site in a country town, you can leverage to that community. You can also leverage to fans of the larger themes.

> Commit to measuring effectively and your leverage program will become immediately more effective.

Figure 9: Markets rightsholders sell you

Figure 10: Markets you can leverage

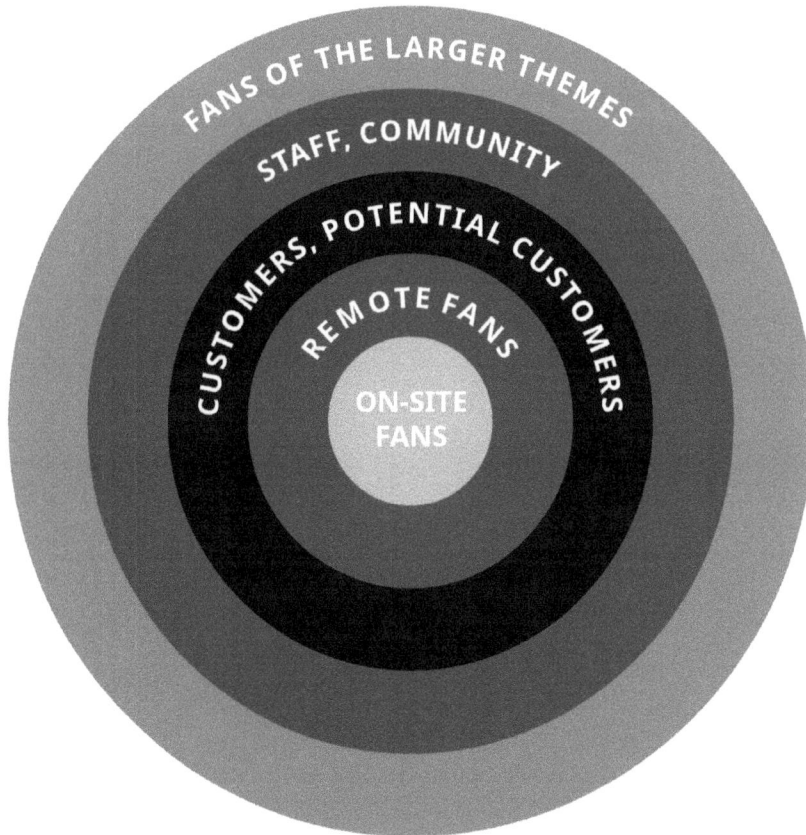

Every sponsorship has larger themes, and some have dozens of them. As an example, you could leverage sponsorship of a conference on emerging green tech to people who are interested in both sustainability and green tech. Even if they've never heard of the conference, there is likely to be credible content from the conference that would be super-interesting to them. Another example would be sponsorship of an anti-bullying charity.

It may serve one geographic location, but parents and kids around the world are interested in credible, authentic advice on dealing with bullies.

Increase the overlap

What the above chart may have made you realise is that a lot of your leverage isn't going to be aimed at the property's market, but at your own markets, through your own channels. This section expands on that.

Take a look at the following graphic, paying attention to the overlap. Most sponsorship is sold based on the overlap — the proportion of a property's fans that a sponsor is targeting. Focusing on this overlap is the same as focusing just on the on-site fans and the property's social/EDM followers, in the previous graphic.

Figure 11: Increasing the overlap

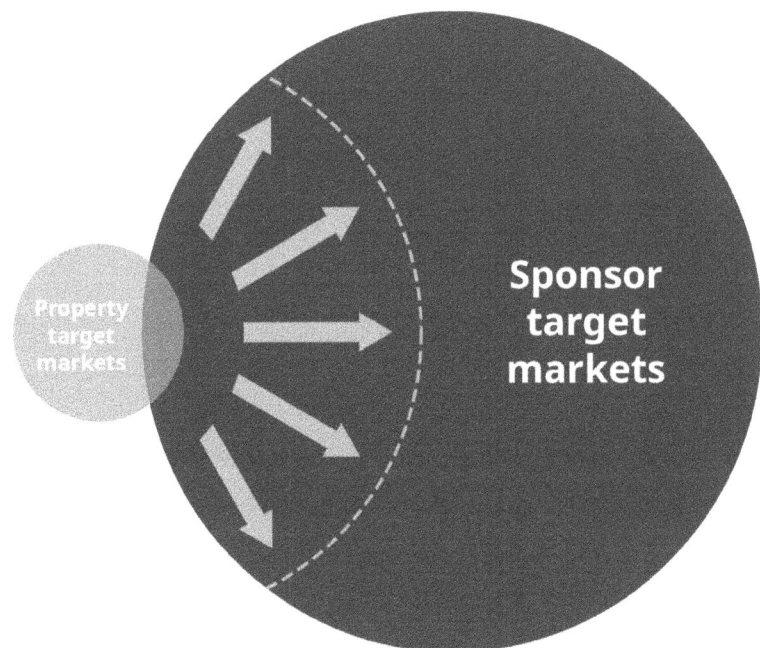

If you are overly focused on the overlap, it's not great for your brand, but it's even worse for the fans, as you (or your boss) might think the right strategy is just to hammer fans with marketing messages and activities in a fevered attempt to achieve your marketing goals within the constraints of that overlap.

For the good of both the fan experience and your own results, learning how to increase that overlap is a winning proposition.

Let's say for a moment that you're a new sponsorship or brand manager, and when you

CHAPTER 11/WIN-WIN-WIN LEVERAGE

review the portfolio, you see that your company is sponsoring a depression charity serving one smaller city. Your first impression might be, "We're a national brand. What am I supposed to do with this?" But you'd be overlooking a potentially great opportunity.

Why? Because although the number of people that the charity serves may be relatively limited, and the donor list the same, the proportion of your brand's national target market that is affected in some way by depression would be substantial. The question then shifts from, "What do we do with this sponsorship?", to "How do we use this sponsorship to help our target markets?". Given the amount of expertise the rightsholder has, chances are, you could do quite a lot.

You could provide credible advice and coping skills in your employee communications, information about how to recognise depression in your socials, or on monthly statements or product packaging. There are all manner of useful angles and advice you could explore. It won't matter that the information is coming from a local organisation, so long as it is authentic, relevant, and credible.

Examples: Adding value

As the official vehicle of the Deutsche Bank Championships, **BMW** offers owners free parking at the event. As title sponsor of the BMW Championship, BMW offers private parking for BMW owners, who also get access to the BMW Owners Pavilion on the 16th green.

This vintage example is from the very start of my career. **Totinos Pizza** was sponsor of the Minnesota Twins. They negotiated with the Twins to hold open tryouts on their home field, with the Twins committing to take at least one person to spring training, to train with the team. This took place in the middle of winter – which is frigid in Minnesota – in their roofed stadium, and had thousands of participants being put through their paces by the Twins' coaching staff. Some people came for the fun of it, while others were real contenders for being recruited. It was free to participate. All you needed to do was sign a waiver and bring two Totinos proofs-of-purchase.

During subsequent COVID lockdowns in the UK, Japan's **NH Foods** used their sponsorship of the Liverpool Football Club to do two rounds of "Cooking with Champions". Both series pitted two players against each other, in a cookoff, the second one designed by Michelin-hatted chef Marcus Wareing. Kits with all the ingredients and every utensil were provided to players at their homes, and they followed along in a real-time Zoom with the chef from his COVID-safe, Michelin-starred restaurant kitchen, creating a bounty of fun content during quite a bleak time.

You can take the same approach when sponsoring a marathon or conference or minor league baseball team. Think about what the property knows or has that would be meaningful to your larger target market. How to choose or train for your first marathon? Industry trends from a heavy-hitting conference keynote? A funny, gritty series of "stories from the road" from that baseball team? Again, the angles are limited only by your creativity.

The upshot is that if what you're sponsoring is both credible and relevant to your market, use well-selected IP and sponsorship-driven content that uses that broader relevance, and direct it back through your own marketing channels. This will increase the *functional* overlap, and even a small, very short-term sponsorship can deliver for your brand and target markets, as if it were much bigger.

Understanding the fan experience

Another important building block for outstanding leverage is really understanding the fan experience. In a perfect world, the rightsholder will provide this background information. But even if they don't, you still need it. You've got two options:

1. Go through the leverage development process with the sponsorship stakeholder group, and fill in the fan experience blanks yourselves. Given how many events you've attended, you'll probably be able to infer a lot. It won't be perfect but should give you enough to find some great ideas.
2. Invite the rightsholder to sit in on that process, bringing more precision to the backgrounding, and potentially unearthing some opportunities you may not have thought of.

The importance of being a fan

While we're on the subject of understanding the fan experience, I need to remind you to actually *be* a fan.

Forgetting what it's like to be a fan is epidemic in our industry. I call this "fan-nesia". We can't go to events without paying more attention to the sponsorships than to the bands or the game or parade. And when we do go to events, we're more often than not ensconced in some private hospitality suite or otherwise getting the VIP treatment. And while we are unbelievably privileged to get that kind of access, it can also be our undoing because we're completely disconnected from the fan experience.

How can you disrespect the fan experience in the name of brand goals, when *as a fan*, every time a sponsor is overbearing at an event you care about, all you can think is, "Oh, would you just piss off!"? How do you insist on a degree of exclusivity that borders on draconian, when *as a fan*, you're outraged when a sponsor suddenly has control of your

> Forgetting what it's like to be a fan is epidemic in our industry.

rights? If you've ever had to turn your t-shirt inside out because it had a sponsor's competitor's logo on it, or been told you can't buy tickets unless you're using the sponsor's credit card, you have experienced that fan outrage.

So, how do you cure fan-nesia? Easy. Get your arse out of the corporate box and into the cheap seats. Go to events with your family and friends, not your work associates. Ditch the champagne reception and take your kids to that museum on a Saturday morning. Cheer and sing and dance with the abandon you can't show in a sponsor function. Take public transport, stand in lines, buy your own beer. And wherever you are, pay attention to what you're there to see; don't overanalyse what all the sponsors are doing.

By allowing yourself to be a genuine fan, your approach to sponsorship can't help but move significantly towards best practice.

Make it win-win-win

Once you understand the fan experience, you can turn it into wins. Creating those "third wins", those small, meaningful value-adds for the target market, falls into two main categories: Amplifying or extending the best parts of the fan experience, and ameliorating the worst parts of the fan experience. There are as many ways to do this as there are aspects to a fan experience, but here are some ideas to get you started.

Amplifying the best stuff – could you:

> Provide sponsorship-driven advice, tools, inspiration, or information?

> Create exclusive content or ways for fans to get a behind-the-scenes info or experience?

> Create ways for fans to have input into the development of the property (content, location, etc.)?

> Create ways for remote fans to feel more a part of the experience?

> Create ways for fans and customers to share their content – photos, videos, stories – where your brand will champion them?

> Create ways for fans to customise their fan experience?

> Create ways for people to post their own related content (eg, they can post their "best bike stack" videos around a mountain bike event), and people might be able to vote on the best one?

> Create ways for people to participate in the pre-event promotion – submit questions for a press conference, participate in a live webchat with a star/expert/whatever?

> Extend the experience with pre- or post-game activities?

> Gamify an aspect of the experience?

Win-win-win is the bedrock of best-practice sponsorship.

Reducing the worst stuff — could you:

> Create an augmented-reality wayfinding app for a large or complex event?
> Offer tickets to your customers before they go on sale to the general public?
> Provide more convenient access or parking?
> Create a VIP area for customers?
> Help remote fans feel like they're part of the experience?

While this is just the tip of the iceberg, the starting place is always having a strong understanding of the fan experience. Exploring this, and what you can do with it, is part of the leverage development process I outline in Chapter 14: Finding the big leverage ideas.

Examples: Adding value

During COVID lockdowns, Australian insurer **QBE** helped fans of Australian Rules football team the Sydney Swans get their fully customised footy fix. QBE created a microsite that housed an intelligent video creation system, allowing fans to create a customised, two-minute highlight film, culled from 30 years of Swans video. Every downloadable/sharable QBE Swans Story video featured a welcome from the fan's favourite player, all of the customised clips, as well as club trivia. (Full disclosure, the Swans are my favourite team in the world!)

When **Audi** sponsored Iron Man 3, they took a hard turn into fan crowdsourcing, co-creating a digital comic book and giving fans a hand in the story. Fans could both vote on the story direction, via social sharing, and draw frames for the eventual finished product. Audi even launched a range of instructional videos on how to draw key parts of the comic, including Iron Man and an Audi R8. **Marvel** judged the winner, and the winner's art ended the story.

For hockey fans, everyone has a grooming ritual if your team makes the playoffs, and you keep it up until they're out. In the lead-up to the NHL playoffs back in 2009, brewer **Molsen** decided to champion this fan weirdness. They created the Molsen Canadian Official Guide to Playoff Grooming, encouraging fans to upload photos and videos of their playoff grooming rituals to the Molsen Facebook page. Rituals ranged from the mundane (blue socks) to the nutty (getting the team logo waxed into one's back hair), celebrating this peculiar and glorious form of tribalism.

Go for many smaller wins

After close to a month off, I went back to the boxing gym and, wow, was I ever sore the day after! Actually, it's not the muscles I used for punching that were so sore, it was the back muscles I used for recoiling after a punch and getting ready for the next one. I was explaining this to a friend and used a line my coach has said to me countless times:

> It's not how hard you punch. It's how accurate you are and how fast you can punch them again.

As I said the words, I realised how pertinent that concept is for sponsorship.

The goal with best-practice sponsorship is that a large proportion of the target markets should receive small, meaningful benefits through a sponsorship, not just the chance for one person to receive a giant prize.

Many sponsors have embraced this idea, which is fantastic. Providing for added-value benefits to go to the target markets brings a level of relevance, relationship building, and even respect and appreciation for the sponsor, which is lacking from earlier generations of sponsorship.

That said, there are degrees. The best sponsors in the world create multiple small wins in each of their leverage plans. This may be comprised of many different wins or one win that is used multiple times by each person over the course of the sponsorship (eg, VIP baseball parking for bank customers). The net effect being that the customers/consumers have an experience that is improved in many small ways by a brand that has obviously thought about their needs.

Examples: B2B added value

In the UK, COVID hit both grassroots football clubs and small businesses hard. Even when lockdowns eased, it was clear that recovery wasn't going to be easy. Alongside their English Football League sponsorship, **eBay** created Small Business United – what's billed as the world's first micro-sponsorship program. eBay encouraged small businesses across the UK to sponsor their local football clubs, and paid for them to do it, helping to rebuild clubs and small business at the same time.

Global bank **ABN AMRO** found their hospitality package at the symphony was losing its appeal to their VVIP clients. The symphony worked closely with the bank to create a series of top-quality, one-of-a-kind events, often in offbeat locations. The clients loved it from the start, and it quickly became the place to be for major decision-makers, and an unbeatable relationship-building opportunity.

Other sponsors have gone the way of the one big gesture — providing one added-value benefit one time — for the target markets. That is absolutely fair, and will be valued by the target market, but you will probably get your best results by surrounding that bigger win with a number of smaller wins. Alternatively, you can provide a string of the big wins across a number of sponsorships. But providing one big benefit one time only tells your target market that you thought about them, well, once.

A more comprehensive group of wins for your target market fosters the idea that you're always thinking about them — that you are providing them with benefits that are pinpointed to their needs, and you're doing so consistently. That you're making meaningful connections and making them often. Just like boxing . . . but friendlier.

Right-sizing your sponsorship leverage activities

With win-win-win, the goal is to provide small, meaningful benefits for all or most of the market, not one big prize for one person. That's all well and good, but what do you do with benefits or leverage activities that are, by their very nature, limited in size? How do you make that a win for everyone . . . and should you even try?

For instance, if there are hundreds of thousands or millions of fans of a team, the perceived difference between you offering one big prize of a pair of grand final tickets or 50 pairs of grand final tickets is almost nil. The fans still don't believe they have any chance of winning, so why bother entering? In the mind of the fans, providing them with a much smaller win that they can easily access is more meaningful and has more impact on deepening your relationship with them.

Understand the size of the markets

Every market you're trying to influence will have a different size. Before you can right-size the wins, you need to understand the size of your markets. These could include markets, such as:

- Your customers (all)
- Your customers (geographic, psychographic, demographic segments)
- Your potential customers (people you actively market to)
- Intermediary markets, such as retailers, resellers, dealerships, or brokers (all, one channel, geographic segment, etc.)
- Major, VIP, enterprise, or institutional customers
- Staff (all or a subset, such as staff in one location)
- Fans who actively participate in the property (attendees, members, donors, volunteers, etc.)
- Remote fans, who love the property but may not attend, donate, etc.
- All fans of the property
- Fans of the property category (professional development, dance music, golf, etc.)
- Fans of the larger theme (conservationists, fitness buffs, avid gardeners, etc.)

Before you can right-size the wins, you need to understand the size of your markets.

Looking at those 50 pairs of grand final tickets, across which of these groups would that constitute a broad win? Most likely, a segment of your intermediary or VIP markets.

How to spread the wins around

Our knee-jerk reaction these days is often to look straight at social media. There is no question that social media is one of our most perfect ways to leverage a sponsorship and provide wins to lots of people. But, it's not the only way.

Think about apps, customisable content, episodic content, and crowdsourcing. Think about your distribution system — your packaging, your retailers, your branches. Think about all of the ways you stay in touch with your customer base. Think about all of the other media you use. Think about where large groups of fans congregate — stadiums, events, pubs, etc.

In fact, sometimes low tech is a thing of beauty. As noted back in Chapter 1, the autograph pen of choice, Sharpie, demonstrates their huge product range while adding value to the fan experience at games. How? They provide stacks of heavy paper and piles of pens so that fans can make their own signs.

What if you have one giant thing to give away?

As noted back in Chapter 7: Negotiation, there are ways of structuring one giant, what-money-can't-buy experience so that it creates lots of those small, meaningful wins. The key is that there are little wins built into the entry and/or decision process and the content created around it.

Allowing people to nominate themselves or others with a video submission on social, or vote on the winner, or be entertained by and share content created by the winner, are just a few of the little wins you can build into the process of someone getting the big win. What you'll find, I'm sure, is that you'll get a lot more traction with fans with those little wins than with the big one!

Examples: Alignment

The **Cadbury** brand is all about being kind and generous, with genuine human connections. Working with Age UK, Cadbury removed the wording from Dairy Milk chocolate bar packaging, bringing awareness to the epidemic of loneliness among the elderly. This was accompanied by a video telling the stories of older people who feel alone, which ran across television and socials, promoting empathy and volunteerism.

In New Zealand, one in eight kids can't play sport because they can't afford to buy the kit (uniform and gear). Generosity-driven chocolate brand **Cadbury** (again!) partnered with KidsCan to create 150 purple kit lockers across the country, where people can donate new and used kits to other kids that need them, with nearly 100,000 items donated.

Demonstrate alignment

There are two ways to use sponsorship to get closer to your target market: Adding value to their fan and/or customer experience, and demonstrating your brand's alignment to their passions and priorities. Adding value is often a sponsor's default position, but alignment can also be a powerful factor.

If you understand your target market — their priorities, motivations, and why they care about whatever it is you're sponsoring — you have the opportunity to show that your brand or company is just as passionate as they are. It's saying:

> *You care about the environment? So do we! And here are all the things we're doing to reduce our environmental footprint and help you to reduce yours.*
>
> *You're concerned about skin cancer? So are we! These are just a few of the things we're doing to support skin cancer sufferers, help find a cure, and encourage our staff and customers to look after themselves when they're in the sun.*
>
> *You love the Minnesota Wild? We're their biggest fans! Have a look at some of the Wild things our people get up to!*

Your messages don't have to be worded in such an over-the-top way, but if your target markets care about something, and you have an authentic company culture that mirrors that passion, do be passionate about how you show it.

Demonstrate what your brand is about

Stop looking around at what other sponsors are doing, and stop referencing how sponsorship has historically been done. Instead, look at your brand and find ways to demonstrate what your brand is really about.

- If your brand is caring and helpful, add value to the fan experience in a way that's caring and helpful.
- If your brand is innovative, do something really innovative.
- If your brand is about understanding the customers, leverage in a way that lets people customise their fan experience.
- If your brand is brash, create at least one win that is a little crazy and over the top.
- If your brand is nostalgic, create a way for fans to share their memories.

This list could go on and on, but I'm sure you get the idea.

Think logo-free

I'm not saying you shouldn't have any signage or logos. What I'm saying is that, beyond brand hygiene, you shouldn't think about them. The preponderance of research categorises logo exposure as a low-value mechanism, with no bearing on changing perceptions or behaviours around a brand.

When you leverage (and measure) a sponsorship, forget that you get any logo exposure at all. This will force you to concentrate on the much meatier aspects of your sponsorships — the ones that will impact perceptions, behaviours, and alignment.

Have a Plan B, then do it anyway

If COVID taught us anything, it's that sponsors either need to have a Plan B, or be nimble enough to come up with one fast, in case something goes wrong. Nimble sponsors found themselves:

> Refocusing leverage on the remote fans (because there were no in-person fans), adding value to that remote fan experience
> Creating leverage strategies to engage with fans, even when events were cancelled
> Proactively creating new and interesting kinds of content around the properties, while not getting super hung up on production values, because we had no choice
> Aligning with fans' frustration and sadness about the impact of COVID on their fan experiences

> When you leverage a sponsorship, forget that you get any logo exposure at all.

Examples: Alignment

Back in 2012, **Procter & Gamble** used their sponsorship of the London Olympics to make it not about the sport but about the incredible hard work and unwavering dedication of the mums who got those athletes there, and celebrating all that mums do to help their kids be all they can be. This rolled out in a series of videos thanking mums for everything they do, and positioning the P&G masterbrand as "Proud Sponsor of Moms". To this day, I can't watch any of these videos without crying. Do yourself a favour and look them up.

Nike leveraged International Women's Day and their incredible roster of sports superstars to champion black women, pointing out that Naomi Osaka, Caster Semenya, Serena Williams, and so many others didn't get where they are because of "magic", but hard work, talent, and perseverance. The "We Play Real" video was interspersed with video of NASA astronaut Mae Jemison, late Congresswoman Shirley Chisholm, and Black Lives Matter activists.

New Zealand's national rugby team, the All Blacks, are almost a religion, and no one loves them more than **Air New Zealand** and its staff. They call themselves a "fanatical sponsor" and take corporate fandom to new heights, with shows of support for the team and the fans that are both grand and genuine. To see how this brand-as-fan positioning works, just follow them on social media.

There are some industry pros that believe all sponsors should now have backup plans for all of their major sponsorships, just in case it all goes pear-shaped. To an extent, I agree. Where I diverge is that I believe sponsors should be doing all those backup activities anyway. I mean, why wouldn't you?

If your leverage plan incorporates all of the scrappy, creative, Plan B things we had to do to keep sponsorships delivering during COVID's darkest days, that's going to be a force-multiplier for your results going forward. And if things do go pear-shaped, and the operations of the property are impacted, you already have a strategy underway that will deliver consistent value to anyone that cares about the property.

Chapter 12

Leverage funding

Before we get into how to create a leverage program, we need to address funding.

How much to budget for sponsorship leverage is a perennial question. And the thing is, that's not even the right question. I mean, sure . . . you eventually have to put a line item on a budget. But the bigger question – the one that drives that figure – is how efficient, resourceful, and creative you're willing to be. Because if you can commit to that, your leverage figure will be dramatically lower.

Most sponsors spend far too much on leverage funding. This is a historic habit that has gone further and further off track as the years have passed. This outmoded approach has become so accepted that some publications and associations encourage overspending on leverage and reward sponsors who spend the most.

This chapter addresses how this overspending happened, why it's usually unnecessary, and a target zone for your leverage funding.

The one-to-one rule

Back when I first got into this industry, the big new thing for sponsors was the one-to-one rule. This rule stated that for every one dollar a sponsor spends on a rights fee, they should spend another dollar leveraging. This was both a revelation and a rod for our industry's back that we're still struggling with.

It was a revelation because prior to the one-to-one rule, most sponsors didn't leverage at all. Sponsorship was ruled by visibility, with exposure being its own reward. The new rule took us from the pointlessness of first-generation sponsorship into second-generation sponsorship. It wasn't sophisticated, but leverage was actually happening, and it completely changed the game.

At the same time, this ratio made a rod for our backs because it was all about how much you spent, not how smart or strategic or creative you were. It also assumed that the sponsorship team was going to initiate all of your leverage, rather than it being integrated into existing marketing channels, so it was very inefficient.

Then, sponsorship started to grow . . . a lot. Properties got cluttered, and sponsors grew preoccupied with "breaking through the clutter", so they spent more. The one-to-one rule

Many leverage budgets have become ridiculously and unnecessarily fat.

became the two-to-one rule, and I've lost count of the number of conferences I've attended where at least one speaker was congratulating themselves for spending three- or four-to-one. Our industry media haven't been much help either, often hailing big leverage spenders as being at the vanguard of sponsorship, whether they're actually leveraging well or not.

As a result, many leverage budgets have become ridiculously and unnecessarily fat, and sponsors with modest leverage budgets lament that they just don't have enough money to leverage well, when in fact, they're both wrong.

Doing more with less

Thinking you need to spend that much on leverage, in order to be successful, flies in the face of everything that makes sponsorship so powerful. As a quick reminder:

- It's meaningful and resonant to your target markets.
- It's supremely flexible — like sculpture, you can make sponsorship into anything you want and out of anything you want, so long as it is structurally sound.
- It's integratable across all other marketing media.

Even if you're only spending one-to-one, you're spending too much, and you're probably doing too little. The best sponsors now spend the least amount on leverage, incrementally — 10–35%, not 100%, 200%, or more. This is because they:

- Centralise sponsorship in their portfolios. It's no longer a piece of the pie but a catalyst that makes already-budgeted marketing activities more effective.
- Work cross-departmentally, getting input and buy-in from across the company before negotiation, ensuring that every department gets the benefits they need to have an appropriate platform for leverage. This is where your sponsorship stakeholder group really comes into its own!
- Start by integrating sponsorship across those existing activities, or replacing already-budgeted activities that won't be as effective.

Incremental leverage funding should be only 10–35% of a sponsorship fee.

Below is that catalyst diagram again. Just imagine how much leverage could be carried out for very little money if all of these stakeholders committed to using the sponsorship in a meaningful way in their own channels.

Figure 12: Sponsorship is a catalyst

By taking this approach, the incremental funding required will drop considerably — although the effective value of the marketing channels impacted by the sponsorship may be many times the sponsorship fee — and your results will skyrocket, as you wring every last drop of value out of the investment.

Two exceptions

There are two exceptions where spending more than 10–35% is appropriate.

One is sponsorship of big, quadrennial-style events (eg, Olympics, World Cup). This is because the leveragable platform for deepening relevance and relationships often outstrips the amount of existing marketing activities. In other words, even if those sponsors integrated it across everything they do — which they should — they still wouldn't have exhausted the potential. In that case, war-chesting some money and spending up incrementally is entirely appropriate.

The other exception is when a larger incremental leverage budget will provide the framework for leverage, or a bank of durable, leveragable content that will serve brand and fan needs for a long time — ideally years.

> Sponsorship is no longer a piece of the pie but a catalyst that makes already-budgeted marketing activities more effective.

Even then, incremental budgets don't necessarily have to be huge. You can be both efficient and effective with a well-chosen sponsorship if you're scrappy and resourceful — and I've taught countless sponsors to do just that. And, if you can significantly expand the small, meaningful wins for more fans, customers, and staff, better demonstrate alignment to fans, and more effectively achieve brand objectives, over a longer period of time — by raising your incremental leverage budget from 25 to 45 or 50%, for instance — then it's definitely worth considering.

Reducing your sponsorship budget by leveraging smarter

You can also use this catalyst technique to reduce your overall sponsorship budget, without exiting sponsorships that are working for you.

As an example, one of my clients brought me in when they got a global head office directive to reduce their sponsorship spend by 25%. Most of their investments were in multi-year deals, so even if they wanted to exit some of them (they didn't), they weren't going to be able to. They thought my job was to work a miracle, but it was very simple.

The original budget looked something like the following. Note: To make the calculations a bit more straightforward, I've altered the budget amounts to nice round figures, but the percentages are close to the actual.

Budget item	Amount	% of budget
Sponsorship rights fees	$390,000	39%
Incremental leverage spend (approx. 150% of fees)	$600,000	60%
Research	$10,000	1%
Total	$1,000,000	100%

My strategy was simple:

1. Create a sponsorship stakeholder group.
2. Teach them how to leverage creatively and consultatively, using sponsorship as a catalyst.
3. Rework or reduce the focus on high-cost, on-site leverage activities that impact only a sliver of the marketplace.
4. Increase the research budget, so they get additional insights to improve leverage even more in the future.
5. Provide some money for contingencies.

This was the resulting budget:

Budget item	Amount	% of budget
Sponsorship rights fees	$390,000	66.5%
Incremental leverage spend (approx. 31% of fees)	$120,000	21%
Contingency	$50,000	9%
Research	$20,000	3.5%
Total	$580,000	100%

As you can see, we did much better than reduce the sponsorship budget by 25%. In fact, we reduced it by 42%, without exiting any investments. The difference was a change in approach, a big injection of creativity, and meaningful involvement by a broad stakeholder team.

Chapter 13

The opportunities and traps of emerging technology

This is your last chapter before I get into exactly how to create your leverage plans, including step-by-step instructions and lots of case studies. For many of you, that's a big focus of why you're reading this book, and I get that. But if you go into it unprepared, your leverage plans will be less creative, less efficient, and, most importantly, less effective.

I'm asked all the time which of the new and improving technologies are best for sponsorship. While I can give an answer in real time about the technologies I think are providing great leverage opportunities, the speed with which tech is changing means that committing to a hot take that's relevant as I write this means it could well be out-of-date by the time you read it.

So, this isn't about how to use tech that's current as of this writing so much as it's about how to think about emerging and improving tech, and how it serves your primary mission.

New tech, old thinking

Back in the 1990s, the internet was exploding, and brands were shouting from the rooftops, "Ooh, yay! Another place to advertise!"

For many brands, this is still the way they look at the internet and all of the jaw-dropping technology that has emerged, and continues to emerge, from it. Where can we advertise? How do we use this to get our messages in front of people? How can we brand the experience?

These brands have missed the fundamental change in how technology has affected the world, and their customers' relationships to it. As a result, they are underusing this amazing marketing platform to such a great degree that they may as well be pounding nails with an iPhone.

People want technology that enhances and enriches their lives. They want tech that gives them more control over their experiences, more information, more insights. They want tech that makes their lives easier, more convenient. They want tech that gives them a sense of community, while valuing and showcasing their individuality. They want tech that makes them feel closer to the action, and closer to the people and organisations that matter to them. When combined with modern, fan-focused sponsorship, using tech to give people what they want is adding enormously to the fan experience.

What don't they want? Ads. You know this because of all the sites, apps, and social platforms that allow you to go ad-free for $X a month. And you know this because you don't like ads in your tech either.

If you want to maximise your sponsorship results, there are a million things you can do to leverage your investments with technology. But the *first* thing you need to do is get out of the branding/ads mindset.

The coolness trap

Technology can be incredibly cool. It's hard to believe some of the things that are possible now that weren't just a few years ago — or even just last year. Unfortunately, that cool factor can blind us to the usefulness and feasibility of a technology for use in sponsorship leverage.

Think I'm wrong? As someone involved in brand marketing, you've likely had the opportunity to strap on a virtual-reality rig, immersing yourself in an experience that isn't really happening. It's so cool, it makes you want to use that technology, but does it comport with best-practice sponsorship? Right now, probably not. Scalability is the issue, and until we're all walking around with VR-enabled glasses, it's unlikely to be effective for markets of more than a few hundred.

The metaverse is another example. You may have been part of a presentation showcasing some of the marketing possibilities in these (potentially) extraordinary worlds. And there is a small percentage of people who live large chunks of their lives online — often gamers. Integrating sponsorship into an existing, accepted, well-used metaverse may be a good plan, if that's your market. But most of the rest of the world isn't ready to adopt Ready Player One as a life strategy, and look at technology as a way to enhance real life, rather than replace it.

This section wouldn't be complete without mentioning NFTs, which went from nothing to a craze worth billions, and back to almost nothing, in the blink of an eye. The blockchain technology sitting behind NFTs is extremely interesting, but NFTs ended up being little more than tech's version of the Macarena.

All this is to say that coolness isn't a good filter for evaluating the efficacy of a technology for sponsorship leverage. Go ahead and appreciate the innovation, but moderate

> Most of the world isn't ready to adopt Ready Player One as a life strategy.

your enthusiasm enough to assess whether a particular technology is really the best option for your needs.

Using tech in sponsorship leverage

Technology options for sponsorship leverage are exploding, but that doesn't mean they're all smart choices. If you change the framing, however, tech that advances your brand will be quickly parsed from the rest.

In order for a technology to be a viable choice for sponsorship leverage, it needs to:

- Add value to the fan experience, demonstrate alignment, and/or demonstrate your brand or company values
- Be scalable, so that all or most of the people in the target market — including remote fans — can meaningfully participate or benefit

This is how you need to look at tech, as it is now, and as it will be. Don't waste money, time, or brainpower using some new, shiny technology just for the sake of it. It won't work.

Examples: Leveraging with tech

In mid-2021, New Zealand brewer **Steinlager** decided to celebrate the "everyday greatness and spirit of rugby supporters". They worked with NZ Rugby and the national rugby team, the All Blacks, to create the Steinlager Alt Blacks, allowing regular Kiwis to don a virtual All Blacks jersey to go head to head with rivals South Africa in a live Rugby Challenge 4 esports game right before the actual All Blacks played an international test against South Africa. All Blacks coaching legend Sir Graham Henry chose 23 players from the thousands of applicants. Once selected, the players were virtually kitted out in 3D-modelled virtual avatars, representing their country on the virtual playing field, and becoming local heroes all over the country.

Heineken Vietnam knows that the Vietnamese are soccer mad, and they love an extra-smooth beer, like Heineken Silver. Launched during the UEFA Champions League (again!) quarter finals, Heineken equated the smoothness of their beer to the smoothness of soccer's celebratory knee-slides. Using AI, the knee-slides were measured, and real-time discounts applied to instant delivery by retailer **GrabMart**. Player does a 2.1-metre slide, the discount is 21%. This led to tens of thousands of organic comments, asking their favourite players to do a slide.

In 2020, Australian Open sponsor **Infosys** created Infosys AI Clips. With the starting point of "How do you decode greatness?", this service used AI to identify and grab real-time highlights clips from any of the courts in play, giving tennis fans the ability to view highlights, using 120 filters, demonstrating their deep tech expertise, while adding value to the fan experience.

Scalability

The point about scalability is critical.

As noted, virtual reality is super-cool but currently hard to scale. That's in contrast to augmented reality and artificial intelligence, where there are myriad ways to add real value to the fan experience AND scale it to a huge fanbase, and there are many other technologies that can deliver that one-two punch.

Below, I've gone out on a limb and listed just some of the emerging and improving technologies, breaking them down by scalability.

Scalable now, in many ways, to on-site and remote fans

- Augmented reality
- Artificial intelligence
- Face mapping/deep fakes
- Mixed reality
- Drones (for drone video content)
- QR codes (often driving games, like scavenger hunts)

Scalable now for primarily on-site fans

- Geofencing
- Holographic projection
- Drones (for drone shows)
- NFC (near-field communications)

Scalable eventually

- Virtual reality
- 3D printing (customised merch?)

This is really just a stake in the sand at the time of writing. By the time this book is physically in anyone's hands, some of these things may have become more scalable. We also may have more amazing new technology at our disposal, each fitting into one of these categories. It's moving fast, but scalability is a lens we need to apply to all of it.

Authenticity

Just like your brand needs to be a natural match, in order for your sponsorships to work, the technology you use should be a logical, natural fit for the fan experience and your brand.

If your brand ethos is all about being helpful, you should be leveraging in a way that's helpful, and there's no reason you can't use tech to deliver on that helpfulness. If your brand ethos is about security or peace of mind, you can leverage a sponsorship to demonstrate that, using tech, if that makes sense. And if your brand ethos is about being brash or edgy, there's certainly a role for tech in your leverage planning.

What you don't want to do is leverage in a way that's at odds with your brand values, or at odds with how people relate to the property you're sponsoring. Artificial intelligence is an amazing tool, but if you're sponsoring a cancer charity, you wouldn't use it to show people what they'd look like after four months of chemo. Obviously, that's a ridiculous example, but you'd be surprised how often technology is used in such a wrongheaded, inauthentic way that it — as we Aussies say — sticks out like dogs' balls.

Fan-centric/win-win-win

As with everything you do with sponsorship, your focus needs to be the fans, and providing those fans with small, meaningful wins.

It's not, "OMG, this new tech is so cool. How can we use it in leverage?" It's, "Now that we understand the fan/customer experience, how can we deliver them some wins?" If technology — existing or emerging — can create genuine wins for them, that's fantastic. By all means, use technology.

Keep in mind that to be fan-centric, people shouldn't have to jump through hoops to use the technology. Asking people to download an app, register with all of their contact details, and confirm their details by email or SMS, before they can avail themselves of whatever win you're providing, is too much. It ceases to be a win.

Examples: Adding value

During the 2023 Women's World Cup, major sponsor **Visa** created the Visa Freestyler global gaming experience. This mobile game mimics an interactive ball-juggle, where players try to keep the ball in the air with increasingly difficult tricks, all while continuing to remember the previous tricks. It uses innovative motion capture and pixel streaming for a top-notch experience. One of the things I love about this is that Visa didn't bolt on extraneous prizes, and just let the game itself – and the game between friends – be its own win.

In 2023, **Snapchat** worked with the NFL to create the "NFL Kickoff Jersey Lens". Fans could customise the lens for their favourite team. They could also create a virtual bobblehead (no thanks, my hair is huge enough), play cornhole, enter a commentator contest, and more.

Like any self-respecting mobile service provider, America's **T-Mobile** wanted to demonstrate the quality and possibilities around its 5G mobile service. They used their sponsorship of Major League Baseball's All-Star Weekend for a series of jaw-dropping demonstrations. Using the official MLB Next app, they did a 5G drone tour of the field, 3D overlays on the field for pitches, and a ball/strike system. They also used a drone to provide aerial shots, feeding into coverage across MLB.TV and socials.

The data acquisition trap

Another aspect of technology we need to address is big data. Sponsors around the world are becoming preoccupied with data acquisition — to the point where it is a primary goal of many sponsorship strategies. This is a big mistake.

I'm not saying data acquisition is a bad thing — far from it. Adding to, and rounding out, your databases is clearly raising the usefulness and value of a major marketing tool. But making it a focal point of a sponsorship program has some major flaws that could damage, not enhance, your results.

Cynicism

Data-driven sponsors around the world continue to run promotions where there is just one winner and require some kind of active connection — some data — from the fan to participate.

➢ Follow us on Instagram and go into a draw to win . . .

➢ SMS your name, address, and email to go into a draw . . .

➢ Use our hashtag and go into a draw to win. Come on, let's get this thing trending!

The problem is, every time you ask fans to part with information about themselves before you have established some real rapport with them, they see it as a one-sided deal favouring you. Whether you have any intent of abusing the relationship or not, we've all been abused enough that we're now cynics, and we regard companies who do this with suspicion.

And how many sponsors are gathering data and likes and follows without any strategy for developing and sharing the meaningful content that will keep the fans engaged? If your plan extends largely (or solely) to bludgeoning these fans with offer after offer, and talking ad infinitum about your brand, you're going to lose them as fast as you got them.

The data detour

The part about this preoccupation with data acquisition that annoys me the most is that it totally misses the point. The point with all marketing media is to change perceptions and behaviours, and build alignment, and sponsorship is one of the most powerful ways a brand can do that.

But the way most sponsors are using all this data acquired through sponsorship doesn't access that power at all. Instead, the acquired data is seen as a result, in and of itself. That data is aggregated with existing data, and at some point in the future will be used in various data-driven marketing campaigns that have nothing at all to do with the sponsorship, or the property people care about. The model looks like the following diagram.

Figure 13: The data detour

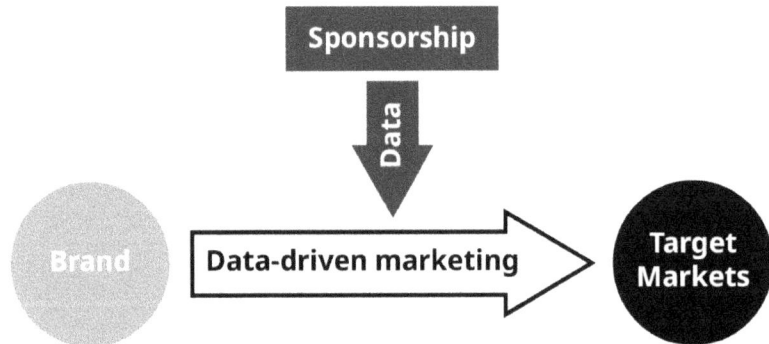

Instead, you should follow the logic that the shortest distance between two points is a straight line. Why would you do anything else but use the most powerful and personally resonant marketing media you have to directly influence perceptions, behaviours, and alignment around your brand? Why make an unnecessary detour to data-land?

Deepening your relationship with a target market does not require their email addresses, mobile numbers, Facebook likes, Instagram follows, access to social profile information, or any other individual piece of data that you may get through a sponsorship. It simply requires you to understand, respect, and add value to the things they're passionate about. And if you do that, they'll volunteer their data to you.

This dramatically changes the model to the one that follows. Instead of one-way marketing, it's a two-way, passion-driven relationship between fans and your brand. Fans volunteer their information to you. You can then use that information, plus your other market intelligence, to guide and fine-tune your leverage program.

Figure 14: Using sponsorship data well

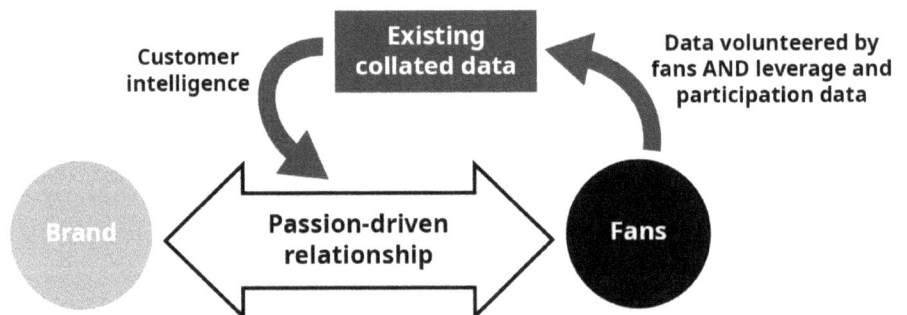

> Deepening your relationship with a target market does not require their email addresses.

It's sometimes illegal

Then there are the sponsors who appear to just say, "Stuff collecting our own data. Too hard. We'll just get the rightsholder to give us their database!"

Despite privacy laws in most developed countries prohibiting the transfer of database information without the consent of the people on that database, sponsors still ask. I've even seen some major sponsors trying to take advantage of that special blend of huge donor databases and a distinct lack of cash that marks many charitable organisations, to muscle them into providing the database as a requirement of a sponsorship.

Listen up, sponsors: They can't give that data to you. Stop asking.

As for getting your partner to send out one after another promotional emails on your behalf to get around those laws? Also not a great idea, as now they think both you and the rightsholder are abusing them. Sure, do it once or twice, but don't abuse the privilege.

Use data to build empathy

In sponsorship, data's most powerful role is to drive empathy; to understand what matters to people and why.

If your markets are segmented by how they relate to your brand, that's super-useful for brand marketing and sales. Likewise, if you use market profiles from a market research company, like Prizm Market Segments, Nielsen Audience Segmentation, or Mosaic Segments, that may be useful for your overall understanding of the market.

But neither of these approaches to understanding markets are very useful for sponsorship as they don't provide any specific insight about why the segment might be interested in the property, how intense their passion is, or the kind of leverage that will have meaning. You might be able to infer it, to some extent, but it won't come close to giving you the information you really need.

Instead, you either need strong fan experience research from the property, or you need to do an exercise of dissecting the property to identify the main motivations for people to care, and extrapolate from there. That's a big part of Chapter 14: Finding the big leverage ideas.

Finding the big leverage ideas

I've spent a big chunk of this book building up to this very chapter. You've got the mindset. You've done all the preparation. This is the chapter where you put all that to work and find the big leverage ideas that will transform your sponsorship opportunities into marketing returns.

Using design thinking for sponsorship leverage

The process we're going to go through is based on design thinking, and that has a few components.

It starts with empathy

When it comes to sponsorship, the deeper the analysis, the better the leverage. "Deeper" doesn't mean more complicated. In fact, it's very simple. Thorough analysis leads to greater insights about the target market, their experience with the property, and experience with your brand, opening up numerous channels for creativity. This is about building empathy, something that's absolutely non-negotiable when you're trying to influence and align with people through something that matters to them.

Analysing your raw materials

Alongside developing empathy for the fan and/or customer experience, you need to analyse what you've got to work with. This is largely about cataloguing all of the marketing channels available to you, so you can leverage across them. This goes back to using sponsorship as a catalyst.

Unleash your creativity

Once you've developed that empathy, as well as a strong understanding of what raw materials you can work with, it's time for creativity.

This is where the leverage ideas flow, but they're not going to flow if you've put constraints on that creativity. Instead, you'll remove all of the normal rules, and reframe the process to foster great ideas.

I'm often asked whether this ends up with a whiteboard full of crazy, unfeasible ideas. The answer to that is . . . mostly no. Occasionally, I'll see an idea that is totally unrealistic. Dropping a dozen pianists playing grand pianos into a stadium with parachutes springs to mind. But most of the time, that background work on empathy and raw materials keeps ideas quite doable and strategic. And even if an idea isn't going to work, for whatever reason, there's every chance it could be fine-tuned or remixed into something that will.

It's consultative

This process won't work if you try to do it alone. The good news is that the process is straightforward, good fun, and it allows you to get your whole team — and your stakeholder group — involved and bought in. They will not only be helping to form your leverage plan, but your measurement plan as well. They will also be instrumental in the seamless implementation of those plans.

In addition, best-practice leverage requires almost a perfect balance between analytic, left-brain thinking, and creative, right-brain thinking. Working with your stakeholder group provides both a variety of perspectives and a group balance between those necessary strengths.

It's structured

Getting super-creative isn't just about saying, "Okay, people, give us some creative ideas!" It's about working step-by-step through a brainstorming process, giving your stakeholder group a range of angles and prompts, designed to elicit a broad range of creative ideas.

It's replicable

The process I'm about to introduce is 100% replicable. You can use these techniques across your whole portfolio of sponsorships, from major consumer sponsorships to industry association awards, to create amazing and totally different leverage plans every time.

You can use this process for:

- Individual sponsorships
- Vertically integrated portfolios
- Umbrella portfolios
- B2C, B2B, and B2G markets

There's more on vertically integrated and umbrella portfolios in Chapter 23: Structuring your portfolio.

When to do leverage planning

This leverage-planning process is valuable at several stages, providing you with ideas to start a new sponsorship off right, reinvigorate an underperforming sponsorship, and assist with renewal planning.

Before you negotiate a new sponsorship

As covered extensively in Part 2: Sponsorship Selection, I strongly recommend you work through this process with your sponsorship stakeholder group before negotiating a new sponsorship. Don't do this with every sponsorship opportunity that comes your way, just with the handful of shortlisted properties that have genuine potential for your brand.

Doing this process prior to negotiation has many benefits:

- You can gauge the degree of buy-in from the stakeholder group. You may think it's great, but if they don't, your leverage plan will be both less effective and more expensive.
- Stakeholders can flag any potential issues, or questions, for the rightsholder.
- You'll create a draft leverage plan, which can be fine-tuned and operationalised, should the sponsorship go ahead.
- You'll know exactly what benefits to negotiate, so that all of the stakeholders get what they need for their leverage plans.
- You'll know what the stakeholders think the sponsorship is worth, which may be more or less than the initial offer.
- You'll create a very preliminary measurement plan, committing stakeholders to nominating benchmarks and measurement mechanisms.

Before negotiating a renewal

This is a great idea for all of the reasons listed above. Plus, this is a good opportunity to work collaboratively with the rightsholder, who may have insights and ideas that you don't.

With existing sponsorships

If you've got existing sponsorships, where you know the leverage is underdone, use this process to overhaul what you do with it. Again, including the rightsholder can work really well.

Two recommendations:

1. Do this process as far in advance as you can, so you have ample time to implement your plan before the next event, season, or year of the sponsorship kicks off.
2. If you come up with ideas that require a different complement of benefits, don't panic. I've outlined how to go about mid-term renegotiations in Chapter 22. If you suspect your current contract doesn't provide for the benefits you need, one of the best things you can do is include the rightsholder in this process. Once they see the benefit to the fans and their property of swapping around a few benefits, they'll often be happy to oblige.

Who should be involved

I'll keep this short as I've addressed collaboration and stakeholders quite a lot already. Below are a couple of lists of the types of people you definitely and maybe want involved with this process. This is just a guideline. If your organisational structure is different, your lists may be different.

Definitely

- Frontline brand and/or sponsorship team members, tasked with managing the sponsorship.
- Your sponsorship stakeholder group. I note that they don't all have to be involved with every leverage-planning session, but you should have a cross-section.
- Regional marketing manager(s) from the region where the sponsorship is taking place. You should have some regional managers on your stakeholder team. This is about ensuring that you're involving the appropriate regional manager(s) for a geographically targeted property; ie, if you're in the home office leveraging a major festival in Gothenburg, you should have at least one frontline person from your Gothenburg region involved.

Maybe

- A senior executive, ideally your CMO or group brand manager. They don't have to be involved often, if they don't want to, but having a senior executive representative in the room occasionally can be very valuable.
- Agencies and consultants, if you're working closely with them on brand or sponsorship strategy or delivery, and you believe they'll be open to the process. (Not all of them are open to ideas that aren't theirs, unfortunately.)
- The rightsholder, if:
  - You've just closed the deal
  - You're in the middle of a contract
  - You're on renewal

Setting up for leverage planning

This process — the backgrounding, the brainstorming — takes up a lot of space, and you need to be set up for it.

The most important thing with the setup is that you have a way to reference all of the background material while you're doing the brainstorm.

My absolute favourite setup is a conference room that has entire whiteboard walls. (I'm a whiteboard nerd.) That way, you can use one section of the vast whiteboard space to capture the background material, and another section for your leverage ideas.

Your group will need a way to reference all of the background material while you're doing the brainstorm.

My second favourite, and how I facilitate this process 90% of the time, is to capture the background stuff on butcher paper, and the brainstorm on a big whiteboard. Just because it's easier to write on, I generally stick a couple of sheets of butcher paper to the empty whiteboard, fill them up, and put them up on the wall. I keep doing that until we're done with backgrounding, at which point there's usually six to eight sheets of butcher paper on the wall. Then we put the brainstorm ideas on the big whiteboard.

If you don't have one of those setups, just get creative. I've done this process plenty of times with just butcher paper, an easel, and some Blu Tack (or similar) to stick the butcher paper to the wall.

If you're doing this remotely, I suggest setting up a PowerPoint deck with a slide for each of the background sections, and lots of slides for ideas. You won't be able to use display mode, as you'll be editing the slides live, but this works just fine. I've done this dozens of times.

How long does this take?

The first time I do this with a client, I usually schedule two hours. After that, 90 minutes will usually suffice. You may want to schedule some extra time, until you get the hang of facilitating this process, but it will eventually speed up.

Working with huge properties, or a very large group, can take a bit longer. You want to budget about half the time for backgrounding and the second half for brainstorming.

Throughout the process, you need to keep it moving at a fast clip. Part of the reason for this is to keep to schedule, and the other part is to keep people from overthinking individual elements of the process. If they start to do that, remind them that this is a brainstorm, you're not committing to anything, and you'll vet everything at the end.

Leverage-planning process

You made it! Yes, I know . . . there was a lot of prep to get to this point, but I promise it will be worth it.

Once you've got your team and the sponsorship stakeholder group together, go through these steps one at a time. I've provided pertinent examples of sponsor leverage at the bottom of the pages, illustrating the types of ideas you're after for each brainstorm angle, noting that some case studies work for multiple angles. You can also use these case studies as thought-starters if you hit a lull.

Please note, none of the background steps needs to be exhaustive. If you get 80% of the way there with each of the steps, that will give you plenty to work with in the brainstorm.

When you get to the brainstorm steps, you're likely to think there's a lot of them, and this is just going to take too much time. Here's the thing: **You don't need to do every single**

step of the brainstorm. My suggestion is to do what I do with clients: Make some of the steps must-do, and add other steps as warranted by the particular sponsorship you're leveraging.

The must-do brainstorm steps are 1—4, 6, and 11. These form the core of the exercise. When you're planning the session, you can keep it simple and stick to these, which you may want to do your first couple of times facilitating it. You can also add in additional steps, as required. Don't be shy about adding steps, particularly as you get comfortable with the process. It's steps 1—4 that take easily the most time. Beyond that, most of them are really quick.

Finally, if your group is finding a particular brainstorm step uninspiring, don't keep pushing. Just move onto the next step. You'll also find that there are fewer and fewer new ideas as you progress, and the process will keep speeding up. This is normal and happens because you're looking at the opportunity from a bunch of angles, which can cross over each other.

Prelim: Introduce the opportunity

The very first step, once you've got your group assembled, is to briefly introduce the opportunity. You want to go through why it's been shortlisted and brought to this group. This will give some context around the target market and attribute or theme matches you've identified.

> The must-do brainstorm steps are 1-4, 6, and 11.

Examples: Adding value

As Brazil prepared to host the soccer World Cup, locals wanted to do all they could to support and inspire the home team. Brazilian bank **Itau** stepped in to help. They toured all over the country with high-tech soccer balls featuring sensors on the sides. Fans could hold the ball, and it would record their heartbeats as sound waves. Families of the team and Brazilian soccer legends also participated. All of the crowdsourced heartbeats were amalgamated into one heartbeat, in one ball, which was provided to the team before the competition, so they could literally hold the heartbeat of a nation in their hands.

Irish newspaper **An Post** used their sponsorship of the Irish Book Awards to re-establish relevancy with young families; an important segment for their new ecommerce and financial services offerings. As part of their sponsorship, An Post worked with the Dolly Parton Imagination Library to deliver 200,000 free books to kids in disadvantaged areas of Cork and Dublin. They also gave away books on World Book Day and launched a teacher-designed schools program called "Brain Busters", building children's literacy and numeracy skills.

You should also touch on any issues you've identified. If, for instance, the initial offer is based around commodity benefits, tell them that.

You also want to quickly overview the goals. You're doing this to:

- Assess the opportunity
- Create a draft leverage plan, so you know what benefits everyone will need
- Capture a preliminary measurement plan
- Understand the degree of buy-in — which business units see value in leveraging across their markets and channels

Backgrounding step 1: Your target markets

Which target markets do you want to influence with this sponsorship?

For consumer markets, try to use psychographic segments. If you use personas, it's fine to use them here.

For B2B and B2C markets, you're not targeting companies because they don't make decisions. You're targeting decision-makers and decision-influencers, so specify the role. You can also specify the size and type of company, if that's pertinent.

For intermediary markets, specify exactly what role(s) you're targeting. Retail buyers (people who decide what products to stock)? Store managers? Dealership managers? Finance broker management? Individual finance brokers?

For internal markets, be specific. Are you influencing all staff? Staff in just one location or one business unit? Are you targeting new recruits?

Backgrounding step 2: Your overall marketing and business objectives

What are you trying to achieve with these markets? You're looking for overall marketing objectives, which all come down to one of three things:

1. Changing or reinforcing perceptions
2. Changing or reinforcing behaviours
3. Building brand alignment

Do NOT let people nominate mechanisms, like "get awareness" or "do hospitality". If they start down that track, pull them up, saying, "That's a mechanism, not an objective. Let's say we do great VIP hospitality; how does that affect how our enterprise clients perceive the brand? Behave around the brand? Align with our brand?" This technique can be used to turn any mechanism into a real objective.

You also want to look at larger business objectives, which could include things like:

- Does your company have a stated purpose or values that legitimately guide how you operate?

> Do you want to underpin your corporate culture or change it?

> Do you have an issue with attracting or retaining talent?

Backgrounding step 3: Brand touchpoints

In this step, you just want to generate a list of all of your brand touchpoints — ways that people come in contact with your brand. This step is generally very fast.

Below is a sample of some brand touchpoints. Again, while these may be different for your type of brand or company, this should provide a good starting point:

> Buying/using your brand

> Social media content and promotions

> Apps

> Ambassadors/influencers

> Brand website

> Brand packaging

> Advertising — above-the-line, social, search

> Promotions — media, retail, on- or in-pack, online, etc.

> EDMs

> Collateral materials

> Retail or branch experience — flagship store, multi-brand retailers, etc.

> ATMs

> Loyalty marketing programs

> Branded vehicles

> Statements/bills

> Cards

> In-flight materials

> Customer service

> Service, maintenance, warrantees

> Corporate culture-building activities

> Staff training, team building

> Shareholder communications, annual reports

> Retail or broker incentives

> Other sponsorships

Backgrounding step 4: Property's larger themes

Now, we're moving to analysing the property.

In this step, I want you to list all of the larger themes around the property that you can think of. For instance, if the property is a women's professional soccer league, the larger themes would include things like:

- Fitness
- Teamwork
- Talent
- Discipline
- Determination
- Empowering women and girls
- Equality/equity
- Heroes
- Role models

Your list may be a little shorter than this, or it could be a lot longer. Either way, this is likely to be another reasonably quick step in the process.

Backgrounding step 5: Property market segments

This is a two-part process.

Part 1: What are the different reasons people care about this property? What is their motivation to want to be involved?

This is about digging into the meaning and passion behind the fans' relationship with the property, and can vary quite a lot between one property and another. Two examples:

National industry conference	Cancer charity fun run
Learn new skills/stay up to date	Personally affected (self or family)
Network with peers	Empathy
Lay the groundwork for a new job	Camaraderie/social
Party (yes, this is a genuine motivation!)	Peer pressure

Examples: Adding value

In 2022, brewer **Carlton Draught** leveraged their sponsorship of the Australian Football League right into the grassroots, by offering eight footy legends that would be "drafted" to local clubs. Clubs could sign up for the chance to have a footy legend play for their local team in one match, followed by a draft day, and then the matches, creating a great match day, plus plenty of content for Aussie Rules fans across the country.

During NCAA Basketball's March Madness, **Nissan** worked with the broadcaster on the NCAA Bracket Challenge. This included providing fans with the opportunity to participate in a call with the **Nissan** Bracket Engineer, former basketball legend, now commentator, Kenny "The Jet" Smith, who provided advice on how to make their picks.

We're capturing the main motivations here, understanding that there could be a lot of cross-over with secondary motivations. For instance, the primary motivation for someone to participate in the cancer fun run might be because their sister is currently fighting cancer, with the secondary motivation around camaraderie.

Part 2: If you gave a representative of each motivation – a flagbearer – a magic wand, what would they want?

This is about getting deeper into the mindset, and will clarify the differences between the motivations. This is critical if you want to accurately hit their hot buttons.

So, what would these flagbearers want, if they could have anything? These things don't have to be realistic and could fall into any of the following categories:

- Their fan experience with the property
- The larger fan experience – outside factors that can impact on their experience
- The larger theme(s)

Backgrounding step 6: Fan experience best and worst

This is a different way of looking at the fan experience, and like the magic wand exercise, can net you a lot of empathy-building information.

I suggest asking both the best and worst questions at the same time, building both lists simultaneously. People tend to jump between best and worst, and this is the quickest way to capture everything.

- What are the best things about this property?
  - The stuff they love?
  - Most desirable or appealing?
  - The things they want more of?
  - What they talk about to others?
- What are the worst things?
  - Least convenient?
  - Least accessible?
  - Most disappointing?
  - Least relevant?
- What about the remote fans? Do they have any specific challenges?
- What about fans of the larger themes?

In some cases, the best things for some people may be the worst for others. For instance, some people love the tribal feeling of being in a likeminded crowd (like at a game), while other people hate crowds.

Importantly, by identifying the worst things, we're not taking the crap out of the property. We're simply identifying things that could be improved, and all fan experiences can be improved!

You may be asking yourself (or your group may ask), what if none of us have ever experienced this particular property firsthand? Honestly, the best and worst things in a particular category — music festivals, professional sports, museums, etc. — are often very similar, so even though you may miss a couple of things, you should still be able to infer a lot.

Backgrounding step 7: Fan experience touchpoints

This is the property version of your brand touchpoints, and should be quite easy to knock out.

In my experience, people around the table often pull out their devices and take a look at the property or rightsholder website and/or socials, looking for touchpoints that may be relevant but aren't indicated in the initial proposal. You also want to keep in mind that some of the fan experience touchpoints may not be controlled by the property.

Below is a list of sample fan experience touchpoints. The property you're working with may have some different touchpoints, but this will give you a starting place:

- Attending in person
- Watching a broadcast (TV, streaming platform, social)
- Social media — rightsholder, participants, attendees
- Property website
- Rightsholder website (the rightsholder may have an overarching website, and a different website for the specific property)
- Advertising — above-the-line, social, search
- Ambassadors/influencers
- Ticketing
- Donations
- Volunteering
- Membership
- Hospitality
- Buying merchandise
- Launch
- Editorial coverage in media
- Newsletters or other EDMs
- Related online communities (eg, Taylor Swift fan pages)
- Street or other signage
- Seeing the venue
- Gambling or tipping
- Transport, parking
- "What's on" listings

If you prefer, you can make up this list on your own prior to going into a leverage-planning session with your stakeholder group. I generally do it with the group as it's quick and encourages participants to be both scrappy and thorough in assessing the property's various marketing channels.

Brainstorm rules

You're now done with the backgrounding. If your meeting room looks anything like when I facilitate this process with corporate clients, you'll have butcher paper with all the backgrounding material all over the walls, and a group of people who are warmed up and ready to brainstorm.

This is the point where you switch from assessing raw materials and building empathy, to unleashing the group's creativity. To do that, you need to remove all of the constraints. This is the way I introduce this to my clients:

- There are no rules.
- You – the people in the room – own the company.
- You have unlimited funds.
- No one will say no to you, and there are no politics.
- Anything is feasible.
- You can have any benefits you want from the rightsholder.

You may get some questions about that last point. I answer those questions like this:

> To get the best, most creative ideas, we're removing that constraint. That said, if we have a fantastic idea that requires a very creative or different benefit from the rightsholder, there's every chance we can get it – or something like it – if we can demonstrate how it's good for the property and the fan experience.

Brainstorm step 1: Magic wand

Referring to the property's market segmentation – and particularly the magic wand part – from step 5 of the backgrounding, ask the group:

- Can we help your target markets get what they want?
- If you can't get them exactly what they want, can you get them closer?

This is about creating small, meaningful wins for lots of people. If you have ideas around giving those fans exactly what they want, great. If it's just about getting them a little bit closer (like the Weet-Bix example below), that's also powerful, as long as it's meaningful. The fact that the starting place is the magic wand exercise keeps it meaningful.

If someone does nominate an idea where just one person – or a relative few people – win some big prize, point out the issue with that, and ask a few questions that can create more wins around the idea:

- Can we ask our customers or fans to nominate potential winners?
- Can they vote on the winner?
- Can they audition to win — video, photo, story, or ?
- Can we create compelling content around the experience the winner has? Behind the scenes? Day in the life?
- Can the winner(s) create content for you themselves, like being a citizen journalist or photographer at an event? Live blogging it? Providing daily updates?

Taking a one- or few-winner prize and adding angles, like those outlined above, creates lots of small wins for fans and customers.

Pro tip: My experience is that either this step (magic wand) OR the next step (best and worst) will net a ton of ideas, while the other is much less fruitful. I don't know why and haven't found any patterns as to why one often works better than the other. If you find the same thing, don't panic. Just move on.

Example: Using the magic wand

New Zealand's leading cereal brand, **Weet-Bix**, is one of the smallest sponsors of the revered national rugby team, the All Blacks. Years ago, I worked with them to make this small sponsorship deliver big on their two main goals: Increasing market share; and getting all New Zealanders – and particularly kids under 12, who are forming their lifelong health habits – to eat healthily and exercise regularly.

The exercise started with giving the kid a wand. What would he (we settled on a nine-year-old boy from Dunedin) want from the All Blacks, if he could have anything? We came up with meeting the All Blacks, being an All Black, running onto the field with the team, training with the team, bringing an All Black to school for show-and-tell, and heaps more in that vein. It was clear that, even in a country with around 4 million people at the time, there was no way to deliver those actual wishes to all or most of the kids Weet-Bix was targeting. So, we looked at the theme, and found that the overarching theme was that the kid wanted to get closer to his heroes.

Weet-Bix then came up with ideas for getting kids that little bit closer. They launched the first-ever All Blacks trading cards, which were so popular they had to limit people from buying no more than 16 boxes of cereal at a time. They did a face-matching app, where you could find out which All Black you looked most like, and half of all New Zealanders participated. There have been many other blockbuster ideas from Weet-Bix over the years – they just keep getting better at this! – but it all started with understanding the dreams of the flagbearer.

Brainstorm step 2: Fan experience

Referring to your list of the best and worst things about the fan experience, ask these questions:

> How can we amplify the best stuff about this property?
> - Make their experience bigger and better?
> - Make them more a part of the experience, closer to it?
> - Extend the timeframe (eg, make a concert experience last days or weeks longer, before and after the concert)?
> - Help the target market achieve their own goals (eg, marathon runners to get a personal best time)?
> - Give them more input, a stronger voice?
> - Give them more information, insights, advice, or inspiration?
> - Amplify their contribution (eg, providing a donation for every staff member that participates in Movember fundraising)?
> - What about remote fans?

Examples: Adding value

In the lead-up to the 2010 Winter Olympics, Canadian brewer **Molsen** undertook a range of activities created to share and amplify Canadians' national pride, including a "Made from Canada Rally Book" with thousands of fan messages from every corner of Canada, and presented to the Canadian Hockey Team before a crucial game. Molsen also created a 4,000-square-foot mural made up of fan photos submitted on their website and displayed on an outer wall of their Vancouver brewery, fronting the Olympic fan zone.

In Sweden, **Adidas** became a hub of information for Muslim athletes trying to stay fit during the month of Ramadan, when they're fasting from sunrise to sunset every day. Adidas used several of their Muslim brand ambassadors to front the video content, providing advice for athletes at all levels who are contemplating having to choose between fasting and fitness.

This isn't a sponsorship, but it really should have been, and illustrates a great angle for sponsors. During COVID lockdowns, Swiss ice hockey team ZSC Lions decided to celebrate and thank the fans that still supported them, even when they couldn't be there in person. Their idea was that, if you can't bring the fans to the rink, bring the rink to the fans. They melted the stadium ice, filling small bottles for each of the 4,000 season ticket holders, gifting them with the "essence of Lions".

How can we improve the bad stuff?
- Improve convenience or accessibility?
- Alleviate annoyances and frustrations?
- Make it easier for them to be there or participate?
- What about the bad stuff for remote fans?

Again, the goal is small, meaningful benefits for all or most of your target market.

Examples: B2B added value around conferences, expos, and awards

If you sponsor conferences, expos, and awards, you've got lots of ways to add real value to target markets. Here are a few, to get you started:

- For expos that cross into a weekend, you often see small businesspeople bring their kids. Could you provide childcare for a couple of hours?
- For destination conferences, where people often bring their spouses/partners, could you offer an expert concierge on-site to make recommendations, bookings, and arrange airport transfers?
- Could you do content curation, so people could answer a few questions, and you could recommend the must-see sessions? Or curate content for your customers that would be interested but weren't there?
- Could you get an international keynote to answer 15–20 questions crowdsourced from your customers and social followers?
- Could you do a VIP Q&A right after a keynote has come off stage? Small group, frank discussion?
- Could you crowdsource a citizen journalist from fans, customers, or followers, who will get to attend at your cost, but will churn out real-time insights and analysis from key aspects of the event?

And here's one that requires a little more than a bullet point: Instead of offering a prize to be drawn at an awards dinner, why not do some maths and make it meaningful? (I've done these actual maths for a great result for a sponsor!) Instead of donating some $10k prize that people don't want, we divided it by the 400 people in attendance. That equated to $25 each. We put a card on every place setting, asking people to nominate which one of a few related charities they want $25 to be donated to, and then put their card in a bowl on their table. For instance, if the awards were for the building trades, charities could be around homelessness or housing. Well, people bloody couldn't stop talking about it because it had meaning to them.

Brainstorm step 3: Sponsor-generated content

This step is all about content creation by your brand. I've listed a bunch of options for creating this content below, and there are examples of most of those options as well.

- Episodic video content:
  - Whose stories can we tell? Who can we champion?
  - Can we showcase different angles for each episode, or different stories, or a single storyline that builds over time?
- Augmented reality:
  - How can we use augmented reality to provide fans with more info?
  - Put people in the picture (eg, like the Dallas Cowboys and AT&T, below)?
  - Enhance the in-real-life experience?
  - Can we integrate something into our app?
- Artificial intelligence:
  - Can we do predictive analysis?
  - Deep fakes, facial mapping?
  - Crowdsourcing and creation (eg, music festival-goers text or hashtag a selfie, which gets amalgamated into a huge picture of the next artist on the main stage)?

    (What you can do with AI is exploding, so this may be a very long list by the time you read this book!)

Examples: Episodic video

With war raging in Ukraine, and Mariupol largely reduced to rubble, FC Mariupol relocated to Brazil, where they were roundly supported by the local community. Brazilian brewer, **Brahma** used their strong soccer credentials to support the move, creating a video series, website, and experiential leverage activities around "The Exiled Team", focusing on the two countries' love of soccer, and keeping the dream going in a time of crisis.

In 2017, **Amazon India** became presenting sponsor of the Indian Premier League – the top professional cricket league in the cricket-mad country. As part of the leverage program, they created "India ke Sapno ki Apni Dukaan", which translates to India's Dream Shopping Store. This all rolled out over a 46-video story arc – 46! – following a cricket coach trying to establish a cricket team in a fictitious city, Chonkpur, to play in a T20 (cricket's shortest form) cricket tournament. The storyline involved a major Indian rapper, women's empowerment, how to eat healthily, merchandise for this fictitious cricket club, and lots and lots of Amazon products. It was incredibly well done, and a massive hit with cricket fans.

≫ Virtual reality:

- What would the fans really like to experience?
- Does it need to be on-site? Could you do a VR-lite experience using an app on people's phones?

  (VR is not applicable to all properties.)

≫ Can we use technology to create personalised content?

- Videos, photos?
- Icons, profile pictures?
- Quizzes or matching (eg, quiz to determine fans' summer style, then matching with team members that share your style)?
- Content curation (eg, answer five questions and we'll tell you which art festival exhibitions you shouldn't miss)?

≫ Gamification:

- Can we gamify part of the fan experience?
- Should it be competitive with other fans, or just for fun?

Any other content we can create for fans or customers?

Examples: Augmented reality

As part of their sponsorship of Wimbledon, **American Express** created a 90-second augmented-reality game, called Champion's Rally, with Andy Murray providing coaching to players. As the game gets harder, people can earn more Wimbledon features, and Amex cardholders can win actual prizes. Because it's AR, fans can play from wherever they like, and at the end of the game, cardholders can post a selfie on the Amex Wall of Champions.

When **Snapchat** users scanned the cover of *Billboard* magazine devoted to the Lollapalooza music festival, an augmented-reality Hot Dog and Robot Speaker came to life in 3D, along with an interactive, 3D map of the festival. This sponsorship also featured a Friend FindAR function, helping people to find their friends in the huge crowd.

Pay particular attention to this Snapchat example, as wayfinding lenses and AR apps are a big trend for helping fans navigate large and/or complex events.

Examples: Artificial intelligence

In one of the first iterations of AI and face mapping with sponsorship, potato chip brand **Lays** created an amazing video generator in the lead-up to the UEFA Champions League. Messi Messages used artificial intelligence for fans to create and send someone a personalised video from soccer superstar Lionel Messi, in any of 10 languages. This was slightly clunky, but with advances in AI, doing this kind of thing is going to be much easier, and with a better result for fans.

At the British Open Golf, IT services provider **NTT Data** used their technology and expertise to create ShotView, allowing fans – attendees and remote – and journalists an interactive platform to access millions of collated data points around thousands of shots, in real time. Considering many of their clients and buyers would surely be golf fans, this was an outstanding demonstration of their capabilities.

Examples: Gamification

In 2019, **Jaguar** created a fantastic – and totally scalable – app to leverage their sponsorship of Wimbledon. They created the Jaguar Ace Pace app, which used the gyroscope and accelerometer on your smartphone to calculate the speed of your serve. If you were on-site, you could use the app in a booth, giving a near-VR experience, showing the speed and trajectory of your serve.

For the 2023/24 US football season, spirits brand **Captain Morgan** rolled out a season-long scavenger hunt. Fans were encouraged to "Follow the Captain" using a series of QR codes, giving them opportunities to win gridiron and brand prizes. The leverage campaign starred rappers, Action Bronson and Aminé, musician Bebe Rexha, and former NFL player Victor Cruz, and the premise was that anything could be a clue – an ad, social post, a person or place, anything – and that fans had to pay attention to win. The game was made to be so much fun that, even if you didn't win a prize, you still got a win.

Examples: Virtual reality

The Victoria & Albert Museum sponsor **HTC VIVE Arts** had created a VR experience for the Alice: Curiouser and Curiouser exhibition, so attendees could experience an immersive, virtual Wonderland. When COVID shut down the in-person experience, HTC VIVE Arts pivoted, creating a home version of that immersive experience.

As amply covered earlier in this book, VR experiences sound fantastic. The issue – for now – is scalability.

Brainstorm step 4: Fan/customer-generated content

This step is about your brand asking fans and/or customers to create content. This tends to be quick, easy, and cheap to do, and gives those fans and customers a lot of ownership. You can also amplify and champion the people who participate, which most people love.

➢ Can we provide ways for our target markets to create content, such as:
  • Telling their stories
  • Crowdsourcing
  • Uploading pertinent photos, videos, artwork
  • Nominations, auditions
  • Providing property-driven feedback, input
  • Voting
  • Q&A, debate
  • Reviews

Examples: Fan/customer-generated content

New Zealand petrol chain **Z Energy** took up naming rights of the brand-new Z Manu World Championships. "Manu" is an NZ specialty – a type of bomb into water, with the goal to make the biggest splash. As part of their leverage, Z created the Z Manu Wildcards, a fast track to the finals of the Z Manu World Champs. Participants shared their best manu on their/Z's socials, with the best 20 going head to head, with NZ voting on the wildcards. The 10 chosen by NZ got fast-tracked into the grand final in Auckland Harbour.

In 2021, Australian Open naming rights sponsor **Kia** created what they called "the world's most innovative tennis rally". Using their ambassador, Rafael Nadal, they invited fans around the world to create a 10-second video of themselves returning a tennis shot, in the most innovative way possible, then post it with the hashtag #MakeYourMove. The most creative entries were featured in a mash-up film of the world rallying with Nadal.

Prior to the 2023 Rugby World Cup, sponsor **Cadbury** asked fans of the Australian national team, the Wallabies, to donate their lucky charms. The charms were collected on the Wallabies' Gold Blooded tour of Australian rugby clubs, and included lucky keyrings, socks, charms, jerseys, scarves, and all manner of other lucky stuff. Donation bins were also located at Wallabies games, in the lead-up to the RWC. These charms were then reworked into a 20-metre-long scarf – the world's luckiest charm.

Nickelodeon Australia partnered with Kids Help Line to create the Dare to be Square initiative. Australian superstar Guy Sebastian wrote the song and invited kids across Australia to submit videos of themselves singing the chorus. Many of those videos were incorporated into his performance at the Nickelodeon Slimefest, and the video was made available on YouTube.

➢ What's the mechanism?
- Social?
- App?
- Website?
- In person (eg, a video booth at an event, or at retail)?

Brainstorm step 5: Branding real estate

If you accept that logo exposure has limited value — and it does — you have the option of using some of the branding real estate you get in your contract to do other things.

It may seem counterintuitive, but this can be very powerful — certainly more powerful than one more logo from an already well-known brand. There are some good examples below:

➢ Could we swap our logo or other branding real estate for:
- Someone's name (eg, crowdsource a bunch of local heroes, and put their names in place of the logo on a team's sleeves)?

Examples: Branding real estate

Since 2007, **Swedbank** had naming rights to Sweden's national stadium. Swedbank is also a longtime partner of anti-bullying charity Friends. In 2012, Swedbank negotiated an additional 12-year naming rights deal, but gifted naming rights to Friends, so the stadium is now known as Friends Arena. This has raised the profile of Friends and created ample opportunity for cross-pollinating the two sponsorships, while Swedbank still has all of the other sponsorship benefits to drive their brand.

State of Origin is a uniquely Australian sports event, pitting teams of professional rugby league players who grew up in the two main rugby league states – NSW and Queensland – against each other in a best-of-three series. Longtime sponsor of Queensland, local brewer **XXXX** (pronounced "four X"), decided to change up their extremely well-known logo. Instead of the distinctive XXXX, they swapped in the 4-digit postcode where each Queensland player grew up, in an initiative they called "We give a XXXX about Queensland this State of Origin". From big cities to regional centres to tiny towns, they were on display on the sleeve of their hometown heroes, reinforcing the parochialism that is so much a part of the XXXX brand.

Same team, different sponsor! When **Personalised Plates Queensland** took up a sponsorship of QLD's State of Origin team, they negotiated rights to the players' training jerseys. But instead of the player names on the back, each player picked a customised licence plate showcase instead, promoting their creativity and humour.

> A charity we crowdsource from customers or fans?
>   • One or a few versions of your logo, drawn by kids (eg, kids in hospital, or little kids playing that sport)?
> If applicable, could we gift naming rights to someone or something else?
>   • Gift it to the fans by reverting a stadium to its original, historic name?
>   • Gift it to a charity?

Brainstorm step 6: Brand experience

This step is about integrating the sponsorship across your touchpoints. As covered in Chapter 12: Leverage funding, taking this approach can dramatically increase your effectiveness, while dramatically reducing the cost of your leverage program.

At this point, you've probably already come up with a lot of ideas in this category, but you still want to do this, ensuring you're thorough.

Example: Brand experience

A few years back, Northern Ireland's Action Cancer charity could have told you that more women died of breast cancer in Northern Ireland than anywhere else in the developed world. They knew a big reason for that was because many of the women most at risk were so conservative that they didn't seek out information on mammograms, self-exams, etc. Basically, nice women didn't talk about tits, and this was a huge problem.

At the same time, local producer **Nambarrie Tea** were under fire from global tea brands, using their resources to try to drive them out of business, so shoring up loyalty was a huge concern.

The two organisations got together and did three major initiatives. First, Nambarrie created a cents-per-purchase cause-related marketing offer, providing a donation to Action Cancer for every purchase. Nambarrie also helped with their Pink Ribbon campaign, getting their box manufacturer to make the donation boxes, using their staff to pack them with ribbons, and using their route drivers to drop the boxes to retailers across Northern Ireland, along with tea orders, and picking them up at the end of the month. This saved Action Cancer an enormous amount of money.

The final initiative was the blockbuster. Without any clue on the outside of the tea boxes, the inside cover featured breast self-exam instructions and a special hotline to book a mammogram. They basically smuggled the info they needed into women's homes. Calls to the hotline skyrocketed, and there's no question this saved lives.

The starting point for this step is your list of brand touchpoints.

➤ Can we use this sponsorship to improve, add value, or add power to the brand experience? Can you:
- Theme an ad?
- Put something in our newsletter?
- Promote a sponsorship-driven customer offer on our monthly statements?
- Do something in-store or in our branches?

Keep going, pointing out touchpoints you haven't considered yet.

➤ Can we take inspiration from the property to change or improve your products or touchpoints? Can we:
- Create a limited edition?
- Get the fans to vote or otherwise crowdsource something brand related (eg, limited edition packaging, limited edition flavour)?

Examples: Brand experience

Convenience retailer **Circle K** was new in Ireland in 2018, making a big splash with sponsorship of the Irish Olympic and Paralympic Teams. In 2019, they launched an initiative where customers could generate digital coins, which would then be provided to athletes, so they could purchase fuel and other items from the shops. When COVID postponed the Games until 2021, it was hard on athletes, including financially, so Circle K did a big final push for coins. In the end, over €1 million was raised and distributed to athletes, and Circle K cemented themselves as part of Ireland.

Hyundai sponsored the hit program *Walking Dead*. To highlight the safety features of their cars, they created an app allowing people to virtually customise a Hyundai Zombie Survival Machine and share with their network.

Brainstorm step 7: VIPs

This step is about adding value to VIP relationships, such as major customers, but going beyond standard (boring) hospitality. Remember, hospitality isn't necessarily about doing something luxurious. Anyone can do that. It's about doing something special, meaningful, and memorable.

> Thinking outside standard hospitality options, can we:
> - Do an inner-sanctum or insider experience for VIPs?
> - Create a what-money-can't-buy one-off experience (eg, private orchestra performance at a lighthouse, overlooking the sea)?
> - Create a day-in-the-life experience?
> - Involve kids or grandkids? (This is a big trend, and always a hit!)
> - Do VIP volunteerism (eg, a Habitat for Humanity build day)?

Examples: VIPs

Cosmetics brand **MAC** sponsored New Zealand Fashion Week. And while they are a consumer brand, their main aim with NZFW was to increase preference and advocacy among makeup artists and stylists. One of the challenges for that market was lugging gear around from show to show to receptions, so **MAC** created secure, VIP, invitation-only lockers for them. Receiving a locker invitation in the run-up was an industry cue that NZFW was just around the corner, and a sign that up-and-comers had arrived in the big league, with recipients sharing their appreciation widely.

As part of their sponsorship of the UK's "home of cultural innovators" Somerset House, financial services firm **Morgan Stanley** has created a series of "Lates" for their VIPs. These take place three times a year, offering a site-wide takeover, featuring exclusive, what-money-can't-buy experiences, and after-hours content and activities hosted by curators and artists.

Red Bull, true to its push-the-boundaries brand, created one of the most epic sports hospitality experiences ever, for their VIP customers, celebrities, and Red Bull athletes. At the 2023 British Grand Prix, and in conjunction with Red Bull Racing, they created a bespoke hospitality mecca. Located on the iconic start–finish straight, it featured a nightclub with famous DJs (also providing music for the grid!), a video wall, driver Q&As, art installations, and a skatepark on the roof. If you're going to do "elevated" sports hospitality, it doesn't get much more elevated than this.

➤ Can we amp-up existing hospitality options?
  • Make them more experiential?
  • Make them kid-friendly?
  • Do literally anything to get away from the same-old hospitality that every company does?
➤ Can we pass through any benefits to them?

Brainstorm step 8a: Intermediary markets

You'll either do step 8a, step 8b, or skip step 8 altogether. If you sell through an intermediary market, you'll do step 8a. If your brand *is* a retailer, you'll do step 8b. If your brand is direct to consumer and sells only your own products or services, such as most parts of a bank, you'll skip step 8.

Example: VIP pass-through

I once worked with a major bank that had too much hospitality. They had boxes at all the stadiums and arenas, receptions at the ballet and opera, and more. They had way too much hospitality, so it was underused, and often not used at all.

I worked with them to reduce their hospitality to only the really good stuff, and pass the other hospitality along to major business customers, who often don't have their own hospitality spaces or opportunities. The bank, for instance, kept the opening night receptions at the art museum, but gave the other receptions to their major customer management business unit, to pass along to *their* customers. So, instead of inviting a VIP customer for beers in a corporate box, the bank literally gave the corporate box to that VIP for the day, so they could entertain their own customers. That was repeated across the whole portfolio of hospitality.

Example: Intermediary markets

At the **Toyota** Owners Hospitality Tent at NASCAR races, Toyota, Lexus, and Scion owners simply have to show their car key to allow access for them and a guest. Inside the tent, owners find a relaxing place to hang out before the race, with complimentary refreshments, giveaways, and a chance to meet Toyota NASCAR drivers. Toyota partners with local dealerships to identify and invite current owners to events, with dealerships reporting multiple sales as a direct result.

Intermediary markets refers to retailers, dealerships, brokers, travel agents, resellers, and anyone else that operates as a middleman between your brand and the end-user. You can certainly use the ideas from step 7 for intermediary markets, but there are a few extra things you can do.

➢ In addition to VIP leverage ideas, can we:
- Bring the property to them (eg, bringing a fan leverage activity to a dealership)?
- Create retail promotions?
- Create ways for them to reward *their* VIP customers (eg, grocery rewards members, frequent purchasers)?

Brainstorm step 8b: Vendors (for retailers only)

For the uninitiated, vendors are the brands a retailer sells. A hardware store sells Dulux paint, Makita tools, and much more. A grocery retailer sells Skippy peanut butter, Old El Paso taco shells, and much more. A telecom sells a variety of mobile phones. They're all vendors.

allowances are pools of money vendors can pay to retailers for involvement in in-store promotions, preferential positioning, and specials. If a retailer can involve selected vendors in a sponsorship, you can often access vendor allowances, reducing your out-of-pocket costs.

➢ With that in mind, can we:
- Create sponsorship-driven in-store promotions, involving vendors?
- Create sponsorship-driven in-store events, involving vendors?
- Recommend a complement of products relating to the sponsorship (eg, asthma-friendly products around the sponsorship of an asthma charity)?
- Create a sponsorship-driven co-promotion with a vendor (eg, a telecom doing a sponsorship-driven promotion with a mobile phone manufacturer)?

Example: Vendors

Stadium naming rights sponsor **AT&T** worked with the Dallas Cowboys and vendor **Samsung** to create a souvenir "Pose with the Pros" AR photo. Fans can choose their favourite Cowboys, and pose with them. A Samsung Galaxy S10 5G smartphone uses AR tech to superimpose the players and capture a photo that fans can then purchase.

Brainstorm step 9: Staff

We're onto your staff with step 9. It's always amazing to me how many leverage plans overlook staff, when it's usually quite straightforward to add value to them.

> Can we:
> - Involve staff in a meaningful way? Participation? Volunteerism?
> - Showcase or hero our staff (eg, showcase volunteers or a corporate triathlon team)?
> - Provide staff expertise to the property (eg, technical, creative, analytics)? Can we profile that expert team and what they do for the property?
> - Extend benefits to staff, families (eg, discounts, parking)?
> - Create a day for families and staff with the property?

Examples: Staff

Swedish sustainable social advisor and tech consultancy **Ramboll** took up naming rights of the Stockholm Half-Marathon. As part of their leverage, they created the first and only app for figure running, called ShapeRunner. It gives runners training routes in various shapes. (Yes, I'm sure someone has created routes in *that* shape.) Ramboll got staff involved in creating the shapes for the app, championing their ingenuity and getting them intrinsically involved in the leverage program.

ESL is one of the world's largest esports organisers, with a streaming audience of over 600 million people annually. **DHL**, well . . . you know who they are. DHL sponsored ESL with a big focus on recruiting staff from ESL's young, talent-rich audience. Working with ESL on three of their biggest gaming strands, and creating a lot of very relevant content on the DHL site and socials. DHL even created an EffiBot game, replete with an ESL World Championship. This was a big winner for recruitment, with 1,600 applications direct from the ESL audience, and a big jump in positive perceptions of DHL as an employer.

Brainstorm step 10: Demonstrating brand attributes

We're starting to wind this brainstorm down now, and these last couple of steps will go super-quick. You may well have ideas that already tick these boxes, but just to be thorough, you should still do these steps:

- How can we use the sponsorship to demonstrate key attributes of our brand? Maybe your brand is particularly helpful, or you don't make people wait on hold or talk to a bot? Maybe you make the world's most efficient washers and dryers, or you're all about wisdom and wise investments?
- How can we demonstrate that your brand cares about the same things as your target markets? Their passions? Concerns?
- How can we demonstrate that our brand is a real fan (just like them)?

Examples: Demonstrating brand attributes

Another mobile provider, but a different angle. Malaysia's **U Mobile** underpinned their overarching strategy of "bringing out the Unbeatable in everyone" with their sponsorship of the Malaysian Special Olympic Team. In the run-up to the Special Olympics World Games, U Mobile created a series of videos showcasing the unbeatable spirit of these Special Olympians, driving support for their efforts, as well as discussion around equality and equity in the intellectual disability community.

New Zealand bank **ASB** has been sponsoring NZ Rugby since 2015, including the All Blacks, the Black Ferns (women's team), and the Māori All Blacks. To demonstrate their commitment to SMEs, they gave away many of their rights to up to 100 SME businesses. This included getting a video ad starring one of the NZ players, which was then distributed through digital billboards, digital media, and socials.

ASB signed on as naming rights sponsor of NZ's home of rugby, Eden Park, for one week. ASB then extended the above initiative, loaning stadium naming rights to a local fish & chips shop, Cooper's Catch, during one of the biggest games on the annual rugby calendar.

Brainstorm step 11: Demonstrating alignment

This step is about showcasing your alignment – your like-mindedness – with fans, customers, staff, and anyone else you may be targeting:

- How can we demonstrate that our brand aligns with target market self-definitions (eg, cool, green, rev head, tech savvy, busy parent, ambitious, local pride)?
- How can we demonstrate that our brand cares about the same things as our target markets? Their passions? Concerns?
- How can we demonstrate that our brand is a real fan (just like them)?

Examples: Alignment

In 2022, **Principality Building Society** invited fans of the Welsh Rugby Union to nominate the "Unofficial Squad" of 15 Clubhouse Champions - people at the grassroots of Welsh rugby who make clubhouses feel like home. Over 800 nominations came in from fans, with the final 15 chosen by a panel including Welsh players. These grassroots heroes were championed in a multimedia campaign from Principality, and given VIP treatment at an international match.

Aussie telecom **Telstra** used their longstanding sponsorships of both the Australian Football League and the National Rugby League to hero local football clubs, players, and their communities. Their "This is Footy Country" ads are long, gloriously Australian and funny, and underpin their genuine commitment to, and affection for, regional Australia.

Promoting gender equality in sport, Equadorian bank **Banco Pichincha** used their major sponsorship of Liga Deportiva Universitaria de Quito football team to make a bold statement about the women's game. During a sold-out men's game, halftime featured an "invisible match", with three refs, *no players*, and a remote-controlled ball. The fans got right into it. Following the game, the men's team captain was shown on the big screen with this message, "Like this match, there are 234 matches that very few people see. It is very important that together we promote gender inclusion and equality in sports."

Brainstorm step 12: Demonstrating core values, corporate culture, and/or purpose

This final step is about the values and culture that genuinely drive your company, and could include aspects of DEI and ESG as well. Sustainability is becoming a key selection criterion for many sponsors:

- How can you use the sponsorship to demonstrate who you are and what you're about? Your brand values, corporate culture, purpose?
- How can we ensure our leverage is sustainable?
- Can we contribute to the property being more sustainable?
- Is there a diversity, equity, and/or inclusion aspect we can explore? (This may not be a natural fit for some sponsorships.)

Examples: Demonstrating values, corporate culture, and/ or purpose

Global sport retailer **Decathlon** created a brand-owned eCycling team for prisoners in a high-security prison in Belgium. Called "The Breakaway", this program gave prisoners a connection to the outside world via Zwift, a virtual world for millions of cyclists to race and ride together. Their training schedule was posted online and promoted on Facebook, so people around the world could join their rides. Prisoners got a personal training program, so they could compete against other teams and pro cyclists, and the whole project was documented in a four-episode podcast. The initiative supports Decathlon's vision of sport for all, and ran with the taglines, "Sport can free people" and, "Better than other riders. Better than themselves."

The University of Reading is a major sponsor of Reading Football Club. With sleeve branding on Reading FC's recycled jerseys, the uni turned the sleeves into climate stripes, showing Reading's average temperature over the course of years, with a series of blue and red (and increasingly red) stripes. This was used to promote the university's "Show Your Stripes" climate change initiative, now rolled out worldwide, with skyscrapers, stadiums, and signs lit up with climate stripes on Climate Stripe Day every year. You can get a set of climate stripes for your location at showyourstripes.info. Sydney's stripes are not good.

While UK men's soccer has plenty of fantasy football leagues, there weren't any for the huge UEFA Women's EURO tournament. As part of their Leveling the Playing Field initiative, **Starling Bank** stepped in and built one. They even provided expert tips for everything from choosing your players, balancing your fantasy budget, and naming your team.

Vetting

At this point, what you will be faced with is a whiteboard, or a lot of butcher paper, full of a vast array of ideas. You will probably also be faced with a room full of stakeholders who have had a lot of fun and are feeling pretty good about what they've just accomplished.

Some of the ideas will be gems — others, not so much — so the time has come to vet them. You'd think this process would be arduous, but you've got your team in a zone, and it tends to go quickly. When I do this with clients, it takes literally 5–10 minutes.

➢ Across all of the ideas you've come up with, ask your group to choose the best several ideas:

➢ You may amalgamate some ideas.

- Don't panic if you pick a lot of ideas. If you're looking at a multi-year contract, you want ideas that will be consistent year-on-year, ideas that will build over time, and ideas that you can snap in and out of the leverage program, keeping it fresh.
- Pro tip: Use a different colour whiteboard marker for vetting.

Once your group has picked favourites, ask them these questions:

➢ Have we achieved, or moved towards, each of our key objectives?

➢ Have we achieved win-win-win for each of our key target markets?

➢ What are the first steps to determine feasibility? Who is going to take those steps? (These should be people from the pertinent areas of the company.)

➢ What benefits will we need from the rightsholder to make them happen? Note, you can do this as a group, or you can work this out later.

You also want to ask these questions. The answers are usually "no", but occasionally, you'll have an idea that isn't so great, once you stand back and look at it in terms of fan and rightsholder wins.

➢ Is there anything here that detracts from the fan experience?

➢ Is there anything here that is bad for the rightsholder?

Measurement

You're on a roll now. You've got the stakeholders to buy-in to the value that sponsorship has to their area of the business, participate in the creative process, and commit to incorporating appropriate aspects of the leverage plan into their operations. DO NOT let them leave the room until you've got a commitment on measurement, as well.

Don't worry, this part is quick. It usually just takes a few minutes.

Say, for example, "Let's say this is all feasible and we make it happen. How will each area of the business measure your involvement? From what benchmarks?"

Tell them they don't have to be super-specific then and there, and that you know you've put them on the spot. If they can each nominate a couple of ways they could measure their involvement, and that they'll look into the appropriate benchmarks, you can always follow up on the specifics later.

Examples: More sponsor-generated content

There are so many great examples of sponsor-generated content that I couldn't fit them all into that section!

Using a combination of insights from their ambassadors and ChatGPT, **Under Armour** created the "most inspirational team talk of all time". The starting point was using ambassadors to hone in on the 12 most effective elements of a good team talk. The result was a powerful, 90-second speech, delivered by UK rapper Ashley Walters. While the result isn't about to replace a human coach (yet!), this opens up yet another way to leverage with AI.

Sports fans in my home state of Minnesota have been treated to the State High School Hockey Tournament "hockey hair" commentary for many, many years. In a state where every game of the high school hockey tournament is shown live on TV, hockey hair commentary is no less than a cult obsession. In recent years, budget haircutting chain **Great Clips** has taken up the hockey hair gauntlet with their sponsorship of the NHL, celebrating this hilariously quirky fixation. There's now a website, memes, videos, trivia, and a quiz, matching you to your #HockeyHair style. Mine is apparently "shaggy salad", which sounds about right.

While still in its infancy for sponsorship leverage, global mobile phone network **Vodafone** demonstrated its 5G technology in the world's first-ever hologram coaching session. Athlete ambassador Emma Raducanu delivered a coaching session live via hologram from Abu Dhabi to teenage tennis players 7,000 km away.

Hong Kong Sevens should be on every sports fan's bucket list. It's at least as much a party as a fast and furious rugby sevens tournament, with costumes, drinking, and lots of streaking on the field … or at least there used to be streaking. When security dictated that the field be secured from streakers, brewer **Carlsberg** took the opportunity to fill the void with a streaking app. Create a virtual facsimile of your naked self (from behind) and streak down the distinctive Hong Kong Stadium, with security in hot pursuit. It was irreverent and entertaining, and ended up going viral.

Investment firm **Charles Schwab** leveraged their sponsorship of the PGA Tour with a microsite featuring a series of golfing tips with Tiger Woods' former swing coach, Hank Haney. The site also featured a Game Tracker, and the novel Mental Game Assessment.

Once they've all committed to some degree of measurement, and you've written down that list, congratulate them on a job well done, and treat yourself to a nice cup of tea, a margarita, or the reward of your choice. You've earned it!

Brainstorm tricks

There are a couple of tricks I use in very specific situations. You wouldn't use these often, but they can work a treat.

Leverage on (almost) no budget

If your sponsorship stakeholder group – or your historic approach to sponsorship – looks at leverage as a huge expense, you can swap this step in. You would make the following changes:

- Don't tell the group they have unlimited funds in the brainstorm rules. You can tell them that after this new first step.
- Put this new brainstorm step in first, before the magic wand.
- Remove brainstorm step 6 as it will be redundant.

Tell the group that the first step in the brainstorm is about being super-resourceful and creative, and that once they've completed this step, they get an unlimited budget.

- With a maximum incremental spend of $3,000, what can we do with this sponsorship to:
  - Add value to our target market relationships?
  - Align with our target markets?
  - Demonstrate brand values, corporate culture, purpose?
  - Achieve brand goals?
- Start by integrating across things you're already spending money on, referencing your brand touchpoints:
  - How can we use sponsorship to make those touchpoints more powerful and relevant?
- New social media initiatives can also be cheap to implement.

When you start this step, I guarantee you that your group will be like a deer in headlights, but they will warm up. I often point to a couple of the channels, saying things like:

- How many new ads do we create a month? Could we theme one or more of them around this sponsorship?
- Are there any sponsorship-related stories we can tell in socials? People we could hero?

It usually only takes a couple of these before people start jumping in with lots of ideas, most of which will cost little to no money. Even if they do have an idea that costs more than $3,000, be sure to write it down. You don't want to waste creativity.

Once you've got a bunch of ideas, move onto the magic wand step.

Short lead time

If you've got a short lead time before the property kicks off, you may need to develop ideas that are super-quick to implement in the first year of the contract. I've got two easy strategies that will help you identify those short lead-time ideas:

> Ask your group which of your brand touchpoints could be planned, approved, and implemented in 4 weeks (put a "4" next to those touchpoints)? Then ask the same thing for 8 weeks (put an "8" next to those touchpoints)?

> At the vetting stage, once you've identified your favourite ideas, go back through and indicate the ones that are fast and easy enough to implement in year one, referencing your fast touchpoints. You can then use the rest of the ideas for years two, three, and beyond.

Creating a leverage idea bank

After you've finished the brainstorm, and the group has left, I strongly urge you to catalogue not just the ideas you've determined are best, but *all* of the ideas. You never know, an idea that's not right for this particular sponsorship could be perfect for another one.

One trick I share with clients is about marking up the ideas so they're sortable. You could do this in Excel or Google Sheets or some other simple, sortable spreadsheet. I suggest marking each idea with the following codes:

> B — This is for the best ideas; the super-strategic ones that add huge value to your target markets, while driving you closer to your objectives.

> E — This is for the easiest ideas; ones that aren't complex at all. Some might call them "no brainers".

> F — This is for the fastest ideas; the ones that can be approved and implemented super-quick. These ideas are great for short lead-time situations.

Importantly, ideas can be marked up with multiple codes. For instance, an idea could be both easy and fast. Or an idea could be fast and best. Or an idea could be all three. Your idea bank could look like this, making it simple to sort on B, E, or F:

Best	Easiest	Fastest	Leverage ideas
	E	F	**Idea #1 name** Outline of idea #1
B	E	F	**Idea #2 name** Outline of idea #2

To this list, add ideas from this book — the examples I give, the case studies. Over time, you'll end up with a robust list, allowing you to create leverage plans much easier and faster. You'll still need to collaborate, but you can start from your idea bank and build out from there.

I will say, however, that if you're looking at a sponsorship that is enormous, super-complex, or way outside of what you've done before, you'll still need to go through the entire brainstorm process. But once you're done, you'll have lots more ideas for your idea bank.

Chapter 15

Other leverage angles

In the previous chapter, I covered a lot of leverage angles. There are a few more that are less common, but that can still be excellent options, for the right sponsors.

Umbrella leverage programs

One option for consistent, cost-effective leverage is to create an umbrella leverage program. This is completely different than an umbrella portfolio, which I cover in detail in Chapter 23: Structuring your portfolio.

An umbrella leverage program includes one or more leverage strategies that you apply to all or most of your sponsorships, creating multiple wins for customers.

If you've got some easy way for people to show they're a customer — a card, a customer barcode in your app, car keys — negotiate every sponsorship so that you get at least one benefit you can pass directly through to your customers. Taken collectively, this can be a huge relationship-builder. A customer could get free entry to a museum for their family one weekend, better parking at the baseball the next weekend, and complimentary bag and pram check at a festival the week after that.

Examples: Umbrella leverage

A great (and somewhat vintage) example is **Bank of Montreal**. They created an umbrella leverage program spanning much of their diverse sponsorship portfolio. Customers who showed their BMO Mastercard or BMO debit card got access to a whole range of "Power of Blue" benefits, such as preferred parking, special event entrances, better seats, discounts, merchandise, celebrity appearances and more, creating a consistent "we're thinking about you" message.

American Express hosts exclusive concert afterparties for cardmembers. Billed as Amex Afters, cardmembers are treated to high-quality, immersive experiences, with exclusive performances, gifts, and other perks.

Because of the number of wins available to your customers, the wins don't have to be particularly big. Just look for something that can be scaled to all or most of your customers that will make their fan experience that little bit better.

People's choice

A natural extension of consumer-generated content is consumer choice — actually inviting your customers to have a say in what you sponsor or support.

On the surface, this would seem to be a brave choice, but the risks are more a perception than reality.

The first time I saw this in practice was quite a while ago, with a regional American telecommunications company — **Broadview Networks**. They allowed their customers to nominate a charity — any charity — and a portion of their bills would be donated to that charity. They then leveraged the whole program as one big sponsorship. On one hand, it seems crazy for a brand to offer the option for customers to donate to organisations that could be divisive — Greenpeace, Amnesty International, Planned Parenthood, Boy Scouts, etc. On the other, putting the choice into the customers' hands changes the rhetoric from "we support this charity" to "we support our customers' passions". The quote below says it better than I could:

> We don't have a social or political agenda but our customers do. We cut checks to churches, Boy Scout troops or the local garden club — as long as it's a 501-c3 not-for-profit group.
>
> Vern Kennedy, President and CEO, Broadview Networks.

Examples: People's choice

After polling music fans in Scotland, **Tennant's Lager** pledged £150,000 to create a series of music events. They then put the fans in charge, giving members of their Tennant's Mutual website voting privileges for key aspects of the gigs, including the bands, venues, and ticket price.

Pepsi Max sponsored the halftime show of the Canadian Football League's Grey Cup, their championship game. They allowed fans to logon to a website to create the playlist, voting for their favourites from halftime band Blue Rodeo, which were then played on the night.

Green Mountain Coffee worked with Changemakers to fund innovative ideas that improve local communities in the northeastern US. Nominations for the Revelation to Action come from those communities with voting for the organisations that receive grants.

The consumer choice trend seems to have more traction in the area of charitable giving but can be seen across everything from music to sports to education. You'll spot elements of consumer choice in many of the examples provided throughout this book.

I do have one warning: If you are going to let people choose whatever they want, as opposed to giving them a set of pre-approved options, you need to be prepared to go with their choice.

Back in 2016, the UK's Natural Environment Research Council conducted a public poll to name their new polar research vessel. The winner — far and away — was Boaty McBoatface. Yes, it was a silly name, but, wow, did it ever make the people of the UK (and the world) sit up and take notice. The name was overruled by the Science Minister, and it was named after Sir David Attenborough instead. More dignified, sure, but imagine how many more people would pay attention to the good work done on that ship if it was called what the people named it.

Property ownership

This is another trend that seems to ebb and flow. With property ownership, a brand isn't a sponsor but an owner of the property. It may be a property the brand has created specifically to suit their needs and target markets, or they may buy an existing property.

The upside is that your brand has a tremendous amount of control over the property and how you can use it. You may also be able to create and own an entire niche, such as Red Bull has done with the Red Bull Air Race.

The downside is that you also get all of the risk. You also get all of the headaches of event management, when running events probably isn't your core competency. You will probably also need to sell sponsorship to other brands to underwrite some of the cost. Just think for a moment about how demanding you can be as a sponsor. Now, multiply that by 20 or so and that is what you will be experiencing, including all of the things they want you to change about your event to suit their brands. Yes, you can hire companies to run your events and sell your sponsorship, but the buck will always stop with you.

If you can stomach the downside, owning property can be tremendously rewarding. Just don't go into it without doing your due diligence.

If you can't find the perfect sponsorship, creating your own property is always an option.

Examples: Property ownership

Red Bull has well and truly taken the event ownership approach pioneered by Vans and upped it to a whole new level. **Red Bull** Street Style, a global phenomenon for soccer ball "freestylers", with national finals in 44 countries culminating in a World Final, has taken ownership of an entire sport, globally and from grassroots to elite.

Rip Curl and **Tourism Fiji** teamed up to create the Virtual Pro – Presented by Tourism Fiji. Rip Curl's Search GPS Smartwatch automatically logs surfing data. During the 10-day virtual competition, 1,600 participants' surf data was analysed for surf time, waves surfed, top speed, distance paddled, and the number of times they went surfing. Once complete, data visualisations were downloadable and sharable, along with a personalised Virtual Pro video.

Red Bull strikes again with the Red Bull Air Race, a global series of high-speed, death-defying races through aerial obstacle courses. In addition to global television rights, merchandise, tickets, hospitality, and other revenue sources, they have created the perfect platform for leveraging their brand. "Red Bull gives you wings", indeed. Local leverage programs capitalise on the immense popularity of the events. They have also created a school-based art project, called the Red Bull Air Brush contest. And apps abound, but not all of them are as much fun as the Red Bull Air Race app.

Weet-Bix, New Zealand's top cereal brand, balances commercial interests with their mission to get New Zealand kids to eat healthily and exercise. Part of that commitment was to create the Weet-Bix Tryathlon, a non-competitive triathlon series for kids aged 7–15, competing either individually or as a team. There are 12 annual events across New Zealand, with a total participation of 19,000 annually, making it the world's largest sporting event for kids – not bad for a country of only 5 million! Their microsite is chock full of great information, including MyTry, where "tryathletes" can track their training and results.

Dove has a long history of promoting body positivity across their platforms, but they took it to another level when they teamed up with Nike to create the "Body Confident Sport Program". This was devised to stop girls from quitting sport because of low body confidence. Interestingly, this tool isn't for the girls, it's for their coaches, giving them the advice and tools they need to build body confidence and help girls stay engaged in sport, and all of its benefits.

During COVID, **ASICS** used the World Health Organization's World Mental Health Day as an anchor for their initiative "In My Shoes". They rolled out a series of audio stories, designed for people to listen to when working out, and centred on the benefits of exercise to their mental wellbeing. They also created a virtual, mass-participation, multi-distance run, so runners from beginners to elite could run together for mental health.

Chapter 16

Ambush prevention

In the first edition of this book, this chapter was reasonably big. Not anymore. Why? Because if you ensure your brand is a strong, natural match to the property, and leverage well, providing plenty of fan and customer wins, it will be difficult to ambush your sponsorships.

What is ambush marketing?

Ambush marketing is when a brand tries to get a marketing return around a property that they don't sponsor, often in direct competition with a genuine sponsor. This is usually done either by the ambusher implying that they're a sponsor, without contravening intellectual property laws; or by attempting to sneak their brand into a fan experience, such as having 50 people wearing a non-sponsor brand behind the goalposts at a game.

The legal stuff

Most ambush marketing is legal. Don't get me wrong, there *are* laws relating to ambush marketing, it's just that they don't prevent an ambusher from giving it a go. Those laws boil down to two main things: IP and proximity.

Intellectual property

An ambusher is not allowed to refer to themselves as a sponsor of something they don't, in fact, sponsor. They are also not allowed to use the intellectual property (logos, images, etc.) of a rightsholder without permission.

IP infringement is illegal and has been for longer than ambush marketing has existed. All anti-ambush legislation does is cast the net wider for IP infringement – adding a few dozen more words and phrases that ambushers can't use. For instance, they can't use "Games", "2032", the word "rings", "Brisbane", etc. in combination. Not to put too fine a point on it, but big whoop. It's easy for ambushers to get around this just by getting creative with wording.

Limiting proximity

A rightsholder can also limit a non-sponsor's access to their event. This means that an ambusher can't be on-site at an event doing a promotion, or Mr Whippy ice cream vans can't

> Laws will not protect you from ambush.

be parked within the perimeter of a festival sponsored by another ice cream company, and for major events, even the airspace is controlled lest an ambusher's blimp makes its way overhead.

Some rightsholders take this to epic, draconian, and patently stupid lengths. These include requiring people attending the event to turn their shirts inside out if they have the logo of one of their sponsors' competitors on it, or not allowing competitor soft drinks into an event where people are encouraged to bring their own food and drink.

The upshot is, the laws are limited and the rightsholder doesn't really control much, so if you want to protect yourself, you will have to *protect yourself*.

What to worry about, what not to

While there are a number of variations, there are two main types of ambush marketing: Cosmetic ambush and strategic ambush.

Most ambushes are nothing more than cosmetic ego trips. Exposure- or proximity-based ambush is very low value, but will likely continue for as long as brands believe that "being there" equates to "being meaningful". It's annoying, but not something you need to worry about.

Strategic ambush is about creating fan wins, without being a sponsor or breaking any laws. Strategic ambushers look at the whole fan experience, not just on-site, and find ways to make that larger experience better for people. Does this work? Yes, I've done it. Is it preventable? Absolutely.

Protecting yourself from ambush

Protecting yourself from a strategic ambush — at least one of a size and scope that could damage your own results — is straightforward, and has the following two components.

Ensure your brand is a natural match

The first thing you need to do, before you commit to any major sponsorship, is ensure that your brand is a natural match to the sponsorship — better than your competitors. This is a big part of the authenticity that's required for strong sponsorship results. I've included a worksheet for this below.

If your brand is clearly the best fit, it will be hard work for any of your competitors to create a strategic ambush. On the other hand, if one or more of your competitors is a much better natural match than your brand, think long and hard before investing.

Be both thorough and creative with leverage

If your brand is a more natural fit and you implement a strong, creative leverage plan, there's very little any non-sponsor can do that's going to hurt your brand or advance theirs.

And *this* is why ambush marketing is in the leverage section of the book.

> If a competitor is a much better match for the sponsorship, don't invest.

◑ Ambush Fit Assessment

The better the fit with the event, the stronger it is as a marketing opportunity. When the fit is weaker — particularly if a potential ambusher is a better fit than your brand — the opportunity for strategic ambush increases dramatically.

Step 1: List all the attributes and values that your brand shares with your competitor:

....

....

....

....

....

Step 2: List the key attributes and/or marketing messages that are unique to your brand:

....

....

....

....

....

Step 3: List the key attributes and/or marketing messages that are unique to the competition's brand:

....

....

....

....

....

Fit continuum

Your brand ⟷ The competition

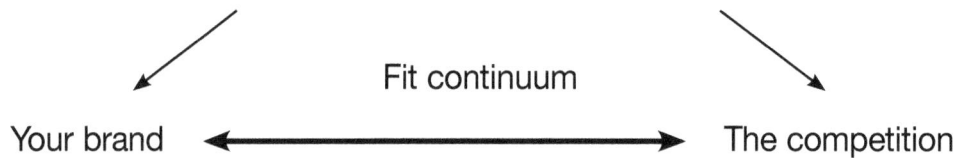

Step 4: List the key attributes of the property you are worried about being ambushed:

....

....

....

....

....

Step 5: Put an X on the fit continuum between your brand's unique attributes and your competitors', where this event would naturally fall. This will show which brand is the stronger, more natural attribute fit.

Chapter 17

Getting senior executive buy-in

Whether you need to communicate your leverage plans to senior executives for their approval or not is usually down to some combination of corporate culture and the size of the investment. If you're making some large sponsorship investments, there may well be an expectation that the leverage strategy around it should get high-level sign-off.

Even if that isn't normally an expectation, if you're changing your approach to sponsorship – and particularly, to leverage – it's often a good idea to keep your head of marketing in the loop. That way, as your sponsorships start to look different, the rigour and rationale behind the changes are clear.

Once your CMO sees that a) some rigour has been put into the decision; and b) the right people are involved, they should be comfortable with you taking the plan forward. They should also be comfortable answering any questions other senior executives may have.

Leverage and measurement brief

I suggest preparing a two- or three-page document overviewing the leverage plan, as well as which stakeholders are involved, and how results will be measured. This document should include the following sections:

- Basics about the sponsorship
- The objectives you intend to achieve with this sponsorship:
  - Perceptions to change or reinforce
  - Behaviours to change or reinforce
  - Areas around which you'll build brand alignment
- The target markets to whom it's relevant
- Your leverage plan – no need to go overboard, but list each significant planned initiative
- Which stakeholders have been involved
- Your measurement plan – how are those stakeholders going to measure results, and from what benchmarks (much more on this in the next section of the book)

Part 4

MEASUREMENT

Chapter 18

The fallacy of ROI

"Return-on-investment" (ROI). Sounds good, right? I mean, we all want returns on our investments, and sponsors are the same. So, why am I calling it a fallacy?

In the context of sponsorship, the definition of ROI has morphed into the expectation that sponsorship returns will be reflected in a neat, dollars-to-dollars ratio. This requires attempting to turn everything into a dollar figure, even things that can't be measured accurately in dollars. For instance, if visitors to a museum you sponsor are 34% more likely to advocate for your brand, that's clearly a good return. But, how much is it worth in dollars? The best you can do is take a wild guess.

This chapter is about dismantling the fallacies and bad habits around sponsorship measurement, so I can outline how it should be done in the next chapter. If you see an uncomfortable amount of familiarity in this chapter, don't despair. First, we've all been there – including me. Second, once you reset your thinking about measurement, your measurement approach is straightforward to fix.

Common but unhelpful measurement methods

Below, I outline a number of common measurement methods, and why they're counterproductive, not only to accurate measurement, but to your results themselves. Sponsors tend to work towards what's being measured, and if that's faulty, you'll be focusing your efforts in the wrong direction.

Exposure-based

Exposure-based measurement is rooted in the first-generation idea that visibility equals results. The sponsorship is measured based on media equivalencies – the advertising value of all the media in which your brand's logo, name, or tagline appears.

As sponsors realised there is a big difference between the value of a 30-second ad that allows them to tell a brand story or create a call to action, and 30 seconds of their logo appearing on television, many simply discounted the media equivalency figure, rather than moving to a more effective measure. Typically, they took the gross media equivalency and multiplied it by 15% to get a lower figure.

While realising that the value of exposure is extremely limited is a good thing, keeping the focus on exposure as the return is inappropriate for sponsors with any degree of sophistication.

Bargain-based

This method of "measurement" compares the à la carte value of the contracted benefits you've paid for (the value if you purchased each of them separately) with the sponsorship fee. If you've paid less than the benefits are theoretically worth, you have a success.

Or not, because all this does is tell you whether you got the opportunity cheap. It tells you nothing about whether you achieved your objectives.

Rightsholder estimates

If you're asking the rightsholder to measure the returns for you, you need to stop it right now. It is unfair to expect that they can measure *your* results, against *your* objectives and benchmarks, across a leverage program *you* have designed and implemented. It's like buying a $400 pair of fabulous shoes, wearing them around for a year and then going back to the shop and asking, "Did I get value for money?" All they know is they sold you a great pair of shoes, beyond that, only you can say whether they performed as expected.

In reality, all a rightsholder can do is provide a bargain- or exposure-based estimate, which doesn't offer you any real insight. Plus, they are motivated to estimate high. There are ways to augment your measurement plan with the rightsholder, which I'll address in the next chapter, but getting them to create a report isn't how you do it.

> Rightsholders can't measure your returns for you.

Justification-based

This sits squarely in second-generation thinking and goes like this:

You invest in a sponsorship. Your main leverage activity is to run a sales promotion. You add up the profit on the incremental sales, and if the amount is higher than the sponsorship fee, you consider it a success.

On one hand, this is a fair way to measure dollar value returns for a sales promotion. On the other hand, it's almost laughably incomplete. It may *justify* the investment, but doesn't come close to fully measuring results.

Any of the above plus "intangibles"

I have seen a number of measurement reports that are based primarily on exposure-, bargain-, or justification-based figures, but with a large dollar figure bolted on the end and labelled either "intangibles" or "good corporate citizenship". Hell, in my early days in this industry, I used to do it myself!

The idea is that the sponsor has identified that changing people's perceptions and

Changing people's perceptions and building alignment is not an "intangible".

building alignment does have some value for a brand, and they are trying to reflect that with a large, arbitrary figure, so it can be reflected in that dollars-to-dollars ratio.

The thing is, changing perceptions and building alignment with your target markets isn't "intangible", it just requires a different measurement strategy, and it simply can't be accurately reflected in dollars.

Formula-based

There are a number of industry players who have come up with formulas for "measuring" your returns. First, all of them have different formulae. Second, the formula invariably measures mechanisms, not results. Finally, anyone who says measurement can be accomplished using a formula is trying to sell you the formula. Avoid these organisations. You can do it much more accurately on your own.

Measure everything

Finally, we've got the "measure everything" approach — if it can be measured, strap a number to it. While not technically incorrect, this wastes a lot of effort on meaningless data.

If you know the degree to which you have shifted target market perceptions, why do you need to know how many impressions your logo got? If you know that the annual spend of customers who participated in a particular sponsorship leverage program rose by 32%, who cares if they can name you as a sponsor when on their way out of an event, after drinking a few ciders?

Just because you can measure something doesn't mean you should.

Keep your measurement comprehensive, but lean. Measure what matters to your company and your colleagues. Don't waste the energy or money measuring inconsequential mechanisms.

Typical ROI report

Below, I have created a typical ROI report. Actually, only the first two columns would appear on a typical ROI report. I've added the third column to point out the common, but old-school, rationale that is driving the figure assigned to the metric. Of all these items, the only real, defensible number is the first one: Profit on incremental sales. That's the only actual result.

Don't feel bad if this is what your reports look like. Early in my career, my reports looked exactly like this, right down to the giant "good corporate citizenship" figure. And if the ROI ratio wasn't good enough, I'd just make the good corporate citizenship, what-money-can't-buy experiences, and logo figures bigger. If social media were around back then, I'm sure I would have fudged that figure, too. I mean, these figures were just made up, so who would know if I inflated them?

Here's the thing: You can measure some things in dollars, but there's also a ton of results — real results — that you can measure, but which don't lend themselves to being reflected in some usually arbitrary dollar figure. So, give it up. Leave anything near this kind of thinking behind you because there is a better way.

But more than that, there's hardly any media that can be measured using a dollar-to-dollar ratio. You can know you spent half a million on advertising last week, but do you know exactly how much that was worth to your bottom line? How about social? Earned media? You know you don't. The exception is direct response, but that's about it.

Sponsorship is more multifaceted than any other single marketing channel, so why would you apply this oversimplified "measurement" strategy to sponsorship when you don't expect it to be a valid measure for any of your many, simpler marketing activities?

Measurement metric	Estimated value	Rationale
Profit on incremental sales (promotion)	$215,000	Result
Hospitality box and other tickets (à la carte value)	$50,000	Equivalent cost (bargain-thinking)
Signage (à la carte value)	$62,000	Equivalent cost (bargain-thinking)
PR/media coverage of logo/name (media equivalency x .15)	$354,000	Mechanism, arbitrary
Ads and mentions in rightsholder/property social media	$135,000	Mechanism, arbitrary
Logos on team materials, website, etc.	$25,000	Mechanism, arbitrary
What-money-can't-buy experiences x 2	$15,000	Mechanism, arbitrary
Good corporate citizenship	$450,000	Arbitrary
TOTAL	$1,306,000	Big fat guess
COST	$350,000	Actual costs
ROI	3.73:1	Good-looking figure, but meaningless

New thinking: Return-on-objectives

The new mindset for sponsorship measurement is return-on-objectives or ROO. This approach takes back the idea that returns are multifaceted. ROO measures:

- Changes in perceptions *and* behaviours *and* alignment
- Financial *and* other benefits
- Short- *and* long-term returns

While there is no formula — every sponsorship measurement strategy is different — there is a methodology to measuring the true results of a sponsorship. Bring on the next chapter of the book, and your measurement strategy!

Chapter 19

Measuring results

This chapter is all about ROO – return-on-objectives – from how to do it, and who needs to be involved, to how to report it.

As you go through this chapter, you'll see clear parallels between doing leverage well and measuring well, and why I referenced measurement over and over in the leverage section of this book. These aren't two separate parts of the sponsorship process, but wholly symbiotic, and if you do one poorly, the other will also fail.

Use experts from across your company

Using your internal experts – your sponsorship stakeholder group – to do the bulk of sponsorship measurement is the non-negotiable first step to doing it right. If you do everything else in this chapter, but don't involve the stakeholders, your measurement reporting will be a fraction of what it could be. Why?

- Those experts "own" the objectives and the benchmarks for their area of business.
- They have many ways to report results against those benchmarks, and can nominate the most appropriate measures for each sponsorship.
- Those measurement metrics are already known and trusted within your organisation.
- They can set appropriate projections or targets against objectives.
- The collective sign-off on the measurement report will have a lot of weight with senior executives.

Having anyone but sales report on sales, retail, or promotion figures is just silly. Having anyone but HR report on employee satisfaction, pride, or retention is in the same category. You have experts in Net Promotor Scores, social sentiment, customer churn, market research, and every other metric your company tracks on a regular basis. Every stakeholder that is using, leveraging, or is impacted by a sponsorship is in the best position to measure against objectives in their area. Period.

Choose your objectives

Note that I didn't say "create your objectives", I said "choose". That's because you don't create sponsorship objectives. There are no such things as stand-alone sponsorship objectives. Each sponsorship should be achieving a subset of overall marketing and other business objectives.

Set the benchmarks

Once your stakeholders have chosen the relevant objectives, they need to specify the existing benchmarks they have, and how they're measured. You can't possibly know what you've accomplished if you don't know where you started.

It's all well and good to say you've moved 10,000 cases of cereal in a given market where you've got a sponsorship, some on-pack or in-store activity, and a social promotion, but if you have no sales benchmark, how do you know if you've actually changed purchase behaviour, and by how much?

I would be delighted to hear that the purchase intent of people who participated in your sponsorship leverage activity had hit 56%, but only if you could show that was an improvement over your ambient purchase intent, as measured in ongoing or recent brand-tracking research.

Projections

Finally, on the objectives selected and the benchmarks nominated, what do those stakeholders think are realistic projections? What would they consider a success? And what mechanisms can they use to measure those results?

What if your stakeholders continue to be fixated on mechanisms?

The solution starts with a question. If someone in your organisation promotes measuring mechanisms, such as exposure, the conversation should go something like this:

> **You:** *Why? What are we trying to accomplish by getting loads of exposure?*
>
> **Them:** *To get front-of-mind awareness.*
>
> **You:** *In a sea of 20 or 50 other logos, that's a big ask. But let's just say we do get front-of-mind awareness. What does that accomplish?*
>
> **Them:** *They'll be more likely to consider our brand. Seeing the brand alongside something they're a fan of will increase their alignment to the brand, and increase their preference.*
>
> **You:** *Then THOSE are the objectives. Increasing consideration, preference, and alignment. We already measure those things and have*

benchmarks. How are we going to take a direct route to achieving them with this sponsorship? How are we going to directly influence how people feel about the brand?

This same conversation can be used to find the real objectives lurking behind all manner of sponsorship mechanisms, so you can focus on those real objectives in your measurement.

What can be measured

There are hundreds and hundreds of things that you could measure against your objectives. I've outlined a number of them below. The important thing to realise is there are four ways to measure:

1. In dollars
2. In percentages
3. In numbers or scores
4. Subjectively

There is a place for every one of these measures, and how you use them is equally dependent on what you're measuring, and what measures your company has decided are relevant and worthy of reporting across the various business units. For instance, some companies are concerned primarily with incremental consumer sales and promotional participation, while others are primarily concerned with wholesale sales and retail support. Both are perfectly legitimate ways of measuring sales, and are reflective of different corporate cultures.

Below, I've outlined a number of things you can measure across those four ways.

Measuring in dollars

When you measure in dollars, it's important that you stick to real figures. The second you start guessing, or attributing dollar values you can't prove, is the second your measurement strategy loses credibility. The areas listed below are some examples of what can be legitimately measurable in dollars:

- Incremental sales
- Profit on incremental sales
- Wholesale commitments
- Direct sales to your partner
- On-site sales
- Profit on upselling to existing customers
- New customer acquisitions
- Average spend
- Acquisition cost

> Customer value
> Loyalty/membership sales
> New or promotional product retail orders (total or average)
> New or promotional product retail reorders (total or average)

Measuring in percentages

There are a myriad ways of measuring in percentages. The key is you won't know how far you've moved the pin unless you know where you started, so it is critical that all percentage measures are done from benchmarks. Examples are:

> Changes in brand perceptions
> Changes in consideration
> Changes in preference
> Changes in purchase intent
> Changes in sentiment and/or alignment
> Changes in advocacy
> Retail promotional penetration/participation
> Increase in wholesale orders
> Increase in retail sales
> Sales promotion participation (as percent of sales)
> Churn/loyalty
> Changes in engagement tracking/social tracking
> Pixel tracking
> QR code tracking (or similar)
> Customer journey tracking (from the property, your app, your landing page, etc.)
> Profitability
> Conversions
> Store traffic
> Staff participation in activities/offers
> Staff retention or intent to stay
> Staff pride
> Staff alignment to corporate culture

In addition, you can add all the dollar measures (above) and number/score measures (below), as long as they can be reflected in a percentage change against benchmarks. For example, AC Milan fans buy an average of $68 a month of our product, which is a 35% increase in our customer average.

Measuring in numbers or scores

Some measures will be in sheer numbers, many of which can also be reflected as a percentage if you have benchmarks, such as:

- Net promotor score
- Social listening
- Sentiment
- Brand engagement
  - Likes, follows, views, shares, comments
  - App or other downloads
- Promotional participation
- Newsletter/membership sign-ups
- Coupon or merchandise redemption
- Staff participation or volunteerism

There is an argument that brand engagement — particularly social activity — is a mechanism, not a result. I have to say, I'm a bit on the fence with that myself. But, it *is* indicative of people moving towards your brand under their own volition, which is one way to try a brand, so worth measuring. I wouldn't measure this one thing in isolation, or overvalue it, but as part of a larger whole it provides useful information.

Subjective measures

While almost everything you want to measure can be measured accurately and objectively, there are a few areas where your measures are likely to be subjective. These include:

- VIP relationship building
- Media relations
- Government/regulator relations

To be credible, reports on these more subjective measures must be completed by the key stakeholders involved — the same people who report on progress against these objectives all the time. Their opinion will be trusted as their jobs are getting these areas of the business to perform.

Sample measurement plan

Below, I have outlined a few measurable objectives around a fake ketchup brand's sponsorship of a professional hockey team. Note, I said "a few". This is just a drop in the bucket of the measurable objectives you could have.

What you will notice is that every objective goes back to an overall marketing or business objective, every objective is measurable, and every objective can be benchmarked. That's your goal, and you're only going to achieve that goal if you are working closely with the business units or departments that "own" the benchmarks and the measurement mechanisms.

Note: I've used the kind of terminology that would typically be used in this type of plan but have included some clarification for readers who may not be familiar with fast-moving consumer goods.

- Profit on direct sales to the Maple Leafs of >$32,000 (box catering).
- Anchor pre-season sales promotion for incremental profit of >$440,000.
- Retail promotion penetration of >50% (the percentage of retailers that run the promotion).
- Increase retail case commitments by >40% in lead up to promotions.
- "Sell out" retailer training day with the team (for their kids):
  - Target incremental sales to those retailers at >10% for following 12 months.
- Launch product extension — Leafs blue ketchup — in second half of year:
  - 45% of fans understand key attributes of new product (Maple Leafs blue, but tastes the same) at launch + 1 month.
  - QR code bounce-back coupon redemption of >10%.
  - >50% retail support at launch (50% of key retailers stock the new product for the launch).
  - Reorders equal to orders (it's easy to get initial orders of a new product, the second order is when you know if retailers think the product is a winner).
- Increase brand-tracking indicators for Toronto-area hockey fans:
  - Healthy 32%→45% in first season.
  - Family favourite 55%→70% in first season.
  - "Canadian family owned" 17%→35% in first season.
- Sentiment:
  - Increase net promoter score by 1.2 among self-identified Leafs fans.
  - Social advocacy, alignment, and sentiment increases of >10% for geotargeted hockey fans.
- Brand engagement:
  - 10,000 incremental "likes" for FB page — season, game times, sustained 1 month.
  - Season participation of 50k for Insta hashtag promo.
- 50% uptake for employee and family day at the Maple Leafs.

Attributing sales to sponsorship

I am often asked the question, "How can I attribute sales to sponsorship?" This is a fair question as the fact of the matter is that most sales are the result of multiple marketing activities over the space of time.

Like so many things about best-practice sponsorship, attributing sales to sponsorship requires a multifaceted approach. Below, I've outlined a number of methods I've used with clients to help them attribute sales to sponsorship.

Get realistic

The first thing you need to understand is that almost all purchases are driven by a combination of marketing messages and channels, and it's not easy to attribute sales to a specific message or call to action. Sponsorship, however, has enough scope and flexibility that you can get closer to that Holy Grail than you can with most media. In other words, it's usually easier to attribute sales to a specific sponsorship than to a specific advertisement or social media activity. The key word is "easier". It's still not easy or exact, as other factors still come into play.

Pick your timeframe

One of the most important things to take into account is the timeframe. Attributing sales to sponsorship is most effective in the timeframe right around and immediately following the sponsorship. After that, it often falls into the category of "one more thing that contributed to this sale", and that is practically impossible to measure. For the purposes of this exercise, we are going to concentrate on a finite time period, and on activities that are most likely to have been the final trigger that evoked purchase.

Retail support

Again, I've used a fast-moving consumer goods brand as an example, but these techniques can be applied across many sponsor categories.

Test marketing

If you are running an on- or in-pack promotion, you can sell both sponsorship-themed and "clean" packages side-by-side in key retailers. This will allow you to see the relative desirability and subsequent sale of sponsorship-themed merchandise.

Retail support

If you are doing a retail promotion, chances are you won't get 100% penetration – that is, not every retailer will participate in the promotion. Use that to your advantage and compare sales figures in retailers running your in-store sponsorship promo to the figures in those retailers that don't.

Revisit history

If you have a reasonably predictable cycle of promotions and special offers, you can compare the uptake of the sponsorship-themed offers to similar offers, with similar marketing weight, in preceding quarters or years.

Create unique "funnels"

"Funnel" is a strange marketing term that basically refers to different ways that someone can enter your customer cycle, eventually becoming a customer and having monetary value to your brand.

There are dozens, if not hundreds, of ways to construct a sponsorship-driven funnel that will not only provide a starting point to your relationship with a potential new customer, but will allow you to track their progress towards becoming a customer. Some of these include:

- Click throughs to purchase from a sponsorship-driven landing page, app, or social media activities.
- Click throughs to do things that are trackable and could lead to purchase from sponsorship-driven landing page, app, or social media (such as booking a test drive, downloading trial version software, etc.).
- Bounce-back coupons or other special offers, distributed via the property or sponsorship-driven leverage activities (links, QR codes, near-field communications, etc.).
- Access to sponsorship-driven promotions, unique content, or other premium that requires purchase.
- Calls to dedicated hotlines, SMS product enquiries, and bot queries.

The starting point is to think of all of your touchpoints with the customer, and all of their touchpoints with your sponsorship, and ask yourself how you can create a unique interaction, leading to sales (or qualified leads) that you can track.

Track customer value

If your company is database-driven (banking, utilities, insurance, travel, etc.), you can track increases in customer value for those customers who have availed themselves of sponsorship-driven benefits or activities. These can be benchmarked against customers who haven't.

You can also track customer value of customers who engage with your social activities, download your app, or sign up for a special offer, promotion, or premium content. Again, these would be benchmarked against your ambient customer value.

In either case, you can measure a lot of things against benchmarks, such as:

- Sales — new product, upselling, incremental sales
- Customer profitability
- Cost of acquisition of new customers
- Referral business (if that is part of your business model and you track it).

Sponsor-generated research

You are probably expecting this to be a long, complicated section. It's not. Sponsorship research is not that complicated!

If your goal is to measure changes in perception, intent, and alignment — and it is — then that is what your research strategy should be about. All you need to know is whether you changed your target markets' perceptions, intentions, and alignment in the way you wanted to, and by how much.

Depending on the size of your company, you probably have either ongoing brand tracking or do market research every couple of years. I've referenced brand tracking below, but either one will provide a good benchmark.

Don't ask questions about sponsorship

"Can you name the sponsors of this event?" "Would you be more likely to buy from a company because they sponsor this charity?"

Please, please, please do yourself, your brand, and our industry a favour and stop asking questions about your sponsorships. They are leading, inaccurate, and tell you nothing about the actual performance of your sponsorship. In fact, a study was done a while back that looked at how people answer the "Can you name all of the sponsors of this event?" question. They concluded that:

> People mentally list the categories of sponsors who typically sponsor that type of property
> To that list, they add airlines, banks, insurance, and telecommunications, because those categories sponsor everything
> Then they list either the category leader or the one they use

In other words, the data that comes from asking that question is useless.

You don't really want to know whether they can remember seeing your branding, you want to know whether their preference has changed, whether they are more loyal, whether they'd advocate your brand to others, whether they believe your brand aligns with their lives and their needs. That's what you need to measure.

If a sponsorship is well leveraged, fans will know your brand is a sponsor. That will have nothing to do with how visible your logo is, and everything to do with how thorough and meaningful your leverage program is. In that case, high awareness is caused by strong leverage, not visibility.

Two ways to use brand tracking in sponsorship research

Depending on the type, size, and scope of the sponsorship, you have two options for using brand tracking in sponsorship research.

> If a sponsorship is well leveraged, fans will know your brand is a sponsor.

Option 1

This option works best on local and regional properties, like a local festival, and properties with a niche market, like a B2B conference.

- Review your brand tracking, pinpointing a handful of questions that most closely align with the perception and alignment goals you're trying to achieve.
- Ask those same questions of fans of the properties you sponsor, the in-person audience, people who get a third win, etc.:
  - "Same questions" is important. Don't change the wording, or even the punctuation, or you won't have an apples-to-apples comparison.
  - Use a variety of survey mechanisms. I've included a section on response options below.
- Compare those numbers to ambient measures.

Option 2

This approach works better for properties with a large, geographically disperse fanbase — likely your largest sponsorships. Doing this for all of your sponsorships would be unwieldy.

- Ask a few framing questions in your brand tracking:
  - Are you a football/soccer fan? Did you follow the Women's World Cup?
  - Do you follow college basketball? On a scale of 1–5, what is your interest level?
- Analyse key brand-tracking metrics against those framing questions:
  - Example: Consideration and propensity to buy are higher for college basketball fans, rising as their interest level rises.

Don't get hung up on statistical validity

If you talk to professional research organisations, many of them will tell you that you need to survey a minimum percentage of your target market in order for the research to be valid. Not to put too fine a point on it, but talk about making a rod for your own back!

You don't need statistical perfection to get the answers you're looking for. Sure, you've got a bigger margin of error if you ask 400 people than if you ask 4,000, but you will still get a strong indication — particularly if you ask several questions across several groups — and it won't cost the Earth.

Use a range of response mechanisms

While you don't need to be hung up on getting huge numbers of responses, using a range of response mechanisms will help you get a critical mass to compare to ambient numbers, such as:

- Online surveys — These are great because you can drop links into newsletters, your website, social media and more, and many are free.
- In-person surveys — Getting a crew to ask a short selection of questions at an event is pretty straightforward, and with the kinds of tablet apps available, compiling the data is simple.
- Phone surveys — If you have access to a database (yours or your partner's), you can arrange for some short phone surveys.
- Piggy-back on partner research — If your partner is doing market research, you should ask if you can include a couple of questions from your brand tracking. You could also add a couple of questions to their forms (eg, a marathon entry form).
- Mini-surveys — There is a trend towards using pop-up mini-surveys to get market info. Use one qualifying question and one or two other multiple-choice questions. It's not perfect or complete but, because it's so fast and easy, you can get quite a lot of responses.

What if you don't have benchmark research?

If you don't have research to use as a benchmark, this approach isn't going to work for you. But rather than falling into old, irrelevant habits, like asking whether people can name all of the sponsors of a given event, think about the value of investing in some benchmark research.

You will be able to use it for at least a couple of years and across your whole portfolio. If you're concerned about the budget, then don't ask 40 questions of 2,000 people. Ask 15 questions of 500 people instead. The figures won't be statistically perfect, but they will certainly be indicative and better than nothing. Plus, anecdotally, if you do a small research program, the figures will be used across the company, and the value of having it identified, you will likely be able to get a bigger research program funded before too long.

Rightsholder-generated research

There are ways to generate good research through your partners. Some of it will assist with measurement, while other rightsholder research will be useful for creating strong leverage plans.

If your partner offers you the chance to include a few questions on one of their surveys, use it to:

- Ask identical questions to your ongoing or benchmark research — If you can only ask two to three, be sure to choose them carefully.

Your partners can be a good source of research.

> Build your understanding of the fans and fan experience. The four best questions a rightsholder can ask are:
>   • What are the three main reasons you decided to attend/donate/join/participate/whatever?
>   • What are the three best things about the experience?
>   • What are the three worst things about the experience?
>   • If you were to describe this experience in three words, what would they be?

Strongly suggest that the rightsholder allow fans to answer in their own words, rather than choosing options provided to them. This will net the best information for you and for them.

Reporting results

Reporting isn't about mashing all of this good, solid, benchmarked information into some kind of neat little ratio just because that's what your senior executives are used to. Reporting is about collating the data into a multifaceted report that tells the real story of the success of a sponsorship.

It's about using the data you've got and reflecting it against both benchmarks and projections, and because that data has come from the stakeholders who "own" those pieces of your business, it will be credible.

As someone who has created many, many of these measurement reports for corporate clients, I can tell you with hand on heart that even the most die-hard, ratio-loving, C-level executives would much rather read a multifaceted report, which reflects the credible results of a multifaceted marketing endeavour, than try to make themselves believe that a nice-looking ratio means anything at all.

What does this look like?

Most of my corporate clients reflect results in terms of benchmarks, projections, and actual results. Often there are multiple actual results, reflecting the impact on different target markets.

You can certainly do this in text, but I find it easiest to digest using bar charts for anything where you have comparative numbers, as shown below.

Figure 15: Reporting results

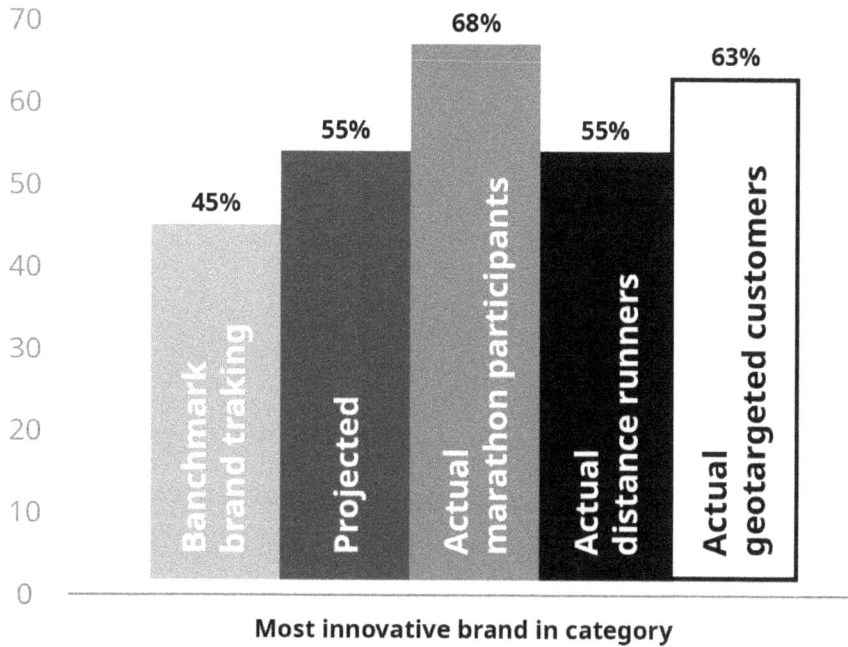

Most innovative brand in category

What if senior executives still want a ratio?

Do both — give them the old-school ratio AND a proper, multifaceted report. You'll only have to do this once. My extensive experience has been that as soon as they see the proper report, they shove the ROI ratio to the side, often claiming that this is the first time they've actually understood what sponsorship accomplishes.

Part 5

SPONSORSHIP & PORTFOLIO MANAGEMENT

Chapter 20

Managing your relationships

To work well, sponsorship relies on ongoing collaboration and cooperation between the sponsor and rightsholder. This chapter is all about setting that relationship up for success, and minimising the potential for issues. If you do have issues with a rightsholder, I address how to deal with those in the next chapter.

Start the relationship right

For the most fruitful partner relationships, it's important to set expectations from the start. Some rightsholders seem to think that if they are on their best behaviour throughout the sales process, the pressure will then be off them once the deal is done. Your first meeting after the deal is done is your opportunity to make it clear that you expect just as much accountability and engagement from them now as you did during the sales process.

Sponsor information kit

One of the easiest and most powerful things you can do in the initial meeting is to provide a sponsor information kit. This will include:

- Your leverage and measurement plan — Leave out anything commercial-in-confidence, but give them the rest.
- Info on your brand, objectives, and target markets. If you've got comprehensive sponsorship guidelines, that's probably sufficient.
- Contact details for their primary contact in your company.
- Contact details for at least one other decision-maker, just in case the primary contact isn't available and there is something urgent.
- A list of your key dates and deadlines.
- Your branding elements and other IP in various formats (usually provided in the cloud).

- ➤ Your brand guidelines — What is and is not allowed regarding the brand.
- ➤ Approval process — Who needs to sign off on any use of branding or other IP, and how long you need to get something approved?
- ➤ Report template and expectations — A short template with all of the information you need from them on a monthly or bi-monthly basis (see the template below).

Most of this will already exist. The biggest inclusion is your leverage and measurement plan, but you need to do that anyway. Once you've got a process for getting this together, creating a kit whenever you need one should be quick and simple to do. This is a great task for a sponsorship admin, if you have one.

The most important part of this process is the message it sends about your expectations of professionalism and engagement.

◐ Reporting Template

Below please find our sponsorship reporting template. We are requesting that you fill this out and email it to us [monthly/bi-monthly], [for the course of the contract/during the following timeframe]. Providing this information in the body of an email is fine.

Report date:

Report period:

Report prepared by:

Contracted benefits provided to [sponsor] during the previous [month/term]:

Added-value (non-contracted) benefits provided to [sponsor] during the previous [month/term]:

Overview of activities to be undertaken by [rightsholder] during the next [month/term]:

Cash payments or contra required from [sponsor] during the next [month/term]:

Key dates, meetings, and activities for upcoming month(s):

Opportunities/issues to address:

Rightsholder information kit

Once you've provided the rightsholder with a kit, you should request a similar kit from them. Suggest that it include:

- Their implementation plan for your sponsorship (who is responsible for delivering benefits, etc.)
- Contact details for the primary contact and at least one additional decision-maker, just in case
- Contact details for any related suppliers (catering, audio-visual, security, etc.)
- Key dates and deadlines
- Dates and details for any sponsor functions
- Contact details for other sponsors
- Rightsholder logos and any other IP, as agreed in the contract
- Guidelines for logo and IP use
- Approval process for logo and IP use

Setting servicing expectations

When I refer to "servicing", I'm referring to how your partners manage their relationship with you after the sale. Below, I outline what you should expect and not expect and what to do if a partner is hopeless.

What you should expect

Rightsholders used to have a reputation for taking the money, delivering the absolute minimum, and barely having any contact with sponsors until the next time they want money. Most rightsholders have moved on from that approach, but some still have a long way to go.

There are a number of things you should expect from your partners through the course of the relationship, and you should be making those expectations clear at the outset.

Delivery of benefits

The number-one thing you should expect is that the rightsholder delivers the benefits they have contracted to deliver. They should do this on time, and without prodding.

Delivering
contracted benefits
in full and on time
is non-negotiable.

If this becomes an issue, be firm in your insistence that they abide by their commitments.

If they still can't be bothered to live up to their legal obligations, I have some suggestions for managing the situation in Chapter 21: Rightsholder management issues.

Adding value to the relationship

You should expect that your partners will go out of their way to add value to the relationship when they can. You should also be looking for some evidence that they think about your brand and needs, and provide you with information, links to interesting blogs or articles, and let you know about new ideas (and not just when they're trying to sell you a new idea!).

You may have noticed that near the top of the Sponsorship Guidelines template is a line reading, "We expect our partners to budget and spend a minimum of 10% of the gross value of the sponsorship to add value to the sponsorship." It is best practice for a rightsholder to have a servicing budget like that. For you to tell them upfront that it is your expectation, you are doing two things:

1. Telling them to charge you 10% more.
2. Making it clear that you will be expecting them to add meaningful value to the sponsorship.

The typical ways a rightsholder can add value to the relationship are:

- Providing additional, non-contracted benefits
- Delivering sponsor networking functions
- Delivering sponsor education forums
- Facilitating sponsor cross-promotions
- Participation in audience research

If they are held accountable for adding that value, it is absolutely worth the extra 10%, but you need to do it. This is accomplished in a few ways:

- Reporting — The Report Template has a section where they can list any added-value benefits that have been provided in the preceding month. If a few months go by and nothing has been reported in that area, feel free to reiterate your expectation.
- Leverage planning — If you involve the rightsholder in your leverage planning and, through that process, identify a couple of benefits that would be ideal, you can ask the rightsholder if they fit within the 10% servicing budget you require. They may stammer around a bit as they struggle to remember what you're talking about, but chances are they'll say yes.
- Communications — In your regular communications, if you ask for any special favours, go ahead and say, "I assume this fits within the 10% you've budgeted for adding value?" This will remind them that you do have that expectation. It will also remind *you* that extra benefits are not going to be endless — there is a budget.

> Your partners should have a budget for adding value.

Flexibility

If you have a big, new leverage plan and need a few new benefits to make it work, you should expect that your partner will be willing to provide these in exchange for some of the contracted benefits that are less appropriate to your needs.

There are circumstances where a rightsholder simply can't provide something you'd like – it may be out of their control or already contracted to someone else – and you need to accept that. What you should be looking for is a willingness to find some way to make it work.

What you don't want is for a partner to be enforcing the letter of the contract simply because they can. You're not trying to change the money or the term of the contract, so this shouldn't be a threatening situation for them. In fact, most rightsholders will see your efforts to improve your results as a good sign that you see value in the relationship.

Staying in the loop

This is both very basic and subjective, but critically important. Your partners need to tell you what is going on with their organisation and the property you're sponsoring, as changes could affect the appeal of the property, the audience makeup, and your results.

There are three main ways that you should be kept in the loop:

1. Meetings and phone calls
2. Monthly or bi-monthly reports
3. Crisis communications

It is a good idea to explicitly tell your partners what your expectations are. You can actually tell them that you expect to be kept in the loop, particularly on issues to do with organisational or property health, their fans, or sponsorship.

You should also be willing to ask the hard questions. For instance, if you're sponsoring a conference, and it comes out that registrations are much lower than projected, you should be asking how they are addressing it, at what point do they decide if the event is not going ahead, and if there is anything you can do to assist.

Reporting

If you request reports based on your Report Template on a monthly basis, you should expect that it will happen. If it doesn't, make it crystal clear that part of your assessment of the sponsorship, and subsequent renewal, will be based on whether they live up to their commitments. That usually does it.

What you should not expect

As a sponsor, you should be expecting quite a lot from your partners. There are a few things, however, that you should not expect.

Endless freebies

Most rightsholders do their best to be responsive to sponsor requests but some sponsors take it way too far.

Every time you request more tickets or an extra appearance or some other extra benefit from a rightsholder, it costs them money. Rightsholders should have a budget to look after you, but you shouldn't be expecting them to do more than that. If you've asked for a few added-value benefits, you may want to preface additional requests with, "I know we've had a few added benefits from you already. Please tell me if we're getting to the limit of your servicing budget. We don't want to do the wrong thing by you."

If you realistically need more benefits to run the sponsorship than you've contracted, you should be talking to the rightsholder about renegotiating to a higher level.

Comprehensive end-of-year reports

End-of-year reports are a lot of work for the rightsholder to produce, and rarely have any information that's meaningful to you. They are usually based on these two things:

1. Media equivalency figures, social metrics, and press clippings — None of these provide any meaningful insights as to the objectives you've achieved through the sponsorship. You need to measure your own sponsorships.
2. Annual recap — You don't need to know what happened with the sponsorship over the past year, you need to know what is happening now and in the future, so you can manage and plan effectively. A monthly or bi-monthly report will have far more value to you.

In my experience, requiring partners to submit end-of-year reports is more about holding rightsholders accountable than accessing useful information. In fact, I know few sponsors that even bother to read them. You are much better off holding them accountable on an ongoing basis — using reporting, meetings, and more — than trying to make up for it all at the end of the year.

ROI reports

Many sponsors also require rightsholders to submit some kind of ROI ratio at the end of the year. I think I covered this sufficiently in the Measurement section of the book but here are the salient points:

> Sponsorship cannot be measured in a dollars-to-dollars ratio. Measures must be multifaceted.
> Only you can measure sponsorship results against your objectives. Expecting a rightsholder to provide you with any substantial measures is unrealistic.

End-of-year reports are more about accountability than useful information.

Maximising results

Moving forward, you should endeavour to make the relationship as collaborative as you can.

Include your partners in leverage planning

If you are going to have a leverage brainstorming session, invite your partner to be a part of it. This will serve a number of purposes:

- They can provide additional insights about the event and event experience.
- They can point out if something is flatly impossible.
- They can provide insight about opportunities you may not be aware of.
- They will be more likely to offer new meaningful benefits, or to renegotiate some of your less effective benefits, if they are part of the planning process.
- They will be much more engaged with your brand and your needs.

You may have to remind your partner that, for the purposes of any brainstorm, your brand can have anything from them that you want. As long as you make it clear that the brainstorm doesn't commit them to anything, they should remain open-minded. In my experience, when they take off the blinkers and see both what is possible and how good it is for them and the fans, they will likely be very open to making adjustments.

Provide expertise to your partners

It is a great idea — and definitely in your best interests — to involve your partners in the planning process. It is an equally good idea to help them out and provide input, if they need it. You could offer to:

- Participate on a marketing advisory committee
- Participate in marketing strategy sessions, such as assisting them with fine-tuning their brand architecture or market segments
- Provide input on planned research
- Provide input on planned marketing activities

The idea is not to try to influence what your partner is doing to suit your needs, but to help them be the best marketers they can possibly be, which will improve their value to you.

This kind of thing doesn't take much time or effort, but can make a big difference to your partner. And keep in mind, if you are adding value to your relationship with them, they will likely reciprocate.

Be proactive with other sponsors

If your target markets intersect with other sponsors, you should definitely explore cross-promotions. You've got a few options:

If you want flexible, responsive partners, include them in the planning process.

➤ Ask the rightsholder for an introduction to the other sponsor.

➤ Contact the other sponsor directly with an idea — even if the idea is rough.

➤ Have a working session with the other sponsor to come up with ideas.

Some rightsholders get a bit twitchy when sponsors meet without them, but that's really their problem. There's no reason you can't initiate an exploratory chat with another sponsor, and if you come up with a strong idea, get the rightsholder involved then.

Debriefs

At the end of every contract year, season, event, etc., schedule a debrief session. In that debrief, you'll go over:

➤ What went well and what didn't

➤ Whether all benefits were delivered as promised

➤ Whether audience/participant numbers, composition, and engagement hit rightsholder projections

➤ Any audience research done by the rightsholder

➤ Any available measurement results from your stakeholders and research

➤ The state of the relationship — any management or communications issues

➤ Whether you want to swap some benefits around, so you have a more leverageable platform, and can add more value to fans

➤ Forward planning

Ideally, you'll go into this debrief with a plan for what you want to achieve and an attitude of cooperation. This should stop it devolving into a mutual gripe-fest.

> If you are adding value to your relationship with a partner, they will likely reciprocate.

Chapter 21

Rightsholder management issues

In the previous chapter, I laid out a number of strategies designed to facilitate a smooth, productive working relationship between you and the rightsholder. Unfortunately, it doesn't always work out that way. In this chapter, I address a range of rightsholder management issues that can have a major impact on your results, and what to do about them.

The rightsholder is hopeless

If you've got rightsholders who really just don't get it, chances are that they simply don't have the skills to be the kind of partner you want them to be. This doesn't mean the sponsorship isn't a good investment. It's just an additional challenge to address.

If you have a partner that really isn't, you could choose to drive the sponsorship, which can be very time-consuming. The other option is to help them improve their skills, which is my favoured approach. You could:

- Provide educational materials — If you find an article, blog, white paper, or book that you think will help the rightsholder raise their game, by all means, send it along to them. There are many resources that can work for this. If you need a starting place, I can suggest a few resources from my website, PowerSponsorship.com:
  - My book, *The Sponsorship Seeker's Toolkit*. It is just as how-to and practical as this book, but for your partners' side of the equation.
  - My white papers — There are a whole range of them for both sponsors and rightsholders.
  - My blog — They are almost all how-to and are searchable, so the likelihood is that you will find a blog that will address nearly any issue you're having with a rightsholder.
  - Recommended resources — I feature links to a number of other great sponsorship bloggers and resources, so don't limit yourself just to my stuff.

- Get partners involved in planning — Another benefit of inviting your partners to your leverage-planning sessions is that it's an effective way of educating them, without any implication that they don't know what they're doing (at least, to them).
- Pay for them to attend a quality, credible sponsorship workshop or online training. I have a number of corporate colleagues who pay to send their less-sophisticated partners to one of my workshops or my online training course for rightsholders: Getting to "Yes". They find that this small investment reaps big benefits in their relationships and results. Obviously, you don't need to use my training. Just find a good, reputable course — get recommendations — and take the plunge.

Nickel-and-diming you

This ugly little game takes place when you pay a fair fee for a sponsorship, but then encounter one after another additional costs — some small, some larger — bringing the sum total of the investment to a level that is no longer commensurate with the benefits provided. I've outlined a few of the classics below.

You may or may not be prepared to go along with these, but at least you should be aware that you're being gamed by an organisation that has shown itself to put greed ahead of partnership. I just hate that, and when it happens to my clients, I always advise them to call the rightsholder on it — to tell them they are taking advantage of the relationship, and that's not what a healthy partnership is all about.

I also believe that sponsors should keep this kind of treatment firmly in mind at renewal time. If it was painful enough, don't even consider renewing, and be sure you tell the CEO of the organisation why. If you still see scope for working together, tell them firmly that their new proposal must include all costs.

Charging additional licence fees if you want to do more with the IP

Let's say you negotiated lots of access to intellectual property. This is a great idea as it offers a huge number of marketing opportunities and flexibility, provided you don't breach any of the rules set forth. Sometimes, however, the rightsholder will decide that you're being too creative and thorough, and go back for another bite of the cherry, claiming that you're going beyond "standard usage".

Unless there was a specific restriction on the amount of IP you can use, tell the rightsholder to get over themselves, and that they should be happy to have a proactive partner who is so willing to showcase their property (and the value it can have to sponsors).

If you did sign a contract with some limitation on the amount of IP you can use, you've really created a rod for your own back. Yes, there will be rules on what you can do, so that

> Educating your partners is one of the fastest ways you can improve your results.

your creative doesn't diminish the rightsholder's brand, but aside from that, you should be able to use it as fully as you want.

Charging sponsors if the rightsholder elects to extend or expand the program

As an example, you sponsor a series of professional development workshops, run by an association, which are taking place in eight cities. It is going so well for the association that they decide to add two more cities to the program — then they turn around and ask for more money from you. I know there will be different takes on this, but I think this is wrong.

If you sponsor a series, you sponsor the series — not individual workshops in eight cities. If demand warrants that the series is extended by your partner, they should not be expecting you to pay for their decision to make it bigger. Frankly, your leverage program — how you get a result from the marketing opportunity — is unlikely to be much different if the program is extended, so your results are unlikely to be a lot different.

Charging sponsors for "extended benefits"

Although this is built into many sponsorship contracts — particularly for sports — it annoys me beyond words when a property enacts it without taking the bigger picture into account.

As an example, a major sponsor sticks with a team sponsorship through a decade of losing seasons and falling fan numbers. Finally, the team has a great year and makes the playoffs, but what happens? The team turns around to this long-suffering sponsor and tells them that, unless the sponsor pays extra for playoff benefits and signage, they won't get any benefits around the playoffs, and their signage will be removed and the space sold to someone else. Yes, that was allowed for in the contract, so technically the team did nothing wrong, but from a strategic point of view, it wasn't the right thing to do.

If you end up in this position and a rightsholder is trying to charge you extra for something that you've basically earned — whether through years of loyalty, providing support for the property above and beyond what was required, or some other commitment — don't take it lying down. You need to have a full and frank discussion with your partner about the appropriateness and, frankly, short-sightedness of asking for more. Tell them about the hardship you've endured, or the added value you've brought to the partner and their fans. If they won't budge, tell them that you will be strongly considering that position at renewal time. That's about all you can do.

> Sometimes, enforcing the contract is counterproductive.

Contravening exclusivity

You require sponsor exclusivity in your category, so if a rightsholder contravenes that, it's a big deal. Although, often when this happens it could have been prevented by having a tight contract.

Some rightsholders just don't understand exclusivity. They don't know that many banks require exclusivity across credit cards as well, and approach Amex. Or they don't get that exclusivity goes across sponsorship levels.

Sometimes, this is your fault. If your company is a hardware chain and you sponsor the home show, you can't complain if other hardware stores have booths if you haven't specified that as part of your exclusivity. You can't assume that exclusivity applies to exhibitors, vendors, hospitality clients, or other non-sponsor relationships, unless you have negotiated it.

To avoid either of these situations, make it crystal clear in both your negotiations and the contract exactly what exclusivity you require, including:

- What categories
- All levels of sponsorship, from the biggest to the smallest
- Whether it applies to non-sponsor relationships (exhibitors, vendors, hospitality, etc.)

If it is specified, and they contravene it, you need to be prepared to enforce the contract.

Non-delivery of benefits

I addressed how you should expect all benefits to be delivered on time, and without prompting, in the previous chapter. But what if it goes beyond that? What if even prompting them doesn't work?

Most sponsors have had to deal with at least a few rightsholders that really don't hold up their end of the bargain. These range from minor annoyances to catastrophic, if core elements of the contracted benefits aren't delivered. If that happens to you, you've got a few reasonable options.

Substitute benefits

If they aren't delivering one or more benefits because for some reason they can't, the easiest and most common way to rectify benefit non-delivery is to substitute commensurate benefits.

You've done your planning and leverage based on the contracted benefits. Depending on what is provided, a change in benefits could require some reworking of your leverage plan. That's more work, time, and resources on your part, so they need to come to the party with something substantial, and worth at least as much as what they haven't delivered.

If you've built a leverage program with an epicentre timed around benefit(s) you've lost, the rightsholder needs to either provide a benefit that will provide the same epicentre during the same timeframe, or they need to give you time to rework.

For instance, if your hospitality activities at a game are abruptly cancelled — let's say the function room is flooded and unusable — they could either put your guests in VIP stadium seating and add a private meet-and-greet with players on the same game day, or provide you with a new function in a few weeks, so you have time to manage invitations, etc.

Under no circumstances should you allow the rightsholder to dictate what constitutes an acceptable substitute. Some rightsholders may even try to put one over on you, providing a few extra mediocre benefits, then claiming they were in lieu of the contracted benefits they haven't provided. Don't fall for it.

If a rightsholder offers you something, while contracted benefits remain outstanding, you should respond like this:

> *You are welcome to provide that benefit as an added value to the relationship, but I'm not accepting it in lieu of the contracted benefits you have yet to provide.*

Extend the contract at no cost

If you can't agree on substitute benefits, or there's no way to deliver equivalent benefits to the ones you've lost during the contract, another option is to extend the contract at no cost.

How long that extension should go will depend on the length of the existing contract, how bad the non-provision of benefits was, and the content of the sponsorship. Of course, all of this is dependent on whether they've rectified the problem and whether you can trust them to deliver.

Withhold payment

If you've got an agreed fee schedule, and the rightsholder hasn't delivered some of the contracted benefits, you could point out that a payment is due in a month, and if the benefits in question haven't been delivered, you will consider holding the payment until they are.

This only works if:

➢ There is no question about the benefits owing – no dispute
➢ You have repeatedly requested that the benefits are delivered, ideally in writing

Be careful, though. This game can get ugly fast, as once you withhold a fee payment, you're *both* in breach of the contract, and if they decide to get self-righteous about it – maybe there's a grey area they're trying to exploit – it can quickly escalate.

Reduce fee

Another option is that the rightsholder could rebate or discount a portion of your sponsorship fee by mutual agreement. They're generally not keen to do this, and even if they are, finding an agreeable figure can be problematic.

The rightsholder may look at it as the à la carte value, while you look at it as reducing your returns. In other words, their position may be that to buy the big hospitality event or scoreboard ads they failed to deliver would sell for $X, so that's what they're prepared to rebate.

But you don't invest in any marketing activities thinking you're only going to get the same amount of benefit for your brand that you paid — that the $15,000 hospitality event will only net you $15,000 in value from the VVIPs you invite. What would be the point of that?

No, what you buy is leveragable into something that is far more valuable than the cost of the raw materials it's built around, and that's what you lose when the raw materials aren't delivered as contracted. In addition, the benefits all work as part of a greater whole, so when components aren't delivered, it can devalue the whole platform. It's like trying to use a ladder with several rungs missing.

So, if they can't offer you equivalent and mutually agreed benefits, and it comes down to negotiating a cash rebate (or discount), it needs to be significantly more than the à la carte cost they'll be espousing. This negotiation can be a real pain in the arse.

If you're convinced of the potential of the sponsorship, and you're at or near renewal, instead of a reduction on the fee for the current contract, you could request a commensurate discount on a renewal. That's often more palatable for the rightsholder, and if you trust they'll get their act together, there's no real downside for you.

Combination

Often, the solution comes in some combination of substituting mutually agreed benefits, extending the contract, and/or reducing the fee (particularly at renewal).

Terminate the contract

We're getting into more drastic measures here.

You are under no obligation to agree to any of the above. I'm not recommending you be a jerk about it, but if you really can't make the sponsorship work with the alternatives presented, you can terminate the sponsorship mid-contract on the grounds of non-delivery of sponsorship benefits.

Before you initiate termination, be absolutely sure the contract is on your side — no grey areas — and you've got ample correspondence showing your good faith effort to resolve the issue. You also need to seek the advice of your lawyer.

Seek a refund

If the rightsholder has failed to deliver a critical mass of major benefits, it may no longer even function as a leveragable sponsorship. And if what you've invested in isn't fit for purpose, should you be paying at all?

Exiting and seeking a full refund of fees doesn't happen very often. Even if there's a strong case for the sponsorship not being fit for purpose, most sponsors will terminate the

> When components of a sponsorship contract aren't delivered, it can devalue the whole platform.

contract and walk away — with a possible parting flourish of badmouthing the rightsholder to industry media, in the guise of a "case study" — because seeking a full refund is likely to be expensive and time-consuming.

We're talking lawyers and settlement conferences and expert reports. You'd really only do it if the breach was egregious, the rightsholder appears wholly incapable of doing the right thing, and you're an idealist (and possibly somewhat of a masochist). But it can be done.

Protecting yourself

I think we can all agree that managing a sponsorship where the rightsholder isn't delivering benefits as promised is far from ideal. So, let's turn our attention to how we prevent this from happening in the first place, and if it does, how to make your course of action as clear and smooth as possible.

Contract

The biggest prevention you can have is a great contract. The contract will spell out in detail all of the benefits to be provided, all the terms, all the conditions. You want no grey areas. None.

Documentation

Your contract will clearly state that it can't be varied except in writing, by mutual agreement. Take this as seriously as a heart attack. Don't substitute benefits, don't change due dates, don't vary the contract terms at all unless both sides have agreed in writing.

If things do start to go awry, start sending clear emails requesting (and eventually demanding) rectification of the non-delivered benefits. Put the date that you expect a response, and if the situation isn't resolved by then, create a schedule and reminders to stay on it until it's resolved or you're prepared to take action.

Be sure to detail in writing how their non-delivery is impacting your planning, as well as the value and cohesiveness of your sponsorship. Part of the reason you're doing this is to convince them to, as we'd say in Australia, pull their fingers out. But part of it is because you're collecting evidence.

Identify red flags early

The first time a benefit isn't delivered in a timely fashion, flag it with them. Be friendly, but firm. It may have been an oversight, which they can fix straightaway. What you don't want them to think is that you're not paying attention.

For me, a much bigger red flag is making excuses as to why they're not delivering contracted benefits. Take this as a red flag the very first time it happens, and respond in writing something like this:

All due respect, but [excuse] is not my problem, and I'm accountable for results against these contracted benefits. I need an undertaking that this will be rectified by [date], or a proposal by Monday with what you're prepared to do to make this right.

Yeah, I know . . . nobody wants to be a hard-arse. But not addressing those red flags — letting them slide — makes it harder to recover that lost value. Sponsorship terms are finite, and every day you don't have the full complement of benefits is a day you can't fully leverage the investment.

Crisis management

I don't pretend to be a crisis management expert, but I do want to address two of the most common crises in sponsorship and some of the things to keep in mind.

Cancellation

If property you sponsor is cancelled, for whatever reason, then straightaway you need to:

- Communicate the situation internally
- Issue a statement (you generally want to do this without vilifying your partner, but if it's a Fyre Festival-type situation, go for your life)
- Be open in social media and responsive to comments
- Contact any consumers, customers, prize winners, etc. who may be affected and offer an alternative.

From a legal point of view, you need to:

- Review the contract clause pertaining to event cancellation
- Get your lawyer to provide notice and get it started, if you want to exit the contract due to cancellation

From a management point of view, you need to:

- Cancel whatever leverage and on-site activities you can
- Embark on renegotiations to either sponsor something else or roll the sponsorship into a future year, if you want to continue your larger relationship with the rightsholder.

Disrepute

We have seen a lot of disrepute in sponsorship, particularly high-profile athletes going well off the rails and leaving sponsors wondering what to do.

The good news is that your target markets are unlikely to hold your brand in any way responsible for the scandal as you will have been just as blindsided as the public. The bad

Rightsholder scandal can diminish your marketing platform, but won't hurt your brand.

news is that scandal could reduce the value of whatever/whomever it is that you're sponsoring.

If one of your sponsorships is hit by a scandal, the first thing you need to do is review your contract, so you know your options. You don't need to make a snap decision, although if it's clear you need to drop the sponsorship, don't drag it out.

In terms of your communications, the stand you should take in a controversy is the one that reflects the values of your target markets, leaving only two real choices:

1. If the controversy is divisive, your best option is not to take a stand and to let the law, rightsholder, or governing body sort it out and back the decisions that are made.
2. If the target market falls heavily on one side versus the other, then taking a stand in controversy is an option. You could risk alienating some of your market, but you could also deepen your relationship with the rest of the market.

The depth of emotion that people have invested should also be taken into consideration. For instance, if a football star is arrested for bashing his girlfriend, the degree of outrage people have against someone who has allegedly committed a serious crime against a woman probably outweighs the ambition of dedicated fans to finish the season well.

Chapter 22

Renewals, renegotiations, and exits

Up to this point, I've provided lots of advice on how to make your relationships with rightsholders work. This chapter is about managing change when you're renewing, renegotiating, or exiting a sponsorship.

Renewals

The process of managing renewals is very similar to negotiating a new sponsorship, but there are some strategies and issues that are unique.

Start early

If you want to explore a renewal, you definitely want to start discussions early. This is good for both you and the rightsholder.

If the sponsorship gets renewed, you've got lots of time to create a leverage plan incorporating any new benefits you may negotiate. And, frankly, if it doesn't work out, it gives the rightsholder time to replace you. That's the fair and right thing to do.

For multi-year contracts, you should be starting renewal negotiations at least six months before the contract ends. You can include a timeframe for renewal discussions in your contract, but there's no issue with beginning discussions earlier.

Getting what you want

The only way to guarantee you *won't* get what you want is not to ask, so I am a big proponent of being upfront with your requirements.

Tell them what you need

Some of your partners have no idea what you need from sponsorship. Maybe you've never told them, or maybe they just don't care. Either way, now is the time to change that.

Before you start any negotiations, provide the rightsholder with your sponsorship guidelines. This may be the first time they've seen them, or you may just be refreshing their memory. Tell them that you need them to understand exactly what you need from sponsorship. Try not to make this sound like a criticism. Rather, refer to it as a "clarification of your needs".

Drive the negotiations

You may elect to drive the renewal negotiations, which can be a lot faster than waiting for the rightsholder to come up with something you like. The approach I recommend is similar to the way you would develop a counteroffer to a proposal.

Assume that your partner is going to offer you exactly what you've got now. This may or may not be true, just put yourself in that head space. What you want to do is create a counteroffer to that.

Do a leverage brainstorm and develop a renewal offer, just as if you were developing a counteroffer to a proposal. Create an offer from that and provide it to them as an opener to the negotiations. Don't wait for them to make the first move.

Collaborate

The other option is collaboration. Renewal is a great time to take the collaborative approach, inviting the rightsholder to a leverage-planning meeting, so they can experience your team, your needs, and your approach firsthand. You will collaborate on a renewal offer on the spot, and all that will be required is some minor fine-tuning and formalising of the agreement.

The outrageous renewal

Most rightsholders are happy to work with you on a renewal, knowing that working together to create something win-win-win is going to benefit them the most in the long run.

On the other hand, there are some properties who are happy to try to game you into paying more than you should, hoping that you either want the sponsorship so much you will agree to anything, or that you are too blasé to care and will pay what they want. I have some strategies for managing those players.

So, here's the scenario: Your sponsorship has had a good run. You are on renewal and ready to give it a virtual rubber stamp on the basis of the fab returns you're getting for your brand. Then you get the proposal — a very similar package to what you've had for the past three years, and nothing major has changed with the property — but the fee has increased by 70%.

This isn't that common, but it does happen, and I know of plenty of sponsors that have dealt with this behaviour. Those sponsors are asking me what the rightsholder is thinking and it could be any number of things.

Your leverage program is so good, they've convinced themselves they're indispensable

This is one of the downsides to being an exceptionally good sponsor. If your leverage program is really great and you're getting fantastic results, some of your partners may be under the illusion that they are indispensable — that it is their property making the sponsorship great.

In fact, their property provided the opportunity, but your leverage is what really delivered the results, and if you can do it with that sponsorship, you can do it with another. I know it's a pain in the bum to change over sponsorships, but no partner is indispensable.

You've got three choices:

1. Tell them they're dreaming and counteroffer at a reasonable fee — something that is commensurate with the value they bring to the table.
2. Tell them that if you're going to entertain any substantial increase, they need to provide a benefits package to match. Make your expectations clear: Benefits must be strategic and creative.
3. Walk away and sponsor someone else.

Always keep in mind that there are a lot of fish in this sea.

They're testing the waters

The rightsholder may have higher sponsorship targets, or they may have financial difficulties, or they may have simply caught wind of another property landing a whopper of a deal and have decided to pump up prices to see what happens. It's a totally different situation than that outlined above, but the advice is the same: Counteroffer — tell them they're not getting any increase without some bloody fantastic new benefits — or walk away.

They were under-priced to start with

If you initially got the sponsorship at some crazy, fire-sale discount, you need to expect that the renewal will be substantially higher.

Do be sure that the benefits offered are still right for your brand, commensurate with the price tag, and fair market value. If so, don't gripe about a price correction that was always going to happen.

No partner is indispensable.

Sponsor renewal games

You don't want to be dealing with rightsholder renewal games, but you also need to do the right thing.

Don't pretend you're renewing

Rightsholders often specify a window for exclusive renewal negotiations in the contract, after which time they can continue negotiating with you, while they also put the sponsorship on the open market.

But some rightsholders don't protect themselves like that, and there are sponsors who will take advantage. They pretend they're going to renew, going on and on about "just one more meeting" or "getting C-level sign-off", as if that's just a formality. They keep this going until right before the exhibition, event, or season starts, then come back with, "Sorry, it's not going to work out this year." By that time, it's too late for the rightsholder to find someone else for that spot.

The result is that these sponsors successfully block their competition from getting involved in some premium property, at no cost to themselves. Could this be litigated? Possibly, but the cost and time involved probably wouldn't be worth it to the rightsholder.

Don't do this. Just don't. It's selfish, unethical, and the rightsholder could have been really counting on that fee. Plus, your reputation as a sponsor that rightsholders want to work with will go right down the toilet and, in some cases, you could end up called out all over the media. It's just not worth it.

Don't be a money tease

Rightsholders want you to sponsor bigger, so when it comes time for renewal, they'll often ask if you'd like to consider a larger sponsorship, such as principal or naming rights. Unfortunately, many sponsors will go ahead and ask for a proposal, mainly out of curiosity as to what it would look like.

I had this happen with a client not long ago. The rightsholder specified the minimum price for naming rights at the outset, then jumped through hoop after hoop pulling a super-customised offer together, only to be told that the sponsor never had budget for anything like a sponsorship of that size.

Here's the thing, if you know the maximum amount of money you have for a given sponsorship, don't feign interest in something bigger than that. Those major proposals take a ton of time and are a huge team effort. Wasting that time and effort on a whim is really bad sponsorship karma.

Mid-term renegotiations

As you embark upon a more creative, strategic way of leveraging your sponsorships, you will inevitably find that you have some investments where the property is right for your brand, but the benefits offered aren't appropriate for what you want to do with the sponsorship.

You could wait around until renewal time and negotiate for more appropriate benefits then, but your opportunity may be reduced while you're waiting. Instead, you should do a mid-term renegotiation. This isn't nearly as daunting as you may think.

When it comes right down to it, your partner's primary job is to help you get the most out of your sponsorship, not to enforce the contract to the letter. That said, rightsholders do tend to get a bit twitchy if you start talking about changing the contract, as they often think what you propose is likely to hurt them.

In order to get what you need, without sending your partner into a tailspin, I suggest these steps:

1. Go in with the reassurance that you're not trying to reduce your financial commitment or shorten the term of the contract.
2. Make it clear that your goal is to get the most out of this sponsorship, but that you don't think the benefits you are currently getting are the most appropriate for your needs.
3. Take your lumps. Admit that you haven't done the best job of leveraging the sponsorship, and that is going to change, but you need the raw materials — the benefits — to support that improved leverage.
4. Be fair. Don't expect additional benefits without giving some back. You are exchanging benefits you don't need for benefits you do, not demanding freebies.
5. Make it good for them. The results of this process should be a highly leveraged, creative sponsorship operating at peak performance. This is as good for them as for you. But go the extra yard and ask if they have any marketing initiatives that they're working on. It's quite possible you can help them achieve one or more of their goals while achieving yours.

> The rightsholder's job is to help you get a good result, not to enforce the contract.

Exits

All things come to an end and, eventually, you will exit every sponsorship you have. Knowing when and how to do it is reflective of your sophistication as a sponsor.

When to exit

There are a number of times when exiting is the appropriate decision:

➢ It was never a good brand or target market fit.
➢ It was a good fit, but your target market or objectives have changed, and it isn't anymore.

- It was a senior executive pet project (and nothing more), and that senior executive has either moved on or is facing more accountability for sponsorship investments.
- The sponsorship has been underused for so long, you no longer have any internal buy-in.
- It is a less-good duplicate of something else in your portfolio.
- You are restructuring your sponsorship portfolio, and it is inconsistent with your new approach (typically, this would be streamlining a portfolio and concentrating on only one or two focal points).
- The rightsholder didn't deliver the contracted sponsorship benefits, and you couldn't resolve the situation.
- The rightsholder contravened the contract (ie, breached exclusivity or disrepute rules).
- The rightsholder wants a significant fee increase at renewal, and you can't justify the expenditure at that level.

The decision may stem from an audit, or it may just be the next logical step. Either way, if you have to do it, do it properly.

How to exit

When it comes to exiting, you're already doing something that could hurt your partner. Being unnecessarily punitive or dismissive is bad karma, and you really don't want that. Instead, you want to be as fair and kind as you can possibly be. There are several strategies I recommend.

Tell them as soon as you know

If you know you're not going to renew, you need to tell the rightsholder as soon as you know, even if you're still a long way from the end of the contract. Don't waffle. Tell them the decision has been made, but you wanted to give them as much notice as possible, so they can work on getting a new sponsor to replace the revenue.

Unless there are mitigating circumstances, let the rightsholder know that you'll continue to leverage the sponsorship until the end of the contract, and hope you can continue to have a fruitful relationship until it's time to say goodbye.

You do need to understand that this means they may be talking to your competitors while you're still sponsoring. You've made your decision. You need to let that go.

Tell them why

If you are not renewing because of some failing on their part, you need to tell them. Put it as nicely as you can, but do tell them as this gives them a chance to fix the issue before they lose more sponsors. You might say something like:

> When exiting, be as fair and kind as you can possibly be.

You need to know that a big part of the reason we're not renewing is that we never hear from you between one sales cycle and another. We don't feel like you care about our brand and our needs, aside from the revenue we provide. It's too late to salvage this relationship, but you should consider revisiting your approach before you lose any more sponsors.

On the other hand, if your departure is not their fault, you also need to make that clear — even if the failure was yours. If the decision was based on a change in strategy for your brand, or some other reason that doesn't have anything to do with them, tell them. Don't let them think they've failed if there wasn't anything they could have done differently that would have led to a renewal.

For instance, if it was a bad fit from the start (hello, chairperson's choice!), or you didn't get enough internal buy-in to mount a strong leverage program, you need to own up. That doesn't mean you will change your mind. It just creates some transparency in the decision-making process.

Offer a reference

If the rightsholder was a good partner, and it just didn't work for your brand, offer to go referee for them. Write a letter and give permission for the rightsholder to provide your contact details to prospective sponsors. It's a little thing for you to do that could make a big difference to them.

Do a joint press release

If the rightsholder was a good partner, I would also strongly suggest that you issue a joint press release, to be located on both websites. It doesn't need to be *War & Peace*; just state the facts and the strategic reasons for going your separate ways. Ensure you have a quote or two from both sides, and say plenty of nice things about each other.

Softening the blow

Here are a few things you could also do, depending on the type of relationship you've had. For instance, if you've been a major sponsor for ages, and you know your departure is going to be devastating, you may want to go above and beyond what is required. Same if your investment has made up the lion's share of their sponsorship revenue. And, frankly, you may want to look at these options when exiting charitable and community organisations.

Educate

If you think your partner may struggle to replace the funds you've been providing due, at least in part, to their outdated skills, one option is that you could provide a small stipend to cover the cost of a workshop or online training.

Consulting/coaching

Along the same lines, you could provide a stipend to cover a limited consulting or coaching package, so they have some expert help getting their offer together. This would be most appropriate if you're exiting a larger sponsorship, or one that makes up a lot of their sponsorship income.

With this option, you help them pay for the specific advice they need to get themselves going in a strategic, confident way. It should cost you no more than a few thousand dollars, which will be a small fraction of the sponsorship you've just exited.

Step-down year

The last option I'm going to give you is to sign on for one additional year, at a much reduced level and price. Generally, I don't recommend this option, but there are times and relationships where it will feel like the right thing to do.

The basic idea is that you will move out of the dominant sponsorship position, allowing them a clean slate to seek sponsorship to replace you, while still providing them with some revenue during the transition.

This is an option you should only use sparsely, if at all.

What not to do

While I have recommended to clients that they do all of the above in various combinations over the years, there are a few things I really don't want you to do.

Beat around the bush

I know you don't want to disappoint people, but it really isn't helping a rightsholder if you're indirect.

Don't imply there's a glimmer of hope if there's not. Don't tell them a renewal is "unlikely", as they'll just redouble their efforts to change your mind. If the answer is "no", just say "no".

Believe me when I tell you that rightsholders would rather know the truth — even if it isn't what they want to hear — than continue to put in effort on a losing proposition. You don't have to be mean, but please be direct. For instance:

> *Despite your assurances that you'd be more responsive, that hasn't happened. There's no internal buy-in left, and we will not be renewing.*

Cave in

If you've made a strategic decision and have been open about it, don't cave in and sponsor them again, no matter how dire the situation. I've seen sponsors give a rightsholder over a year's notice that they won't renew sponsorship of an event, then step back in a month before the event because either they felt bad or were trying to do the "white knight" thing. The result created confusion and didn't give them nearly enough time to leverage the sponsorship.

If you make a decision and exit nicely, you need to stick to that decision.

Badmouth

Don't ever badmouth a partner at the end of a contract. Even if you have privately told them that there were a lot of problems, making their future revenue harder to get is punitive and unnecessary.

Dealing with rightsholder bad behaviour

Most of the time, your partners will take an exit in their stride, particularly if you've done everything you can to ease the transition. Only the rare rightsholder resorts to threats when faced with an exit.

Threats to go to your CEO

This is a specialty of charities when a renewal isn't going their way. Don't get me wrong, only a small minority of charities pull this stunt, but most of the rightsholders who do it are charities.

This happens when the sponsor informs the partner that the sponsorship will not be renewed – for whatever reason – and the partner decides not to take "no" for an answer. They threaten to go straight to the CEO for an approval and that'll show you!

Here's what you tell them:

> Go ahead. The CEO is aware of the strategic reasons behind our decision not to renew, and we'll now make her aware that you are trying to strong-arm us. So, good luck!

Nine times out of ten, they will poop their pants. The tenth time, they will leave 16 messages for the CEO and never get an answer. The number of times this strategy will actually get a positive result for the rightsholder is negligible.

Threats to go to the media

This is another tactic employed at renewal time by a small fraction of rightsholders. Again, it is mainly used by charities, who threaten to position your company as the big, mean corporation cruelly pulling critically needed funding from their humble, deserving organisation. Blah blah blah.

Here's the thing: When you spend marketing money, you need to get a strong marketing return. If you no longer get a marketing return, you need to exit. And when an organisation seeks sponsorship and accepts that marketing investment, they sign onto the same deal.

> Never buckle to rightsholder threats.

Threats to go to the media are the ultimate in lacking grace. Not only are they unlikely to net any kind of positive response from the media (coverage of these deals are rare), if they do, they have essentially told every other sponsor in the marketplace not to sponsor them because they don't know how to say goodbye!

How to exit a senior executive's pet sponsorship

While most sponsorship exits are relatively straightforward, exiting a senior executive's pet sponsorship can be fraught with in-house complexities and politics. There's every chance your normal exit strategies won't work at all in this situation, so I'm providing a roadmap to exit — or at least mitigate the damage — from these white elephants. Once you've dealt with the politics, then you can use some of the previously mentioned strategies to manage the rightsholder.

Do a stakeholder group leverage session

You may be thinking, "Not this again!", but this is a very different use for the process.

Get your sponsorship stakeholder group together and give them the brief. Tell them that the sponsorship didn't go through the normal selection channels, and hasn't been providing good results for the brand, and before making a group recommendation about the disposition of the sponsorship — to exit or keep — you're going to give leverage planning a red-hot go. The goal is to see if there is enough relevance and leveraging potential to justify the investment.

This part is key: Actually give leveraging it a red-hot go. Throw yourselves into the leverage brainstorm process. If there's hidden value, you'll find it. If not, that will become very apparent.

Make exiting a stakeholder group recommendation

If you determine that there's just not enough there to warrant keeping it, make a recommendation from the whole stakeholder group. A tactful recommendation from this cross-section of decision-makers is likely to be taken seriously, with no repercussions on the individuals involved.

Importantly, don't be unnecessarily nasty. Telling the CEO that your group has had a look and determined the sponsorship is a crock of crap is unlikely to do anyone any favours.

Instead, use wording something like this:

> The sponsorship stakeholder group conducted an intensive exercise to determine the appropriateness and leveragability of the sponsorship, and we found very limited scope for leverage going forward. For this reason, we're recommending not renewing this sponsorship at the conclusion of the contract.

You could also substitute "target market relevance" for "scope for leverage", if that's more accurate.

You could add some additional wording, contrasting this sponsorship with similar-sized sponsorships that are performing better, such as:

> *When compared with our sponsorships of [property] and [property], which are very similar in scope to this one, both of the others are consistently delivering measurable results against multiple objectives, whereas this sponsorship isn't.*

Use a consultant

Depending on the temperament of the senior executive in question, and the political situation in your company, there may not be any good way (for your career) to tell a senior executive that their pet sponsorship sucks. This is when a strong sponsorship consultant can come in handy. As a consultant, I can confirm that a big part of the job is delivering bad news!

If you're going to go this direction, hire someone good and well-credentialled, and have them facilitate a leverage brainstorm session, as suggested above. Once that session is complete, the consultant then provides the assessment and recommendation to the senior executive, completely insulating group members and absorbing any hits that may come.

What if you can't get rid of it?

If there's just no way to rid your company of this white elephant, you've still got a few options.

Let it languish

Honestly, this is often the best option. If the sponsorship is a bad fit, throwing good money (and time and effort) after bad is unlikely to improve the situation.

Go hospitality-only

One option that may get the senior executive what they want, while getting you out of a bad investment, is to shift from being a sponsor into doing really outstanding hospitality. For example:

➤ Instead of sponsoring the senior executive's old rowing club at some ridiculously high level, could you invite major customers to a rowing clinic, rowing against each other at the end, or some other creative, immersive experience?

➤ Instead of sponsoring a major public music event with your strictly B2B brand, could you do an exclusive backstage experience for your most valued clients?

This way, you're showing the senior executive that you see some value in the sponsorship and have put some real creative effort into focusing the investment on the specific area that will net the best results.

Provide alternatives

If you can identify why this sponsorship appeals to the senior executive, you may be able to provide some alternatives that still push their buttons, while providing a more appropriate platform for leverage. For example:

- Rather than sponsoring a sport that doesn't work, could you shift to endorsement by a legend of that sport?
- Rather than sponsoring the opera, would sponsoring the opera's schools program, or their school holiday program for kids, be more appropriate for your brand?
- Rather than trying to do consumer leverage around an ill-fitting local charity in your company's hometown, could you repurpose it into an employee engagement program?

Chapter 23

Structuring your portfolio

Most of this book has addressed the management of individual sponsorships. What is just as important is ensuring your entire portfolio works well together, so we're going to go through a number of portfolio structures that work, and a few that don't.

Portfolio structures that work

Portfolio structures that work have a few things in common:

- They're effective against a broad range of your objectives
- They're cohesive and consistent platforms for your brand
- They're efficient to manage, leverage, and measure

Fewer, bigger sponsorships

As the importance of leveraging your sponsorships in a creative, meaningful way has gone mainstream, so has the realisation of how much time and effort goes into doing it well. Many a sponsor has looked at their vast, fragmented portfolio and thrown up their hands in exasperation, realising that they will never be able to do them all justice with the resources they have.

Enter the "fewer, bigger" mindset. There has been a definite trend towards rationalising and streamlining portfolios so that sponsors have fewer investments, and shifting towards larger and/or more comprehensive sponsorships. These sponsors are looking for the sponsorship multi-tools referenced back in Chapter 5 – sponsorships that can be used across many objectives, business units, and target markets, and across time and geographies.

This structure can make your life a lot easier, and can certainly be effective, but unless you are very selective about what you invest in, it can lack in flexibility.

Figure 16: Fewer, bigger sponsorships

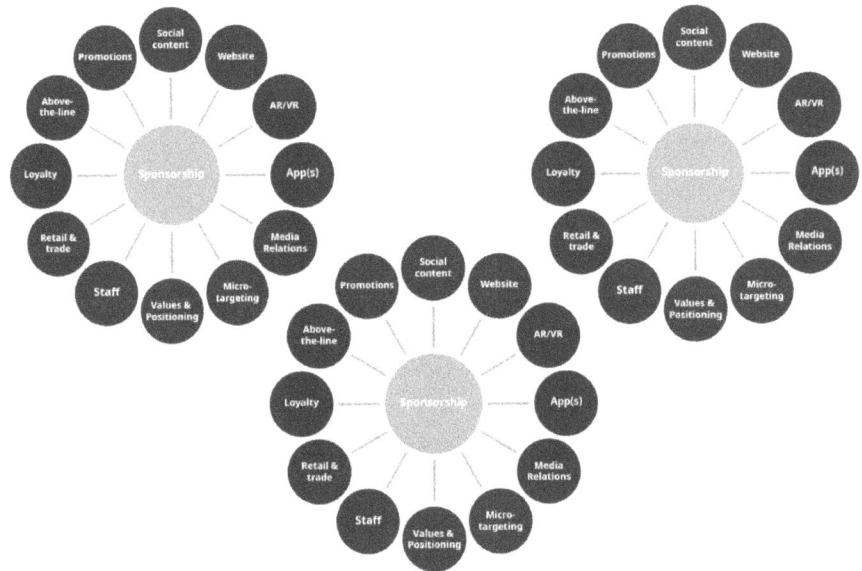

Umbrella portfolio

With an umbrella portfolio, you are essentially creating one large sponsorship around a theme, rather than an individual sponsorship. The whole thing has to work, but the individual components can be a mix of strategic and tactical, national and local, and of varying sizes and shapes. Even sponsorships that are ridiculously wrong can work as part of a larger umbrella, if they fit the theme.

The theme is up to you and could be anything from K-Pop to literacy to your commitment to local communities. As long as it is meaningful to your target markets, and is consistent with your brand, you can have any theme you want.

An umbrella portfolio can be made up solely of sponsorships, but some of the best umbrella portfolios include a whole range of initiatives, such as:

- Sponsorships ranging from tiny to large
- Investments made for purely tactical reasons (for example, sponsoring a small town parade to keep the local government on-side after an issue)
- Staff programs
- Awards programs for that sector (None exist? Create one!)
- Cause-related marketing programs (donations with purchase)
- Other donation programs
- Community grants
- Staff programs — volunteerism, fundraisers, employee giving

> Trade exhibitions
> Brand ambassadors
> Owned events and programs
> Themed product lines

You could give your staff or customers some control over what you sponsor — earmarking a dollar figure and putting it out for nominations and voting.

The list could go on for pages, but the general idea is that if there is an obvious, consistent theme, it can go under an umbrella. And whatever the composition, an umbrella portfolio is a way of making the whole much more than the sum of the parts.

Figure 17: Umbrella portfolio

You only have so much time

One of the biggest reasons to consider an umbrella portfolio is efficiency. It is unrealistic to think that one or two people are going to be able to negotiate, manage relationships, leverage, and measure 200, or even 100, individual sponsorships. That's not to mention dealing with all of the unsolicited proposals and voicemails. Streamlining the workload is the only way this is going to work. Well, either that or a wand.

One of the biggest efficiencies you will be able to create is to bundle related sponsorships into an umbrella portfolio and leverage them as if they were one huge sponsorship. You'll still have to negotiate and manage the relationships, but developing and implementing leverage and measurement plans is time-intensive, and with an umbrella portfolio, you only have to do it once.

No one investment has to be perfect

Have you got a few legacy sponsorships that really don't work, but for political reasons you can't drop? Maybe some senior executive pet projects? Or a couple of badly negotiated deals, where the partner doesn't give a crap whether the benefits really work for you or not? Or maybe you've got a few dozen (or a few hundred) little rats-and-mice sponsorships — those tiny, local sponsorships that you have to do for whatever reason, but that don't have the critical mass to be leveraged properly on their own?

The fact that, as long as the theme is leveragable, no one investment has to be perfect, is one of the best things about an umbrella portfolio.

Creates consistency

Once you've decided on a workable theme for your umbrella, it's a good idea to give it a name or a tagline. It could be as simple as "[Sponsor] in your community" or "[Sponsor] means adventure". Then, instead of just using your logo in any branding opportunities, you'd use your logo with that tagline, or a theme-logo lockup, making it clear that individual sponsorships are part of a larger commitment to that meaningful theme.

You can also create consistency over time. Within that broader umbrella framework, you can do a whole host of leverage activities, which can be rotated through, keeping it fresh year round for years and years, such as:

> Exclusive content provided by the properties
> Content created by your brand, especially durable and/or episodic
> Content created by your staff

Example: Umbrella portfolio

Jack Daniels has managed to use live music to connect with fans around the world, creating a number of events and series keyed to the interests of different markets and customers. The UK version of their JD Set featured some of Britain's hottest bands covering three music legends. The Studio No 7 Series features invitation-only live music events for their customers and up-and-coming bands competing for discovery. They also sponsor selected tours and host seminal music nights in key markets.

Under Armour has made a commitment to remove barriers to participation in youth sports. They started in the US, with equipment and tools for over 50,000 schools. They've now expanded this commitment across a number of global regions, exploring the barriers and how to remove them in these overseas markets. This initiative may look different in different markets, and with different sports, but operates as one giant sponsorship for purposes of leverage.

An umbrella portfolio is the easiest and most efficient way to leverage a collection of related investments.

- User-generated content (created and submitted by fans and customers)
- Aggregated content around your theme (tour dates, list of local hotlines, etc.)
- Interactive elements – games, polls, contests, podcasts, web chats, etc.
- Newsletters, alerts, invitations, memberships
- Themed brand and product promotions, special offers, launches, etc.
- Special edition products

Allows you to create national/global results from local/regional sponsorships

Your brand may need grassroots opportunities. Positioning your brand as having local understanding and relevance could be very important to you. And sometimes, national organisations just aren't a great fit for your specific needs. Don't get me wrong, they can also be great partners, but some struggle to provide valuable benefits, or administer them, on a local level. And a few national organisations are so big that they have fallen into the category of extremely self-important and inflexible.

There are lots of reasons you may favour localised sponsorships, but if your brand is national or global, how you benefit on that broader level can be a challenge. Again, an umbrella sponsorship can be a strong answer.

Imagine you created an umbrella themed around helping teens in crisis, and put that umbrella over the top of a whole group of charities and projects assisting teens. If there is good, credible content that is useful to a national audience, it doesn't matter if it came from a teen crisis hotline serving only Cardiff. If one of the organisations you sponsor has a groundbreaking program to deal with bullying, and they're willing to share advice with your larger audience, it doesn't matter if the program currently runs only in Leeds. If your home office employees participate in a teen homelessness "sleep out" charity event run by your local homeless mission, wouldn't it be great to feature that to your larger audience?

Using an umbrella program, you don't have to look for the one or two major national teen crisis charities, who may or may not be doing anything particularly interesting. You could, instead, make a point of seeking out innovators and outliers who are seeing success.

Importantly, it's not a national versus local either/or. I've done some umbrella portfolios that include hundreds of tiny little community investments, as well as a few larger causes. In those cases, we have leveraged the bigger ones individually, as well as within the umbrella portfolio. This brings an element of vertical integration to the umbrella and that's not a bad thing.

Vertically integrated

A vertically integrated portfolio is a type of umbrella sponsorship. Rather than a simple collection of related sponsorships, however, a vertically integrated portfolio features

A vertically integrated portfolio features sponsorships in one category.

sponsorships in one category — one sport, for instance — from grassroots all the way to the elite or professional level.

A vertically integrated portfolio has all of the positive attributes of an umbrella portfolio. It also offers a multi-level conduit to the target markets, providing the ability to leverage individual components of the portfolio, such as a national team or league, to target markets ranging from elite-level fans to local clubs and players.

Figure 18: Vertical integration

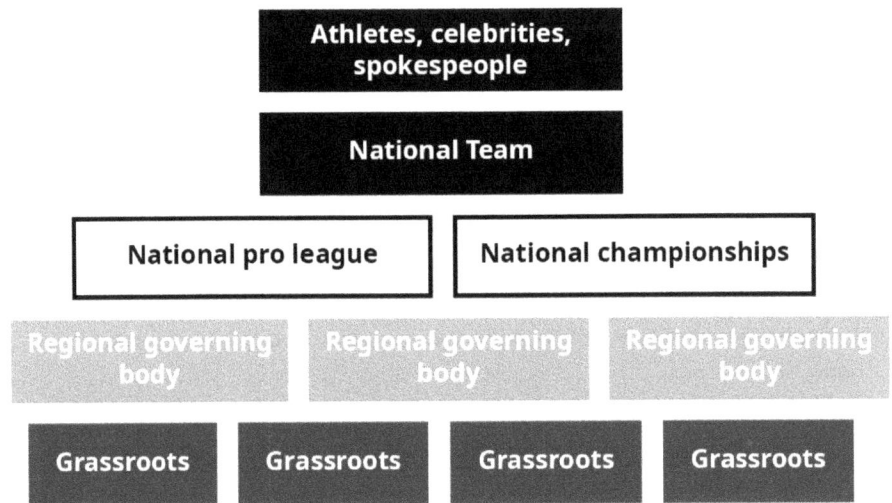

Decentralised

Some companies take a decentralised approach, allowing regional or local areas as well as different business units control over the selection and management of their sponsorships. This works particularly well if your brand operates across a number of geographic areas, where the interests and needs of your target markets are different from one area to another.

The key with making this work is to have a strategy with a firm direction and guidelines, but allow for flexibility and empowerment on the local or regional level. It also helps to provide quality training, tools, and templates, ensuring that both the mindset and method are consistent. Without that framework, this approach is destined to the ignominy of a poorly thought-out, ad hoc portfolio.

I've included comprehensive advice on managing a decentralised portfolio in the next chapter.

Figure 19: Decentralised sponsorship management

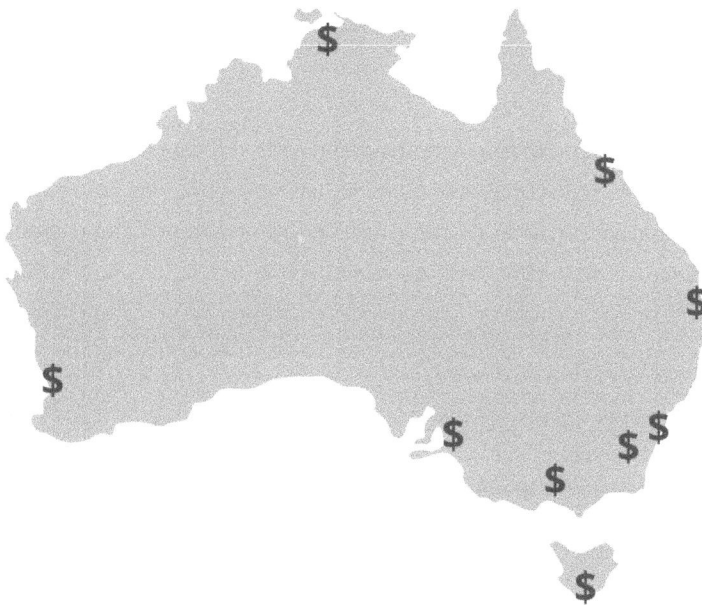

Combination

With few exceptions, most of my clients' portfolios represent a combination of the above approaches. For instance, a portfolio could look like this:

- World Rugby Sevens tour stop (big)
- National ballet (big)
- Netball state associations, national pro netball league, national team, two star players (vertically integrated)
- Fifty-four local, regional, and national literacy organisations, events, and programs (umbrella)
- $25,000 to each regional office for locally managed sponsorships (decentralised)

The result is just four major leverage and measurement programs to manage (plus subprograms) at the national level, while maintaining a year-round, flexible platform for the brand.

I'm not saying your portfolio has to look like this, or that you have to take a combination approach, simply that it's okay if you do. In fact, it's okay to take any of the approaches outlined above. They all have their roles and one or more will suit almost every brand.

Portfolio structures that don't work

There are a few portfolio structures (or lack of) that I don't recommend at all. No matter how talented your team, or how good some of the individual investments are, falling into any of these traps is just creating extra work for you, while diminishing your returns.

Fragmented

This approach is typical, and represents the starting place for many of my clients. The basic idea is that they are choosing individual investments to meet specific needs or that'll work for specific situations. While that's better than making investments for no good reason at all, it is destined to underutilise the sponsorships. Why?

- If your investments are all unrelated, it means you have to leverage them all individually, which is a lot of work.
- If your investments are all unrelated, you may be providing too many or confusing messages about your brand.
- If your investments are chosen only for a concise situation, they may or may not have any relevance across other business units, across time or other geographies, or for other objectives. Even if they do, it's unlikely it's being accessed, making this type of portfolio a chronic under-performer.

Having a fragmented approach is a bit like having an unsolved jigsaw puzzle. It lacks cohesion, and without that, doesn't tell a clear, consistent story about your brand. A well thought-out sponsorship portfolio is that jigsaw put together, with all of the pieces interrelating between multiple business units, objectives, and target markets.

> If your investments are all unrelated, it means you have to leverage them all individually.

Ad hoc

While the fragmented portfolio is like having an unsolved jigsaw puzzle, an ad hoc portfolio is like having a pile of random puzzle pieces from a dozen different puzzles. Not only are they not working together, they never will.

Most ad hoc portfolios need a major overhaul, and the best place to start is with a zero-based audit, which will get you focused on the possibilities. Read more about zero-based sponsorship audits in Chapter 3.

Based on percentages

I'm often asked about the appropriate percentages of sponsorship spend on various categories. In other words, what percentage of the sponsorship budget should be spent on sports, what percent on the arts, etc.

I am all for applying rigour to the sponsorship selection process, but putting arbitrary parameters around the percentage to be spent in the various sponsorship categories is counterproductive. This is marketing money, and your goal needs to be to invest in the most effective sponsorships possible for your target markets and objectives.

Target market relevance, meaning, and passions should be the driving force behind your sponsorship choices. Attribute and value fit will also be a big component. Don't create issues for yourself by starting from some arbitrary percentage.

Chapter 24

Managing a decentralised portfolio

Although I addressed why you may want a decentralised sponsorship portfolio – or a component of one – in the last chapter, actually managing one requires some specific skills and tools, hence having a chapter of its own.

Whether you're looking at decentralised portfolios managed by regional offices, or by various business units, the strategies are basically the same. You want sponsorship to be more effective, more seamless, more consistent, and easier for these stakeholders. This shouldn't be something that corporate marketing is inflicting on them, but something that helps them manage what is always an effort-intensive undertaking.

Know what's out there

The first thing you need to do is try to get a handle on all of the sponsorships these disparate stakeholders have in their portfolios. You at least need to know what they are, how much they cost, and when they end.

Chances are, you won't get all of them, as some regional management (in particular) may not want you to know about some of the lame and/or personally biased sponsorships they've done. I've found that if you tell them that this exercise is to help them make the most of their sponsorships, not take anything away, they're more likely to provide the info you're looking for.

Another option is to centralise sponsorship payments, so decisions are made in the business units or regions, but payments go through home office. By doing that, you can create a sponsorship logging mechanism as part of the payments process, collecting the property name, amount, and timeframe of all new and renewing sponsorships.

However you collect the data – or at least most of it – you will probably be surprised at how much it all adds up to. I've worked with many clients that don't worry much about regional or business unit expenditures, as they're often relatively small and home office doesn't have to manage them. But when they pull together a list and see how much it adds up to, their jaws hit the floor. I've seen figures in the hundreds of thousands to many millions, making it abundantly clear how important it is to get these sponsorships working at peak performance.

Given the power of sponsorship to either build brands or waste money, with very little middle ground, ensuring every dollar is well spent, well leveraged, and well measured is absolutely critical.

Educate

Stakeholders can't make strategic decisions about their decentralised portfolios if they don't understand modern sponsorship, so education is often a big part of elevating their approach.

I harp on about education a lot. I know I do. But that's because effective training is primarily about changing people's mindsets, and that's the fastest way to evoke change in an organisation. There's always more to do, but it starts with education.

For regional marketers, if they're ever in the same place, hire a good facilitator to teach them best-practice skills. You can make it into a workshop format, or you could structure it more as a learn-by-doing session, where a facilitator takes the group through the process of developing leverage and measurement plans for one of their sponsorships right there on the spot.

You can do the same thing with brand teams and business units that are managing their own portfolios.

If gathering stakeholders in one place isn't feasible, you could hold one or more private webinars. The upside is that they don't have to travel, they can attend live, they can review or share the webinar recording later, and the content can be divided into 60–90-minute chunks.

Create a set of tools

This whole book is full of templates and tools, which can be provided as-is to stakeholders or adapted for specific situations. I suggest providing them with:

- Sponsorship guidelines — You'll note that the template I provide is less stringent for sponsorships under $5,000. Whatever figure you use for the cut-off, this ensures that even smaller sponsorships are strategically aligned.
- Proposal evaluation criteria — This is about doing their due diligence. Again, you can provide the standard criteria, or you can alter the criteria to better reflect smaller and/or regional sponsorships.

- Contract/letter agreement templates — This will ensure that these stakeholders are formalising relationships, reducing grey areas, and protecting themselves.
- Email templates — Providing a range of email templates can help streamline their workflow.
- Negotiation checklist — Your working list of all the benefits a rightsholder can provide.
- Inventory of assets — Your working list of non-cash benefits you can provide to a rightsholder, reducing the required sponsorship fee.

All of these templates are found in the book, and are downloadable, so you can customise them for the needs of all of your disparate portfolio managers.

Create a portal

If you've got a lot of regions, different brands, or business units that are running their own sponsorship portfolios, it may be worthwhile investing in a comprehensive sponsorship portal.

Normally sitting on your staff intranet, this kind of sponsorship portal combines the whole gamut of tools, checklists, tutorials, idea banks, templates, and more, all fully customised for your range of brands, regions, and types/sizes of sponsorships, and held together with enough pertinent theory to give it context. People throughout your organisation can then dip in and out of the resource as needed.

If you need assistance in getting this right, this service is a specialty of mine. You can find out more on PowerSponsorship.com/sponsorship-systems-design.

Part **6**

SPECIAL SPONSORSHIP TYPES

Chapter 25

Cause and community sponsorship

Way back in Chapter 2, I addressed *who* should manage cause and community sponsorships. Now, it's time to talk about *how* to manage them.

Cause and community sponsorships work exactly like every other sponsorship. They need to be selected based on relevance, meaning, and fit, negotiated well, leveraged thoroughly and creatively, and measured. There is almost nothing in this book that doesn't pertain just as much to cause and community sponsorships as to any other type.

So, why the special section? It's not because cause and community sponsorships require a different approach, or that you should expect any less of them. Not at all. In fact, cause and community sponsorships are natural multi-tools, offering you *more* options, more ways to leverage, and potentially more power than the rest of your portfolio. This section is about harnessing that power.

Busting the myths

There are a number of myths about cause and community portfolios that will stop you cold in your quest to get a result from these investments.

The corporate social responsibility (CSR) myth

The myth? That a company can "tick the CSR box" by sponsoring causes and community organisations.

The truth? Cause and community sponsorships have nothing to do with CSR. Both are positive activities for a company and absolutely recommended, but they're not related!

CSR has a very specific definition, and it has to do with a company's behaviour — how they make money, not how they spend it. If they make their money in an ethical, responsible, and sustainable way, then they have already "ticked the CSR box". Embarking on cause and community sponsorships does not further the effort — once the box is ticked, it's ticked.

By the same token, if a company doesn't do business in an ethical, responsible, and sustainable way, there is no amount of money they can give to charitable organisations — no amount of self-congratulatory press releases they can issue — that will "tick the CSR box".

Cause and community sponsorship is a beautiful thing in its own right, harnessing the relevance, resonance, and power inherent in this type of organisation to create marketing value for a brand. The sponsor's leverage program often provides even more benefit to the rightsholder — more income through cause-related marketing programs, more communication of key messages, access to a larger, broader audience, and so much more. Because it can provide such a strong return to brands that use their investments well, it is financially sustainable while being meaningful to the community. It is the epitome of that industry catchphrase, "Doing well by doing good".

So, what's the answer?

1. Put CSR back into the governance box where it belongs. CSR is an operational and human resources threshold issue, not a marketing imperative.
2. Make the cause and community investments that provide the best marketing opportunities for your brand, and leverage them for great results for your brand, the rightsholder, and your target markets.

There, now that wasn't so hard, was it?

Money equates to "community engagement"

There is a common myth that paying money to a cause or community organisation equates to "community engagement". Sorry, but since when does giving money to a local charity "engage the community"? It may benefit the community, sure, but it doesn't "engage" them.

If you want to really engage the community, you have to listen to the community, include the community, and reflect the needs and desires of the community. Sponsoring community organisations can provide a powerful platform for doing those things, but just spending the money and issuing a press release is not engagement.

Causes don't know how to be a real partner

Realistically, this isn't always a myth. There are some charitable organisations that used to seek donations but have realised that corporate marketing budgets are a potential source of income. They then swapped the word "donation" for the word "sponsorship", and sent the same-old letter about their worthiness. They changed the words, but not the approach.

Thankfully, causes have become much more commercially oriented and sophisticated, realising that being a genuine marketing partner is much better for them than relying on their need and worthiness to attract corporate money.

> CSR is about how a company makes its money, not how they spend it.

Since when does
giving money to a
local charity
"engage the
community"?

The issue these days is not the intent but in skill level, which can still be a bit patchy. You may need to be extra clear with your needs, drive the negotiations, and do some education along the way. Don't automatically dismiss a potentially great investment because it looks more like a grant request than a sponsorship proposal. Once you've made your needs and rationale clear, most charities are delighted to work in this more advanced, mutually beneficial way.

Cause and community sponsorship options

Cause and community organisations tend to inspire deeply held passion and admiration in their supporters. The potential for providing a sponsor with an emotional added-value benefit for their customers is outstanding.

The biggest thing to keep in mind, however, is that non-profits — and no one else — can provide a sponsor with an opportunity to make their customers and staff the heroes. Say that to them. It's very powerful.

Registered charities have more options for partnering with sponsors than any other type of rightsholder. The most common structures are outlined below, but the key is that any of these can and should be leveraged by the sponsor as if it were a standard sponsorship.

Examples: Cause-related marketing

Ritchies Supermarkets, an Australian regional retail group, offers customers a Community Benefit Card (now an app). Combining both customer choice and cause-related aspects, cardholders can nominate a charity or school, and 1% of their total purchase will automatically be donated every time they shop. 50% of purchases attract the card. Although not a traditional sponsorship, with AU $53 million in card-related donations paid to 5,000 schools and charities to date, the platform and leveragability make it operate as if it was one large sponsorship.

Bank of America new customers can sign up for Pink Ribbon cheque accounts and credit cards, with a donation to the Susan G. Komen for the Cure every year, plus a small percentage donation for every dollar spent through the account. Cheques, cards, and statements feature Susan G. Komen for the Cure branding.

In the US, **Target Stores'** Circle Card and Circle Membership give customers the opportunity to choose which local non-profits will receive grants in their local communities. Members get one vote for each Target visit, with US $26.9 million donated through this program since it rolled out nationally in 2019.

Cause sponsorship

This is the standard sponsorship structure, where you make a marketing investment and receive leveragable benefits in return. This option can work as a stand-alone investment, or in concert with the other sponsorship options below.

Cause-related marketing (CRM)

This is a common option, where you make a donation every time a customer makes a purchase. For instance, you donate 10 cents to the Wildlife Conservation Society every time someone buys your brand of eco-friendly cleaning product.

There is often, but not always, a flat sponsorship or licensing fee paid to the non-profit, and the total cause-related donation is almost always capped.

Another way to structure this is to reverse-gear the cents-per-purchase donation. To do that, you agree on an amount with the charity and pay it upfront. They are often in need of funding, and this can be very helpful to them. Then, you do the maths. How many units are you likely to move during the CRM window – a month, quarter, year, etc.? How much donation per unit does that work out to be? That's your figure.

Round up (or down)

This is an option for financial services organisations, retailers, and any company that bills customers, particularly those with online payments.

The idea is simple: You're appealing to customers to donate their change to benefit a charity. Because these amounts are less than a dollar, many people will opt to do it. Some examples:

> If you're shopping at a retailer – in-person or online – you can round up your total, so if your groceries are $136.24, you can round up the total to $137, with $0.76 to the charity.
> If you're paying a utility bill online, you could check a tick-box that rounds up your total to the nearest dollar, with the excess going to charity.
> If you're using an ATM, and your balance is $540.63, you have the option of rounding down your balance to $540, with that $0.63 going to the chosen charity.

While the individual amounts are small, it can add up to a lot of money for a charity, and a lot of small, meaningful wins for your customers.

In any of these cases, you could:

> Opt to benefit a different charity every month, and those charities could be chosen by the brand team, staff, or customers (for even more wins!)
> Benefit a topical charity every month, such as a breast cancer charity during Breast Cancer Awareness Month, an LGBTQI+ charity during Pride Month, etc.
> Give customers the option of which charity to benefit (for ease of admin, this is usually kept to a small number, so people can choose quickly).

One of the big benefits for sponsors is that the money is being collected from customers, but the actual donation is made by the company, making it a tax write-off you don't actually pay for.

Donation facilitation

This is where you create an easy funnel to collect donations.

An example is Qantas collecting loose change from passengers, in any currency, and donating it to UNICEF. Since this initiative started in 1991, UNICEF has benefitted to the tune of $37.7 million Australian dollars. Like the previously mentioned round-up, Qantas customers are contributing the money, but the donation is coming from Qantas, making it a tax write-off for the company.

Another example is the Ronald McDonald House Charities donation bins in McDonald's restaurants and drive-throughs. You may throw your change in the bin, but McDonald's makes the donation.

Workplace giving

This is another version of donation facilitation. To do this, your company sets up a facility for employees to make regular donations from their earnings.

Because it's the staff making the donations, they get the tax benefits, not the company. That said, these programs are very popular with staff, so it's still a huge positive for companies.

Donation matching

This takes one of the above options, but adds sponsor matching. In other words, your brand would match all donations made, often to a capped amount.

Make it personal

One of the major factors for success that we've seen over the years is that the more individualised and real you can make the investment, the more relevant it will be — even to people who may not be fervent supporters:

> "Every dollar donated will vaccinate X children from all major childhood diseases."
> "In 2024, our staff planted more than 20,000 native trees with their own hands and donated enough to plant 55,000 more. That's almost 500 acres and three times as many trees as there are in Central Park!"
> "A $20 donation could pay for the doorknob this family turns every time they walk into their first real home."
> "We didn't see a doctor to minimise scarring, we saw Green Plan. They showed us how we can cost-effectively rejuvenate retired mining sites, create new habitats, and dramatically reduce the long-term impact of mining on Canada."

The more individual you make the win, the more impact it will have.

Cause and community umbrella

As noted back in Chapter 23, umbrella portfolios are powerful, efficient, and flexible, and a lot of sponsors use an umbrella for their cause and community portfolio. In this section, I'm providing some advice and options that are specific to this type of umbrella.

Even small organisations can provide leveragable benefits

The key to making it work is that you still need leveragable benefits from them, even though some brands are reticent about asking little charitable and community organisations to provide them. Don't be. Even the smallest charities and community organisations can provide benefits that you can leverage into wins.

Some examples:

- Video Q&As with experts — You provide a template or customised questions, they produce the video, you edit the answers into footage you can use.
- Ask-Me-Anything sessions on your social — Video, real time, or you crowdsource questions from your customers and followers, and create a video Q&A answering those key questions.
- Virtual tours of facilities and video explainers about what the organisation does.
- Exclusive advice/expertise you can share with customers and communities.
- Access to stories and profiles (as appropriate) of the need they fill, how they work, and as the sponsorship progresses, what your partnership has helped them — and the people they serve — to achieve.
- Staff volunteer and/or secondment opportunities (then, tell those stories).

If you're looking at that list and thinking, "We won't get the kind of polished content we're used to producing," you need to get over it. That kind of thinking is just making a rod for your back. If content is meaningful to customers and fans, don't worry if it's scrappy. At this point, we're all used to people joining Zoom meetings from their kitchens or a park, and we're not going to forget all the topical DIY content that came out of COVID restrictions.

Turning grants into sponsorships

A lot of companies have a community grants program. More often than not, this is based on grant applications during a fixed window, that the amounts provided are small, and that investment isn't leveraged. This is a big waste for both your brand and the rightsholder's.

Instead, I strongly suggest you provide these cause and community rightsholders with a copy of your sponsorship guidelines. Your guidelines should have an easier option for smaller sponsorships, so if an organisation is looking for sponsorship of less than $5,000 (or whatever cut-off you set), they don't have to provide as many benefits. In the template I've provided, they have to provide three of the specified benefits, instead of six.

Make it clear that by shifting this from "grant money" to a "marketing investment", it's

> Even the smallest charities and community organisations can provide benefits that you can leverage into wins.

better for them. By providing leveragable benefits, it's easier to justify a larger investment, and your leverage program could well bring them additional fans, volunteers, and/or donors.

Use community choice

You've probably worked out that I'm a big proponent of putting some degree of control into the hands of your customers, staff, or fans.

In this case, you could ask for help in choosing either individual investments or the larger theme of a chunk of your investments in a particular year. For instance, you could allocate $X or X% of your umbrella budget every year to community choice. It could then be allocated to STEM education for disadvantaged youth, environmental innovation, local mental health services, or any other topic that your target markets support.

Optional: Set a fixed length for contracts

If you're concerned that it might be difficult to eventually exit all of these cause and community sponsorships — particularly if they've become dependent, over time — you have an option: You can limit all community sponsorships to a fixed term, such as for two years. If you do that, a few things will happen:

- There will be no pressure on you to renew. The terms are the terms. You could make it possible to sponsor an organisation again after a time, such as five years, but at the end of a two-year term, it's over.
- You can do larger, more impactful sponsorships and still spread the money around. For instance, if you provide 50 organisations with an average of $20,000 over two years, that could help smaller organisations jump-start or scale a program. Contrast that with providing $1,000 a year to 500 organisations, over a longer timeframe. Providing small amounts every year is fine, but it's simply not going to spark big change. It's also a lot easier managing fewer partnerships.
- At the end of two years, you can reallocate that money to other organisations. If you really want to be organised — and I always do — have half of your umbrella budget come to an end each year, so you're keeping the overarching umbrella sponsorship fresh every year.

Chapter 26

Government sponsors

More and more governments are getting into the sponsorship business — both as sponsors and rightsholders. This chapter deals with the special considerations and issues that government sponsors have to contend with. Not a government sponsor? Feel free to skip this chapter.

How sponsorship works when you don't have a product to sell

Most of the sponsorship case studies we see have to do with sponsors who have a product or service to sell. Because those are the dominant examples, it would be easy to believe that sponsorship is an inappropriate marketing media for government. Not true!

If we go back to the basics of sponsorship (and all marketing), it is about:

- Changing or reinforcing perceptions
- Changing or reinforcing behaviours
- Engendering alignment

Government marketing is about exactly the same thing. Sure, the things you're trying to change may be different. It could be, "Exercise 30 minutes a day", or, "Keep rubbish out of our waterways", or my personal favourite, "Get your hand off it" (don't use your phone when driving), versus, "Try our new energy drink". But the mechanics of selecting, leveraging, and measuring sponsorship are exactly the same. You have objectives, target markets, touchpoints, stakeholders, and benchmarks.

Rules and expectations

Where government sponsorship diverges from corporate sponsorship is in the rules and expectations that wrap around every decision you make. Manage those, and sponsorship is a powerful tool for any government organisation.

Perception management

As a government organisation, you are spending public funds, and it is absolutely critical to spend those funds wisely. Unfortunately, people who are not in the sponsorship industry — which will include almost all of your constituents — often don't understand what a powerful and cost-effective marketing tool it is, instead classifying it as a frivolous expenditure.

Rather than caving in to that incorrect perception and deciding not to sponsor, you need to proactively manage those taxpayer perceptions. This comes down to three things:

1. Transparency
2. Measurement
3. Reporting

Transparency

What you spend on a sponsorship will probably be part of the public record. It's very easy for someone to latch onto that and protest, without understanding what you're trying to accomplish with the investment.

To the extent that you can, you need to augment the information about the investment level with:

- Your rationale for the investment
- The objectives you will be achieving
- The basics of how you are going to achieve those objectives (your leverage plan)
- How the results will be measured

The perception you want to engender is that your sponsorships are well-chosen, well-used marketing investments.

Measurement and reporting

Every sponsor should measure against benchmarks, and government sponsors are no exception. The difference is the level of public accountability required.

Government sponsors should be measuring the impact against the stated objectives, and making those results available to constituents.

> Transparency is critical with government sponsorship.

Examples: Government sponsorship

Back in 2012, the **Brazilian Health Ministry** teamed up with Vitória FC for a blood donation drive, called "My Blood is Red and Black". The normally red and black, horizontally striped kit was temporarily turned white and black. As fans donated, the red started returning to the jersey, one stripe at a time, until the target was met, and the shirt was once more red and black.

Political management

At the top of every government organisation is an elected minister, mayor, council, or cabinet member who is directly accountable to the taxpayers who voted them into office. Some of them — not all — use sponsorship to curry favour with voters. They will commit sponsorship money to programs with broad appeal, whether there is any marketing benefit beyond garnering votes.

Managing this can be difficult and your best option is to fall back on policy — a specialty of government!

If you don't have a sponsorship policy, you need to create one straightaway. There is a whole section on how to create a sponsorship policy in Chapter 2. Once created, you will need to go through the exercise of getting it signed off by your senior executives, as well as whoever is at the top of your organisation chart.

Once you've got a policy, stating clearly what your sponsorship objectives are and the process by which sponsorships are selected, negotiated, and managed, making those kinds of broad promises becomes more difficult. And if they do make promises, it's a lot less likely to come out of your budget!

Balancing marketing needs with policy

Government is full of policy, and there are times when a potentially good sponsorship runs counter to policy or political rhetoric around an issue.

An example would be a city that is making big investments in being one of the greenest cities in the world, then sponsoring the biggest fireworks extravaganza in the Southern Hemisphere. The positives, in terms of positioning the city to tourists, may or may not outweigh the environmental damage, but if the sponsorship went ahead, you would need to manage any political or constituent fallout.

You may also have a policy of capping the amount of sponsorship you will provide any one organisation. This makes sense, from the point of view of fairness across various community organisations, but poses problems if there is major marketing mileage to be gained by embarking on a much larger, one-off sponsorship.

Another example would be if your organisation has a policy against freebies — free tickets, hospitality, etc. If you are sponsoring something where the ability to influence corporate decision-makers is important, you need to be at those functions.

I could go on and on. Suffice to say that government organisations have a tendency to put policies in place that pose issues when trying to wring the greatest amount of value from your investments.

Once again, policy and transparency are your best friends. In your sponsorship policy, you will need to include a section about message management. In that section, you should include wording like this:

> *When assessing the most cost-effective sponsorship options for [your organisation], we accept that there may be aspects to some of the options that run counter to our larger messages. In this instance, we will collaborate with the stakeholders who oversee those areas to determine whether this is a critical fault or, if not, how any potential issues can be minimised.*

In terms of the public, being clear about why you're doing a particular sponsorship — and acknowledging any areas that may be issues — will be critical to perception management.

The target market conundrum

The final area that government organisations struggle with is in segmenting their marketplaces.

On one hand, any government organisation's job is to meet the needs of their entire constituency — national, regional, or local — so it is understandable that a big factor in sponsorship selection is how broad the appeal is.

On the other hand, one event with "broad appeal" will probably be a lot less powerful than a series of events targeting specific segments. There really is no event, no sponsorship that is going to be equally relevant across all target markets. The solution to this is partly education and partly policy.

Education

In order to educate key people about segmentation and how events have specific appeal across different segments, one of the best things you can do is get them involved in the leverage brainstorm process. It leads off with a discussion on who the target markets of the event are and then how you are going to connect with them. It's a gentle way to educate, but very effective.

Policy

In your sponsorship policy, you should ensure you have some wording like this near the beginning:

> *We accept that no one sponsorship will serve the needs of all our constituents. Our approach is to sponsor a range of properties that, as a whole, serve all the segments that make up our constituent base.*

There is no such thing as a target market of "everyone", even for government.

Chapter 27

Venue naming rights

Not every sponsor will consider venue naming rights. It's a huge commitment, both in dollars and time, and the benefits you receive may have very limited value to building relationships with your target markets.

It is possible to extract a strong marketing return, but it requires sponsors to get over the visibility and sexiness, put corporate ego aside, and work it just as hard as any other major investment. It's not the name on the building that's going to do the marketing job for you, it's your leverage program.

The benefits of venue naming rights

There are two major benefits of venue naming rights that set it apart from other sponsorship options. The biggest has nothing to do with marketing.

Market capitalisation

In my experience, this is the number-one reason companies get into stadium naming rights, but they never, ever talk about it.

According to a *Journal of Advertising Research* study in 2002, of 49 American stadium naming rights deals, market capitalisation for stadium naming rights sponsors rose an average of 1.65% on announcement of the deal. Higher and more sustained rises were attributed to hometown company sponsorship, contract length, and the winning record of the team. This outstripped the market capitalisation rises seen upon Olympic TOP Sponsorship announcements, and marquee sportsperson endorsement. The research attributed the naming rights rises to the perception that such huge, long-term commitments are a sign of senior management confidence.

On the other hand, many companies have undertaken major arena and stadium sponsorships and then failed within a couple of years. Some call this the "naming rights curse", while the more reasonable assessment would be that these naming rights sponsorships were taken up by companies that already had issues, and were using the sponsorship with the specific aim to prop up share prices.

> Market capitalisation increases drive many stadium naming rights deals.

There are other studies that show a much smaller, or even negligible, increase in market capitalisation, so the actual impact is up for debate. I do believe, however, there is a strong perception that market capitalisation increases will be substantial, and that drives many naming rights deals.

I did a research project in 2009 looking at 73 naming rights deals of stadiums and arenas across North America. This was just after the Great Recession. The dominance of financial services companies (40% of the 73 deals researched), car manufacturers (7%), and airlines (7%) taking up naming rights – with many of them committing between 2007–2009 – supports all of the above points.

It is up for debate how many of these underused or badly used stadium naming rights deals weren't really meant to be marketing investments at all. But I hate wasted opportunity, and if the stadium is a half-decent brand fit, it is a crying shame not to leverage it properly.

Cross-event access

The other major benefit that having venue naming rights gives you is access across a potentially huge lineup of events, particularly in a multi-use facility. Depending on the level of benefits (besides visibility) you get, the results could be similar to if you had sponsored all those events individually.

You could get access to a wide array of target markets, and have the ability to add value to your relationships with them. You can create umbrella leverage programs, creating consistency across the whole calendar. You can also create leverage programs for individual events, sports seasons, or types of events, like concerts or family shows.

Venue sponsorship could be an amazing platform for you, but it all rests on the benefits you negotiate.

Naming rights in name only

If you are going to negotiate a venue naming rights sponsorship, it is critically important to negotiate benefits that are incorporated into the experience of people attending the events happening there. I know of venue naming rights sponsors who get absolutely no access to any of the events, except for a luxury box. They don't even have access to the big screen, can't run promotions, sample, or do anything at all with any of the events. Unless all you are looking for is a bump in market capitalisation, please do not agree to that type of sponsorship!

The downside to venue naming rights

There are some significant upsides, but there are also many downsides to venue naming rights. Before you embark on any negotiations, be sure you're aware of the potential issues. Some may not worry you. Some may not be pertinent. But it's better to assess the possible downsides than be blindsided by them.

Cost and length of contract

This is a biggie. Venue naming rights contracts routinely run into millions of dollars a year, over the course of decades. It is a huge commitment for an investment that you can't be sure will still be right for your brand in 8 or 10 years, much less 25. It may be exactly right for your brand right now but by entering into a venue naming rights contract, you could be limiting your flexibility for a long time.

Just think about how much your portfolio has changed even in the past five years, mostly to keep pace with changing brand and target market needs. Even better, think of the annual cost of the naming rights sponsorship. Let's say for a moment that it equates to $5 million a year. If, for some reason, you weren't allowed to do any venue naming rights but could spend that $5 million on sponsorship right now to create the best possible result for your brand, what would you sponsor? Do you think that ideal portfolio would be the same in five years? Ten?

What you should be looking for in a venue naming rights deal is a comprehensive complement of benefits that stretch across the events taking place there. They need to be comprehensive enough that you will be able to create a fantastic leverage plan this year, and it may be entirely different a few years down the track. In other words, with the right deal, you can create some flexibility with your leverage program.

On-selling: One option for reducing your costs

Some naming rights sponsors of new venues have reduced their costs substantially by taking up additional, smaller sponsorships as part of their deal, and on-selling them to other companies.

This has been done primarily by retailers and other companies with vendors who want to keep them on-side. For instance, a major hardware retailer could take up venue naming rights and 20 hospitality suite and signage packages, then on-sell them to manufacturers of the tools and garden supplies and barbecues they sell.

The reason this works primarily for new stadiums is that they don't have all of the hospitality suites, signage, etc. already committed.

One in a long line

As already mentioned, there has been a spate of companies that have taken up naming rights and then gone bust early in the contract. It happened a lot in the first dot com boom, as companies tried to increase their value before their IPO. And it's happened in cycles ever since, creating a revolving door of naming rights sponsors at many venues.

If you are looking at stadium naming rights, and are following a lineup of short-term sponsors, you will need to accept that it will take a while before your brand becomes part of the fabric of the stadium. There will be a degree of sponsor fatigue, and to show that you are the real deal, you will need to be particularly diligent about creating those third wins for your target markets.

The situation is similar if you are following a very long-term incumbent. You need to reassure the target markets that your brand's involvement is going to be even better than the previous naming rights sponsor, and that means being involved, enthusiastic, and emphasising the fan experience.

It's just a vessel

One of the biggest challenges for venue naming rights sponsors is that you are not sponsoring the things people care about – a concert, a family show, a team – but the vessel that holds them. There are a few exceptions, but people don't tend to have real passion for stadiums and arenas. Think about it this way: What is more important, the Dom Perignon or the bottle it's in? You are, essentially, sponsoring the bottle.

By negotiating benefits that go across the events themselves, even if they are limited, you can create leverage programs that reach into those events that people care about. If you don't, your results are destined to be limited as your meaning to the event experience will be limited.

Remote fans get left out

Venue naming rights is, by design, almost entirely about the in-person audience. Naming rights sponsors don't get access to content or other IP around the events and games that happen at the venue, so angles for adding value to remote fans is almost nil. So, even if there are a ton of people attending events at the venue, there's a much bigger marketplace you're not going to be able to add meaningful value to.

Community backlash

This is not an issue with new venues, but a big problem with historic ones.

If people do love a venue, particularly one with historic significance, there could be major community backlash if you change the name. Think: Madison Square Garden, the Melbourne Cricket Ground, or Twickenham.

I don't generally recommend taking up naming rights to historic venues where there hasn't previously been a naming rights sponsor. There is a huge risk of people seeing it as disrespectful and, as already covered in this book, being a respectful sponsor is a threshold need if you are going to use the sponsorship as a platform for forming and deepening relationships with your target market. Starting a big, expensive sponsorship from a deficit like that is just not worth it.

Wringing strategic benefit from venue naming rights

My lack of love for stadium naming rights isn't about its lack of value as a marketing opportunity — there are huge opportunities to make returns — but because so many sponsors spend millions doing it and get virtually no real marketing value from the investments.

Yeah, yeah, yeah . . . I can hear people grumbling about the "massive exposure" all the way down here in Sydney. But as I've been harping on about since Chapter 1, exposure isn't a marketing objective. Changing people's perceptions and behaviours are marketing objectives, aligning with people is a marketing objective, and being huge and loud and having a blimp take pictures of your neon name on the stadium doesn't change people's perceptions, behaviours, or alignment.

Anchor your leverage plans on the fan experience

As we've covered since the start of this book, the most basic premise is that it is win-win-win. That third "win" is about creating a series of small, meaningful wins for their target market(s). Sponsors have any number of ways to achieve these wins and so do venue naming rights sponsors:

- Adding real value to the fan experience — Think about the best and worst things about the experience and then figure out ways to lessen the worst and amplify the best. And, no, crappy giveaways and interruptive in-stadium promotions do not constitute real value.
- Adding real value to the brand experience — Is there anything about the stadium sponsorship that would make your customers' interactions with you better, improve your products, improve the online experience on your site, whatever?
- Aligning with the beliefs, priorities, and self-definitions of the target markets — In the simplest possible terms, this is about using a sponsorship to say, "We understand you and we feel the same way." This is especially powerful when the sponsor uses the sponsorship to amplify a target market's voice.

The mindset is that the name on the building is nice, but a sponsor's real job is to sponsor the fans: To make the experience better, easier, more convenient, more amazing; to make it about the fans, the kids, the communities; to share the celebrations, commiserations, and

> Buying naming rights to a historic venue is a ticket to community backlash.

keeping the faith. If you are able to put your corporate ego on hold and concentrate on putting the fans first, your brand will enjoy a bigger win than if it had all the logo exposure in the world.

Be consistent and flexible

If you are sponsoring a multi-purpose venue (not just the home for one team), creating separate leverage programs for every event that uses the facility is probably unrealistic. Instead, I suggest you take a two-pronged approach:

1. Consistency — Create leverage activities that are consistent across all events that take place in that venue. Think about the parts of the event experience that are the same — excitement, anticipation, sharing with friends, parking, crowds, uncomfortable seats, etc. — and work out ways you can add value across one or more of these aspects.
2. Flexibility — For key events or event categories, such as music events or basketball games, you will want to leave room for the creation of specific leverage strategies to make the most of them for your brand.

Use your access to infrastructure

As the naming rights sponsor, you will get greater access to infrastructure than any other sponsor. For example, you could:

> Create a flagship store or display on-site
> Create an express lane entry for your customers
> Create a zone or lounge
> Create an interactive play area (ie, Citizens Bank participates in an interactive "Games of Baseball" park at the stadium and provides "Citizens Ballpark Bankers" around the stadium, providing customer service)
> Use your major electronic signage to showcase and/or hero the fans

Brainstorm what you want and how you would use it, and don't be shy about asking. When you spend that much money on a sponsorship, it shouldn't just be a stock-standard sponsorship with a big name on the building. You need to make it work for you, so demand access to infrastructure that works for you.

Conclusion

You did it! You've just made it through all of the best advice I have for sponsors, gathered over decades of consulting and capacity building in this industry.

It's a jam-packed read as I want it to be the most complete guide it can be. If I've done my job, you have a deeper understanding of what sponsorship can do for your brand, dozens of ideas for how to put that into practice, and at least the beginnings of a plan. You are ready to join the ranks of best-practice sponsors.

I know it might seem daunting, but you don't have to start big. Just put a few strategies into place, build buy-in, and watch your organisational culture around sponsorship change. Best-practice sponsorship is a bit like a snowball on a mountain. It may start small, but it will pick up pace and keep growing.

My goal is to make you confidently self-sufficient, and ready to respond to any changes this industry throws at you. But if you ever do need expert help, I'm here. Whether it's training or consulting or an audit or sponsorship systems design, just let me know.

Thank you so much for reading *The Corporate Sponsorship Toolkit, 2nd Edition*. I encourage you to drop me a line and let me know how this book and best-practice sponsorship techniques have changed what you do, and the results you get.

Cheers,

Kim Skildum-Reid
Power Sponsorship
www.powersponsorship.com
admin@powersponsorship.com
AU: +61 2 9559 6444
US: +1 612 326 5265

> You did it! You're ready to join the ranks of best-practice sponsors.

Working with me

My goal with *The Corporate Sponsorship Toolkit, 2nd Edition* is that you will have the mindset, strategies, and tools to be able to move forward with a best-practice sponsorship strategy on your own.

But if you do need help — your situation is complex, your team is inexperienced, or you have intractable politics to deal with — just let me know.

I offer the following services:

- Strategic sponsorship consulting
- Sponsorship strategy sessions
- Sponsorship Systems Design (for large and/or diverse organisations)
- In-house training
- Partner training
- Sponsorship coaching

I also provide comprehensive online sponsorship training for both sponsors and rightsholders.

When you hire Power Sponsorship, you're hiring me as I personally handle all strategy, training, and coaching work. Unlike many consultancies, your project will never get passed along to a junior staffer.

You can find details on all of these services on my website: PowerSponsorship.com. If you'd like to discuss any of these options, or if you have questions, please don't hesitate to drop me a line.

About the Author

Kim Skildum-Reid is unquestionably one of our industry's most influential thought leaders. Her inspired yet practical approach, and refreshing, irreverent style have won her legions of fans for her books, industry-leading blog, white papers, and media contributions.

She has decades of experience in corporate sponsorship and is one of very few professionals credited with defining and setting the best-practice benchmark for the sponsorship industry. She has a list of blue-chip consulting and training clients spanning six continents.

Kim provides content and commentary to business and industry media around the world, including *Harvard Business Review*, CNN, CNBC, Bloomberg, *Marketing News* (US), *Marketing Africa*, *Marketing Russia*, *Sponsor Magazine* (Netherlands), Brand Republic (UK), *National Business Review* (New Zealand), *Adnews* (Australia), *Marketing* (Australia), *South China Morning Post*, *China Business Review*, *Australian Financial Review*, and far too many more to list.

Kim spends a lot of time on planes, working with clients around the world, from her home base in Sydney, Australia. She's had the privilege of seeing some amazing places and doing some amazing things. From Lagos to Helsinki, Papua New Guinea to Montreal, Shanghai to New York, plus Durban, Dublin, Dubai, and so many more.

She was a member of two CMO Council advisory boards and author of one of the industry's best-read, most reprinted, and most often quoted blogs. In 1993, Kim was a founder of the Australasian Sponsorship Marketing Association and served as president for its first four years.

On the personal side, Kim is a retired rugby second rower and has been boxing for well over fifteen years. She sings alternative, grunge, and punk with a band, and has a yellow lab, named "Kevin L7", who spends most afternoons snoozing and snoring next to her desk. She loves the Sydney Swans, hot laps, a good cheeseburger, and an icy cold cider.

She'd love to meet you someday.

APPENDIXES

Recommended resources

To ensure the list of recommended resources stays current, I've opted not to publish them here. Instead, please visit this page:

powersponsorship.com/recommended-sponsorship-resources/

On this page, you will find my go-to resources, podcasts, bloggers, sponsorship-related publications and associations, and sports law associations.

Sponsorship Agreement Pro Forma

Guidance notes

1. **WARNING** – this document is provided as a sample only for educational purposes and is not legal advice or a substitute for it. You should seek the advice of a suitably qualified and experienced lawyer before using this document.

   In particular, you or your lawyer should:

   > check the law in your jurisdiction – make sure this agreement works there.

   >> check for changes to the law – law and practice might have altered since this document was drafted or you last checked the situation.

   >> modify wherever necessary – review this document critically and never use it without first amending it to suit your needs. Remember, every sponsorship is different and the parties may agree to allocate risks and responsibilities differently from this template.

   >> beware of limits of expertise – if you are not legally qualified or are not familiar with this area of the law, do not use this document without first obtaining legal advice about it.

This warning is governed by the laws of New South Wales, Australia.

2. This sample agreement may be a useful starting point for a sponsorship agreement. However, it is very general because it is impossible to draft a document that accounts for all situations or for legal differences in all countries. The agreement therefore cannot be relied on for any specific arrangement and must not be signed unless first approved by your lawyer after they check the drafting, change it to suit the law of the relevant place, and better outline the rights of the parties in the context of their specific circumstances.

3. **How this agreement works**

The agreement assumes that there are standard clauses that should be in every agreement and special clauses needed for your sponsorship. The standard clauses that should apply all the time are called the "Standard Conditions". The parts that relate to your specific sponsorship are the "Schedules" and the "Special Conditions".

The Schedules and the Special Conditions have precedence over the Standard Conditions. In other words, what you insert is more important than what is already written. This is why it is vital to use a lawyer or know about what you are doing.

4. **Read the agreement**

Before doing anything, read the agreement and see how it might apply to your situation. There might be Standard Conditions that are unsuitable. There might be new conditions you need to add. Do not just assume that the agreement, or the template risk profile, is right for you.

The agreement is for an _exclusive_ sponsorship for the relevant sponsorship category. If your sponsorship is non-exclusive, consult a lawyer about inserting a special condition and making other changes to the document to reflect your requirements.

5. **Completing the schedules**

You should complete each schedule following the guidance notes in that schedule.

For example, schedule 23 is called "Sponsor's termination events". The guidance note tells you to see clause 9.2. You should read clause 9.2 and understand the circumstances in which the sponsor has a right to terminate the agreement. You should then insert in Schedule 23 _any other circumstances_ peculiar to your sponsorship (for example, the sponsor might want to terminate the agreement if the team being sponsored loses its licence to play in the Major League or if the contracted lead performers for the musical withdraw their services).

6. **Adding Special Conditions**

The Special Conditions (at the end of the Schedules) enable you to insert other conditions that are not dealt with by this sample agreement.

7. **Changing Standard Conditions**

You should not change the Standard Conditions without consulting a lawyer. The agreement is drafted as a package, and changing the Standard Conditions might have an unintended, "domino effect" on other terms.

If you have to change the Standard Conditions, do so by adding a _Special Condition_ such as "clause 18 of the Standard Conditions does not apply".

8. **Signing**

    The parties sign and date the document on the last page. Make sure that the person with whom you do the deal is authorised to sign.

9. **Need more space?**

    This agreement also is supplied in digital form. Obviously, if more room is needed to complete the schedules this can be adjusted on screen.

10. **Need help?**

    You should always consult a lawyer practising in your jurisdiction and experienced in sponsorship matters.

Date	This agreement is dated on the date it is signed by the last party to do so.
Parties	
1.	[*] incorporated in [*] of [*] (the Sponsor)
2.	[*] incorporated in [*] of [*] (the Owner).

This Agreement comprises the Standard Conditions, the Schedules and the Special Conditions.

IT IS AGREED as follows.

Schedule 1

"Sponsor"

Title: ....

Address: ....

....

....

Representative: ....

Telephone: ....

E-mail: ....

Schedule 2

"Owner"

*(Identify the sponsee – the legal entity receiving the sponsorship. This must be the proper name of the company or association receiving the funds and controlling the team, event or venue being sponsored, **NOT** the name of the team, event or venue etc)*

Title: ....

Address: ....

....

....

Representative: ....

Telephone: ....

E-mail: ....

Schedule 3

"Commencement Date"

(insert when the sponsorship starts)

....

Schedule 4

"End Date"

(insert the date on which the sponsorship will end, ignoring any option extensions which are covered in Schedule 5 below)

....

Schedule 5

Option to Renew

(see clause 1.5)

Does Sponsor have an option to renew?   Yes/No

If yes: for what "Period" (specify an extended finishing date or further term, eg. 3 years)?

....

....

will the sponsorship fee and other Owner Benefits be the same after renewal ? If not, list
the new benefits.

....

....

Schedule 6

First Right of Refusal

(see clause 1.6)

Does Sponsor have a first right of refusal?   Yes/No

Schedule 7

"Property"

(identify the event, team, venue or other property the subject of this sponsorship)

....

Schedule 8

"Sponsorship Category"

(identify the nature of the sponsorship eg title/category/official supplier etc)

....

Schedule 9

"Territory"

(specify the area in which the sponsorship operates eg. state, region, country, continent, worldwide etc)

....

Schedule 10

Sponsor Objectives

(see clause 2.1)

(be specific – list bottom line sales objectives, measurable promotional activities, business development targets etc)

1. ....
2. ....
3. ....

Schedule 11

Owner Objectives

(see clause 2.2)

(be specific – list expected leverage from Sponsor in developing event/sport, target participation or attendance numbers, entry fee and merchandise income, measurable business development targets etc)

1. ....
2. ....
3. ....

Schedule 12

"Sponsor Benefits"

(list, in detail, the signage/tickets/hospitality/advertising credits/merchandising rights and other benefits that Owner must provide to Sponsor – be precise about amounts, timing etc)

1. ....
2. ....
3. ....
4. ....
5. ....
6. ....
7. ....
8. ....
9. ....
10. ....

Schedule 13

"Owner Benefits"

(list, in detail, the sponsorship fee, Contra/in kind benefits that Sponsor must provide to Owner – be precise about amounts, timing etc)

11. ....
2. ....
3. ....
4. ....
5. ....
6. ....
7. ....
8. ....
9. ....
10. ....

Schedule 14

Evaluation criteria

Is Media analysis required and, if so, by whom, at whose expense, how regularly and what details must be provided?

....

Is Owner obliged to provide reports on mutual marketing activities, demographic information, samples of printed and promotional materials, reports on digital activities and, if so, what and when?...

....

Specify, in detail, the level of performance (and how it will be assessed) which is regarded by Sponsor as unacceptable: ....

....

Specify the consequences of failing to achieve this level (for example right of termination, reduced fees or benefits): ....

....

Specify the level of performance (and how it will be assessed) above which Sponsor's reasonable expectations are exceeded: ....

....

Specify the consequences of this level of performance (for example increased sponsorship fee or benefits): ....

....

Specify any other relevant evaluation criteria, information or consequences: ....

....

....

....

Schedule 15

"Applicable Law"

(identify the country or state the laws of which will apply to this Agreement)

....

Schedule 16

Owner Marks

(insert here all trade marks, names, logos and other artwork which Sponsor is entitled to use under this Agreement. Include artwork. If nothing is listed, Sponsor may use all Owner Marks.)

Schedule 17

Sponsor Marks

(insert here all trade marks, names, logos and other artwork which Owner is entitled to use under this Agreement. Include artwork)

Schedule 18

Use of Owner Marks

(list here the specific purposes for which Owner Marks can be used by Sponsor)

1. ....
2. ....
3. ....

Schedule 19

Use of Sponsor Marks

(see clause 5.1)

(list here the specific purposes for which Sponsor Marks can be used by Owner)

1. ....
2. ....
3. ....

Schedule 20

Promotional & Media Objectives

(see clause 6.3)

(be specific – eg. list target media outlets, promotional events, nature of coverage etc)

1. ....
2. ....
3. ....
4. ....
5. ....

Schedule 21

Competitors of Sponsor

(see clause 7.1)

1. ....
2. ....
3. ....

Schedule 22

Competitors of Property

(see clause 7.2)

1. ....
2. ....
3. ....

Schedule 23

Sponsor's termination events

(see clause 9.2)

(insert here the circumstances in which Sponsor can terminate this Agreement)

1. ....
2. ....
3. ....
4. ....
5. ....

Schedule 24

Owner's termination events

(see clause 9.3)

(insert here the circumstances in which Owner can terminate this Agreement)

1. ....
2. ....
3. ....
4. ....
5. ....

Schedule 25

Insurance

(see clause 16)

(insert here the amount of public liability insurance required to be maintained by Owner and full details of any other insurance required for the purposes of this Agreement)

1. Public liability – amount ....
2. Other: ....
....
....

Schedule 26

Ambush strategies

(include here specific strategies designed to minimise the likelihood of Ambush occurring, such as obligations on Owner to:

- prevent or minimise Competitor involvement;
- exercise control of venue access and signage;
- impose contractual obligations on bidders for commercial rights not to engage in Ambushing should the bids be unsuccessful;
- negotiate broadcasting agreements to provide Sponsor with a first right of refusal to take category exclusive advertising time during broadcasts of the event;
- impose ticketing restrictions;
- prevent the re-use of tickets or licensed products as prize give-aways;
- provide sponsorship fee rebates (be very specific) if serious Ambush occurs etc).

1. ....
2. ....
3. ....
4. ....
5. ....

Schedule 27

"Prolonged Force Majeure Period"

(see clause 18.5)

(insert here the length of force majeure period the parties can tolerate before triggering termination rights – this will likely depend on the length of the sponsorship term; a longer term, a longer period may be agreed. Strike out as applicable.)

1 month/3 months/6 months/12 months/Other (specify) ....

Special Conditions

(insert here any changes to the Standard Conditions and any special conditions not referred to in the Standard Conditions or the Schedules)

Standard Conditions

1. Sponsorship

1.1 Exclusivity

Sponsor shall be the exclusive sponsor of the Property, in the Sponsorship Category, in the Territory.

1.2 Term

Subject to this Agreement, the sponsorship starts on the Commencement Date and is effective for the Term.

1.3 Consideration

The consideration for this Agreement is the mutual conferring of benefits referred to in clause 1.4.

1.4 Benefits

(a)   Sponsor must confer Owner Benefits on Owner; and

(b)   Owner must confer Sponsor Benefits on Sponsor,

at the times outlined in, and in accordance with, Schedules 12 and 13.

1.5 Option to Renew

(a)   This clause applies if the parties specify "Yes" in Schedule 5.

(b)   Sponsor has an option to renew this Agreement for the further Period specified in Schedule 5 if:

    (i)   Sponsor is not in breach under this Agreement; and

    (ii)   Sponsor gives notice in writing to Owner no fewer than 3 months before the end of the Term stating it intends to exercise the option.

(c)   If Sponsor exercises the option, the provisions of this Agreement (except for this clause 1.5) shall continue in full force and effect for the further Period, subject to any differences in fees or Owner Benefits specified in Schedule 5 for the further Period.

1.6 First Right of Refusal

(a)   This clause applies if the parties specify "Yes" in Schedule 6.

(b)   Owner must not enter into an agreement with any other person to sponsor the Property in the Sponsorship Category at or immediately after the end of the Term without first offering the sponsorship to Sponsor on the same terms as it proposes to offer to (or as have been offered by) other parties.

(c)   If Sponsor declines within 30 days to accept the new sponsorship terms, Owner may enter into an agreement with a third party, but only on the terms offered to, and rejected by, Sponsor.

(d)   Sponsor's first right of refusal extends to any revised terms offered to or by third parties after Sponsor declines to accept the initial terms.

1.7 No assignment without consent

(a) Sponsor must not assign, charge or otherwise deal with Sponsor Benefits without the prior written consent of Owner.

(b) Owner must not assign, charge or otherwise deal with Owner Benefits without the prior written consent of Sponsor.

(c) This clause does not apply to Owner Benefits or Sponsor Benefits that the parties, on signing this Agreement, agree may be conferred on third parties.

2. Objectives

2.1 Objectives of Sponsor

The primary objectives of Sponsor in entering into this Agreement are:

(a) to associate Sponsor's brand with the Property;

(b) to promote the products and services of Sponsor;

(c) to encourage brand loyalty to Sponsor;

(d) to assist in raising and maintaining Sponsor's corporate profile and image;

(e) to provide to Sponsor marketing leverage opportunities related to the Property;

(f) to promote community awareness of, affinity for and (if relevant) participation in the Property;

(g) to continually review and evaluate the ongoing success and performance of the sponsorship for maximum commercial advantage to all parties; and

(h) the objectives outlined in Schedule 10.

2.2 Objectives of Owner

The primary objectives of Owner in entering into this Agreement are:

(a) to secure sponsorship funds and other benefits;

(b) to increase the profile, standing, brand value and (if relevant) participation in the Property;

(c) to promote the profile and corporate image of Sponsor and the use of Sponsor's products and services;

(d) to continually review and evaluate the ongoing success and performance of the sponsorship for the maximum commercial advantage to all parties; and

(e) the objectives outlined in Schedule 11.

2.3 Fulfilment of Objectives

The parties must act at all times in good faith towards each other with a view to fulfilling the objectives outlined in clauses 2.1 and 2.2. This Agreement is to be interpreted in a manner that best promotes the fulfilment of those objectives.

3. Warranties

3.1 Owner Warranties

Owner warrants that:

(a) it has full right and legal authority to enter into and perform its obligations under this Agreement;

(b) it owns the Property (or, if the Property is not legally capable of being owned, it holds rights which effectively confer unfettered control of the Property);

(c) Owner Marks do not infringe the trade marks, trade names or other rights of any person;

(d) it has, or will at the relevant time have, all government licences, permits and other authorities relevant to the Property;

(e) it will comply with all applicable laws relating to the promotion and conduct of the Property; and

(f) it will conduct itself so as not to cause detriment, damage, injury or embarrassment to Sponsor.

3.2 Sponsor Warranties

Sponsor warrants that:

(a) it has full right and legal authority to enter into and perform its obligations under this Agreement;

(b) Sponsor Marks do not infringe the trade marks, trade names or other rights of any other person;

(c) it will comply with all applicable laws in marketing and promoting its sponsorship of the Property; and

(d) it will conduct itself so as not to cause detriment, damage, injury or embarrassment to Owner.

4. Disclosure

4.1 Initial Disclosure

Owner warrants that it has disclosed to Sponsor:

(a) the substance (other than financial details) of all agreements entered into or currently under negotiation with Owner for sponsorship, exclusive or preferred supplier status or other like arrangements relating to the Property; and

(b) all other circumstances which might have a material impact upon Sponsor's decision to enter into this Agreement.

4.2   Continuing Disclosure

Owner must from time to time keep Sponsor informed of:

(a) new sponsorship, exclusive or preferred service or supplier status or other like arrangements conferred by Owner in respect of the Property;

(b) significant marketing programs and other promotional activities which might provide leverage opportunities for Sponsor; and

(c) research and demographic information held or commissioned by Owner about the Property and its participants.

5.   Marks and title

5.1   Authorised use

(a) Sponsor may use Owner Marks:

    (i) for all purposes reasonably incidental to obtaining the Sponsor Benefits; and

    (ii) as permitted in Schedule 18.

(b) Owner may use Sponsor Marks;

    (i) for all purposes reasonably incidental to obtaining the Owner Benefits; and

    (ii) as permitted in Schedule 19.

5.2   No unauthorised use

(a) Sponsor must not use, or permit the use of, Owner Marks or any other trade or service marks, logos, designs, devices or intellectual property rights of Owner; and

(b) Owner must not use, or permit the use of, Sponsor Marks or any other trade or service marks, logos, designs, devices or intellectual property rights of Sponsor,

unless:

(c) authorised by this Agreement; or

(d) with the written consent of the other party.

5.3   Merchandise

(a) Unless permitted in Schedule 18, Sponsor must not manufacture, sell or licence the manufacture or sale of any promotional or other merchandise bearing Owner Marks without Owner's prior written consent.

(b) Unless permitted in Schedule 19, Owner must not manufacture, sell or licence the manufacture or sale of any promotional or other merchandise bearing Sponsor Marks without Sponsor's prior written consent.

(c) All authorised merchandise bearing Owner Marks or Sponsor Marks permitted under this Agreement must be:

    (i) of a high standard;

    (ii) of such style, appearance and quality as to suit the best exploitation of the Sponsor, Owner and Property (as the case may be); and

    (iii) free from product defects, of merchantable quality and suited for its intended purpose.

5.4   Image

The parties must ensure that any authorised use by them of the other's marks or intellectual property rights:

    (a)   is lawful;

    (b)   properly and accurately represents those rights;

    (c)   strictly complies with the other party's trade mark and logo usage policies current at the relevant time;

    (d)   is consistent with the other's corporate image; and

    (e)   (if used in connection with the provision of goods or services) is associated only with goods or services of the highest quality.

5.5   Enforcement Protection

The parties must provide all reasonable assistance to each other to protect against infringers of Owner Marks or Sponsor Marks in connection with the Property.

5.6   Title

Despite any rights to use another's marks conferred under this Agreement:

    (a)   Owner holds all legal and equitable right, title and interest in and to the Property and all Owner Marks;

    (b)   Sponsor holds all legal and equitable right, title and interest in and to the Sponsor Marks;

    (c)   naming, title and other rights conferred by this Agreement merely constitute licences to use the relevant Owner Marks or Sponsor Marks (as the case may be) for the purposes of, and in accordance with, this Agreement and do not confer any property right or interest in those marks; and

    (d)   the right to use another's marks is non-exclusive and non-assignable.

5.7   Infringements incidental to television broadcasts etc

This clause 5 does not prevent any person holding rights to televise or reproduce images associated with the Property from incidentally broadcasting or reproducing Sponsor Marks appearing as or in signage on premises controlled by Owner and relevant to the Property.

5.8   No alteration to broadcast signal etc

Owner must not authorise or permit any media rights holder contracted in respect of the Property (for example, the official broadcaster of an event or an authorised Internet site manager or multimedia provider or rights holder), in the exercise of those media rights, to alter any images associated with the Property (for example, by the artificial electronic insertion, removal or alteration of signage or other images) without the prior written consent of Sponsor.

6. Media, branding, leverage etc.

6.1 Media Exposure

At all reasonable opportunities:

(a) Owner will use its best endeavours to obtain public and Media exposure of the sponsorship; and

(b) Sponsor will use its best endeavours to obtain public and Media exposure of the Property.

6.2 Approval

Media releases relating to the sponsorship must:

(a) be issued jointly by the parties; or

(b) not be issued by one party without the consent of the other.

6.3 Promotional Objectives

Owner and Sponsor must use their best endeavours to achieve their promotional and Media objectives outlined in Schedule 20. Sponsor licences Owner to use Sponsor Marks, and Owner licences Sponsor to use Owner Marks, for these purposes.

6.4 Leverage

Sponsor has the right at its cost to:

(a) promote itself, its brands and its products and services in association with the Property; and

(b) engage in advertising and promotional activities to maximise the benefits to it of its association with the Property,

provided that it will not knowingly or recklessly engage in any advertising or promotional activities which reflect unfavourably on the Property, the parties or any other sponsors of the Property.

6.5 Social Media policies

Owner must comply, and must procure its employees and contractors to comply, with Sponsor's Social Media policies from time to time in relation to any direct or indirect references to the sponsorship or the Sponsor in Social Media content created or exchanged by or on behalf of Owner, its employees or contractors.

7. Exclusivity

7.1 Exclusivity within Territory

(a) If the Sponsorship Category is designed for only 1 sponsor (for example, naming rights or principal sponsorship):

(i) Sponsor's rights under this Agreement are exclusive within the Territory; and

(ii) Owner must not enter into any sponsorship or supply arrangements for the Property in the Sponsorship Category within the Territory with any other person.

(b) If the Sponsorship Category is designed for multiple sponsors (for example, official suppliers or Gold Class sponsors) Owner must not, without the prior written consent of Sponsor (which must not be unreasonably withheld), enter into any sponsorship or supply arrangements for the Property in the Sponsorship Category within the Territory with any other person.

(c)   The sponsorship categories for the Property must not be redesigned without Sponsor's prior written consent if to do so might affect adversely Sponsor's rights under this clause.

7.2   Competitors

Owner must not within the Territory authorise or permit to subsist:

(a)   the provision of any products or services to the Property, in any sponsorship category; or

(b)   any association with the Property,

by any Competitor of Sponsor.

7.3   Sponsor Restraint

Sponsor must not enter into any sponsorship or supply arrangements with any Competitor of the Property or the Owner during the Term or within a reasonable time after the end of the Term.

7.4   Injunctions

The parties acknowledge that the restraints referred to in this clause 7 cannot adequately be compensated for in damages and consent to injunctive relief for the enforcement of these restraints.

8.   Marketing and service delivery

8.1   Marketing Committee

Owner and Sponsor will establish a marketing committee to meet quarterly (or otherwise, as agreed) for the purposes of:

(a)   reviewing the progress of the sponsorship and the mutual rights conferred under this Agreement;

(b)   evaluating the success of the sponsorship against its objectives;

(c)   discussing further opportunities for leverage and cross promotional activities;

(d)   maximising the ongoing benefits to the parties, implementing promotional strategies for the parties and identifying new, mutual opportunities; and

(e)   maximising the Sponsor Benefits by:

    (i)   identifying actual or potential Ambush activities;

    (ii)   using their best endeavours to prevent Ambush or minimise its potential impact on the sponsorship; and

    (iii)   directing implementation of the strategies outlined in Schedule 26.

8.2   Service Delivery

Both Sponsor and Owner must designate a representative to be primarily responsible for the provision of the day to day service and support required by the other party under this Agreement. Until otherwise nominated, the representatives will be the representatives named in Schedules 1 and 2.

8.3 Evaluation

The parties must evaluate the success of the sponsorship in accordance with the criteria outlined in Schedule 14 and with the consequences (if any) outlined in that Schedule.

9. Termination

9.1 Expiry

This Agreement, unless terminated earlier under this clause or extended under clause 1, will continue until the end of the Term.

9.2 Early Termination by Sponsor

Sponsor may terminate this Agreement if any of the following occurs and has not been remedied within 10 days after Owner receives written notice from Sponsor to do so.

(a) Owner fails to provide a Sponsor Benefit.

(b) Owner is Insolvent.

(c) any event outlined in Schedule 23 occurs.

(d) application of the evaluation criteria in Schedule 14 permits termination.

(e) any laws come into operation which in any way restrict, prohibit or otherwise regulate the sponsorship of, or association by Sponsor with, the Property or the Owner so that:

(i) the benefits available to Sponsor are materially reduced or altered; or

(ii) Sponsor's obligations under this Agreement are materially increased.

(f) any major, public controversy arises in connection with the Owner, the Property or this Agreement which, in the reasonable opinion of Sponsor, reflects adversely and substantially on Sponsor's corporate image.

(g) any material statement, representation or warranty made by Owner in connection with this Agreement proves to have been incorrect or misleading in any material respect.

(h) the rights conferred on Sponsor under this Agreement are directly or indirectly diminished, prejudiced or compromised by the reckless acts or omissions of Owner.

(i) Owner has not used its best endeavours to ensure that the exclusive rights conferred on Sponsor under this Agreement are not directly or indirectly diminished, prejudiced or compromised in any way by the acts or omissions of third parties (for example, by Ambush).

9.3 Early Termination by Owner

Owner may terminate this Agreement if any of the following occurs and has not been remedied within 10 days after Sponsor receives written notice from Owner to do so.

(a) Sponsor fails to provide a material Owner Benefit.

(b) Sponsor is Insolvent.

(c) any event outlined in Schedule 24 occurs.

(d) any major, public controversy arises in connection with the Sponsor or this Agreement which, in the reasonable opinion of Owner, reflects adversely and substantially on Owner's corporate image or upon the Property.

(e)   any material statement, representation or warranty made by Sponsor in connection with this Agreement proves to have been incorrect or misleading in any material respect when made.

(f)   the rights conferred on Owner under this Agreement are directly or indirectly diminished, prejudiced or compromised by the reckless acts or omissions of Sponsor.

9.4   Immaterial Breaches

Nothing in this clause entitles a party to terminate this Agreement for trivial or immaterial breaches which cannot be remedied, however this does not prevent termination for regular, consistent or repeated breaches (even if they would, alone, be trivial or immaterial).

9.5   Method of Termination

A party entitled to terminate this Agreement may do so by notice in writing to the other at the address specified in Schedule 1 or Schedule 2, as the case may be.

9.6   Effect of Early Termination

Termination of this Agreement for any reason shall be without prejudice to the rights and obligations of each party accrued up to and including the date of termination.

10.   Re-branding

10.1   Change of name, logo, product etc

If at any time Sponsor changes its name or logo, or wishes to change any Sponsor's product associated with Property, Sponsor may re-brand the sponsorship of the Property provided that, in the reasonable opinion of Owner, to do so will not affect the good name and image of the Property or Owner.

10.2   Costs

Re-branding must be at Sponsor's cost. This includes:

(a)   direct costs to Sponsor; and

(b)   any costs incurred by Owner directly or indirectly resulting from the re-branding.

11.   Governing law and jurisdiction

The Applicable Law governs this Agreement. The parties submit to the non-exclusive jurisdiction of the courts of the country or region of the Applicable Law and courts of appeal from them for determining any dispute concerning this Agreement

12.   Relationship of parties

The parties are independent contractors. Nothing in this Agreement or in the description of the Sponsorship Category shall be construed to place the parties in, and the parties must not act in a manner which expresses or implies, a legal relationship of partnership, joint venture, franchise, employment or agency.

13.   Ongoing assistance

13.1   Assist parties

Each party must promptly:

       (a)   do all things;

       (b)   sign all documents; and

       (c)   provide all relevant assistance and information,

reasonably required by the other party to enable the performance by the parties of their obligations under this Agreement.

14.   Costs

14.1   Agreement costs

Each party must pay its own costs of and incidental to the negotiation, preparation and execution of this Agreement.

14.2   Implementation costs

Unless otherwise specified as a Sponsor Benefit or Owner Benefit, each party must pay its own signage, advertising, leverage, general overhead and incidental costs related to the performance of its obligations under this Agreement. Despite this, all signage, artwork, photography, digital and similar expenses incurred under this Agreement must be met by Sponsor unless otherwise provided for in the Schedule or Special Conditions.

14.3   Transaction taxes

Sponsor must also pay all transaction taxes (such as GST, VAT or similar goods or services taxes) applicable to this Agreement.

15.   Notices

15.1   Notices

Notices under this Agreement may be delivered or sent by post or e-mail to the relevant addresses outlined in Schedules 1 and 2 and will be deemed to have been received in the ordinary course of delivery of notices in that form.

15.2   Electronic communications

The parties consent to the use of electronic communications as a means of communicating about this Agreement and the matters contained within it.

16. Insurance

16.1 Liability insurance

Owner must effect and keep current:

(a)   a public liability insurance policy for an amount not less than the amount specified in Schedule 25 for any single claim for liability of Owner or Sponsor or both for death, personal injury or property damage occasioned to any person in respect of the Property (including a contractual liability endorsement to cover the obligations of Owner under clause 17);

(b)   such other insurance as is specified in Schedule 25; and

(c)   if Property is a one-off event (or if the parties specify in Schedule 25), event cancellation insurance in an amount equalling or exceeding the value of Sponsor Benefits.

16.2 Product liability insurance

If:

(a)   Owner is authorised under this Agreement to manufacture, sell or licence the sale or manufacture of any merchandise bearing Sponsor Marks; or

(b)   Sponsor is authorised under this Agreement to manufacture, sell or licence the sale or manufacture of any merchandise bearing Owner Marks;

the party so authorised must effect and keep current a product liability insurance policy for an amount not less than the amount specified in Schedule 25 for any single claim for liability of Owner or Sponsor or both for death, personal injury or property damage occasioned to any person in respect of the manufacture or sale of the merchandise (for example, for claims relating to a defective product).

16.3 Terms of Policies

All insurance policies effected under this Agreement must:

(a)   be wholly satisfactory to Beneficiary;

(b)   identify Beneficiary as a named insured;

(c)   remain enforceable for the benefit of Beneficiary even if invalid or unenforceable by Payer; and

(d)   include full, automatic reinstatement cover at all times during the Term.

16.4 Other Obligations

Payer must:

(a)   not violate, or permit the violation of, any conditions of these policies; and

(b)   provide insurance certificates and copies of the policies to Beneficiary on its reasonable request.

17. Indemnities and liability limitation

17.1 Owner indemnities

Owner must indemnify Sponsor and Sponsor's officers, employees and agents from and against all claims, damages, liabilities, losses and expenses related to:

(a)   any breach by Owner of this Agreement;

(b)   the inaccuracy of any warranty or representations made by Owner;

(c)   any wrongful act or omission by Owner (including negligence, unlawful conduct and wilful misconduct) in performance of this Agreement;

(d)   Sponsor's involvement with the Property (other than losses and expenses incurred solely as a result of Sponsor's decision to invest in the Property);

(e)   liabilities for which insurance is required under clause 16.

17.2 Sponsor indemnities

Sponsor must indemnify Owner and Owner's officers, employees and agents from and against all claims, damages, liabilities, losses and expenses related to:

(a)   any breach by Sponsor of this Agreement;

(b)   the inaccuracy of any warranty or representations made by Sponsor;

(c)   any wrongful act or omission by Sponsor (including negligence, unlawful conduct and wilful misconduct) in its performance of this Agreement; and

(d)   all liabilities for which insurance is required under clause 16.

17.3 Limitation of liability

To the extent permitted by law, Sponsor's liability to Owner under this Agreement (whether for breach of warranty or otherwise) is limited to the payment of sponsorship fees as and when due.

18. Force Majeure

18.1 Notification and diligence

A party which is, by reason of a Force Majeure Event, unable to fulfil its obligations under this Agreement must:

(a)   notify the other party as soon as possible giving particulars of the Force Majeure Event, its effect on that party's ability to fulfil its obligations under the Agreement, and its proposed steps to remedy or abate the Force Majeure Event;

(b)   keep the other party informed as to progress in remedying the Force Majeure Event; and

(c)   resume performance as expeditiously as possible after termination, remedy or sufficient abatement of the Force Majeure Event.

18.2 Consultation

Following notification under clause 18.1, the parties must consult in good faith to assess the Force Majeure Event and any ways in which it might be avoided, its effects mitigated, or in which alternative arrangements (such as extending the Term or renegotiating or substituting payments, benefits or obligations) might be agreed for mutual benefit.

18.3 Consequences

(a) Subject to paragraph (b), a party's obligations under this Agreement are suspended during the time, and to the extent, that their performance is prevented, wholly or in part, by a Force Majeure Event, and no liability to the other party accrues for loss or damage of any kind arising out of, or in any way connected with, that non-performance.

(b) Suspension of any obligations pursuant to this clause 18.1 does not affect:

    (i) the obligations in clause 18.2 to consult;

    (ii) any obligations which accrue prior to the suspension; or

    (iii) (if the Force Majeure Event affects only some obligations of the affected party) any other obligations of the affected party.

(c) The period of suspension of any obligations under this clause 18.3 excludes any delay in the performance by the affected party of those obligations which are attributable to a failure by the affected party to comply with clause 18.4.

18.4 Mitigation

The affected party must use reasonable endeavours to avoid or remove the circumstance constituting the Force Majeure Event and to mitigate the effect of the Force Majeure Event, provided that the affected party has an unfettered discretion in how it deals with any Force Majeure Event that results from a labour dispute or a cyber-attack. The other party must cooperate and provide such assistance as the affected party reasonably requests.

18.5 Termination for prolonged Force Majeure Event

If a party gives notice under clause 18.1, the same Force Majeure Event prevents or inhibits the performance of any obligation or condition required to be performed under this Agreement for the Prolonged Force Majeure Period, and the parties are unable to agree alternative arrangements, then a party that has complied with clause 18.2 may terminate this Agreement by written notice to the other party, upon which neither party is under any further obligation to the other in respect of matters arising after that time.

19. Dispute resolution

19.1 Mediation

Any dispute or difference about this Agreement must be resolved as follows:-

(a) the parties must first refer the dispute to mediation by an agreed accredited mediator or, failing agreement, by a person appointed by the President or other senior officer of the Law Society or Bar Association in the jurisdiction of the Applicable Law;

(b) the mediator must determine the rules of the mediation if the parties do not agree;

(c) mediation commences when a party gives written notice to the other specifying the dispute and requiring its resolution under this clause;

(d) the parties must use their best endeavours to complete the mediation within 14 days; and

(e) any information or documents obtained through or as part of the mediation must not be used for any purpose other than the settlement of the dispute.

19.2   Final Resolution

If the dispute is not resolved within 14 days of the notice of its commencement, either party may then, but not earlier, commence legal proceedings in an appropriate court.

19.3   Contract Performance

Each party must continue to perform this Agreement despite the existence of a dispute or any proceedings under this clause.

19.4   Exceptions to mediation

Nothing in this clause prevents:

(a)   a party from seeking urgent injunctive relief in respect of an actual or apprehended breach of this Agreement;

(b)   Sponsor from exercising its rights under clause 9.2; or

(c)   Owner from exercising its rights under clause 9.3.

20.   Data and privacy

20.1   Compliance with laws

Each party must comply, and ensure its agents and contractors comply, with all applicable Privacy Laws in respect of Personal Data collected, handled or transferred by it in connection with this Agreement.

20.2   Warranty

A party providing Personal Data to the other party warrants that it is authorised to provide the data for the purpose for which it is provided.

20.3   Notice of data breach

A party receiving Personal Data in connection with this Agreement must promptly notify the other party in the event of any data breach or potential data breach affecting the Personal Data handled by it.

21.   Confidentiality

The commercial terms of this Agreement are confidential to the parties unless they otherwise agree. However, this does not prevent:

(a)   Sponsor or Owner disclosing the existence or the sponsorship to the general public; or

(b)   any promotional, marketing or sponsorship activities authorised or required under this Agreement.

22.   Definitions and interpretation

22.1   Composition

This Agreement comprises these Standard Conditions and the attached Schedules and Special Conditions.

22.2 Precedence

The Special Conditions and the attached Schedules have precedence over these Standard Conditions to the extent of any inconsistency.

22.3 Definitions

In this Agreement, unless the context otherwise requires, terms defined in the Schedules or Special Conditions have the meaning set out there and:

Agreement means this Agreement as amended from time to time.

Ambush means the association by any person, not authorised in writing by Owner, of the person's name, brands, products or services with the Property or with a party, through marketing or promotional activities or otherwise, whether or not lawful, accurate or misleading.

Beneficiary means the party for whose benefit an insurance policy must be effected under clause 16.

Competitor means:

    (a)   in the case of Sponsor:

        (i)   any person who conducts any business which competes (other than incidentally), directly or indirectly, with any business conducted or services provided by Sponsor or any company related to Sponsor or whose products or services are antithetical to or incompatible with the business, products or services of Sponsor; or

        (ii)   any person listed in Schedule 21 or who conducts a business in the industry, or of the nature, described in that Schedule.

    (b)   in the case of Owner:

        (i)   any person who conducts any event or offers any product substantially similar to the Property anywhere in the Territory or whose operations are antithetical to or incompatible with the Property; or

        (ii)   any person or property listed in Schedule 22 or any property or event of the nature described in that Schedule.

Force Majeure Event means any event or circumstance, or a combination of events or circumstances, which is beyond the reasonable control of a party, which by the exercise of due diligence that party is not reasonably able to prevent or overcome and which has the effect of preventing the party from performing an obligation under this Agreement.

Insolvent in respect of a party means one of the following events has occurred:

    (c)   the filing of an application for the winding up, whether voluntary or otherwise, or the issuing of a notice summoning a meeting at which it is to be moved a resolution proposing the winding up, of the party;

    (d)   the appointment of a receiver, receiver and manager, administrator, liquidator or provisional liquidator with respect to that party or any of its assets;

(e)   the assignment by that party in favour of, or composition or arrangement or entering into of a scheme of arrangement (otherwise than for the purposes solely of corporate reconstruction) with, its creditors or any class of its creditors.

(f)   something having a substantially similar effect to (a) to (c) happens in connection with party or its assets under the Applicable Law.

Media means any of communication to the public at large, whether by radio, television, newspaper, digital media (such as the Internet) or otherwise.

Owner Benefits include additional fees or benefits that accrue to Owner by application of the evaluation criteria in Schedule 14.

Owner Marks means Owner's name and trade or service marks, labels, designs, logos, trade names, product identifications, artwork and other symbols, devices, copyright and intellectual property rights directly associated with the Property. If Schedule 16 is completed, the term is limited to the Owner Marks depicted or listed in that schedule.

Payer means the party obliged to effect an insurance policy under clause 16.

Privacy Laws means the requirements under the Applicable Law, the Territory, (for Sponsor) the laws of places in which Sponsor conducts business, and (for Owner) the laws of places in which Owner conducts business, relating to the collection, processing, storage, transfer or security of personal data (such as the General Data Protection Regulation (GDPR)), including applicable industry standards in those jurisdictions.

Personal Data means personal information or data the subject of the Privacy Laws.

Social Media means a digital application that facilitates the creation and exchange of user-generated information, whether for personal or business purposes, including (for example and without limitation) blogs, wikis, social networks (such as Facebook, YouTube and X) and on-line media.

Sponsor Benefits may be reduced by application of the evaluation criteria in Schedule 14, and if reduced must be construed accordingly.

Sponsor Marks means Sponsor's name and the marks and other symbols outlined in Schedule 17.

Term means the period starting on the Commencement Date and (subject to clause 1.5) finishing on the End Date.

22.4 Currency

References to currency are to the lawful currency of the country or region of the Applicable Law.

22.5 Examples

Examples given in this Agreement do not limit or qualify the general words to which they relate.

Signing page

By signing, you indicate acceptance of this Agreement (including the standard conditions and the special conditions) on behalf of the entity you represent and you declare your ability to sign this Agreement on behalf of the Sponsor/Owner (as the case may be).

Signed for and on behalf of Sponsor

_____   _____
Name   **Signature**

_____   _____
Capacity   **Date**

Signed for and on behalf of Owner

_____   _____
Name   **Signature**

_____   _____
Capacity   **Date**

www.ingramcontent.com/pod-product-compliance
Lightning Source LLC
Chambersburg PA
CBHW052340210326
41597CB00037B/6203